INTO UNKNOWN SKIES

ALSO BY DAVID K. RANDALL

INTO UNKNOWN SKIES

An Unlikely Team, a Daring Race,
and the First Flight Around the World

DAVID K. RANDALL

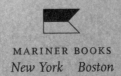

MARINER BOOKS
New York Boston

HarperCollins books may be purchased for educational, business, or sales promotional use. For information, please email the Special Markets Department at SPsales@harpercollins.com.

FIRST EDITION

Designed by Emily Snyder

Map by Mapping Specialists, Ltd.

Library of Congress Cataloging-in-Publication Data

Names: Randall, David K., author.
Title: Into unknown skies : an unlikely team, a daring race, and the first
   flight around the world / David K. Randall.
Description: First edition. | New York : Mariner Books, 2024. | Includes
   bibliographical references and index.
Identifiers: LCCN 2024017069 (print) | LCCN 2024017070 (ebook) | ISBN
   9780063371408 (hardcover) | ISBN 9780063371422 (ebook)
Subjects: LCSH: Flights around the world. | Aeronautics—History—20th
   century. | Aeronautics—Records. | Air pilots—United States—Biography.
Classification: LCC G445 .R36 2024 (print) | LCC G445 (ebook) | DDC
   910.4/1--dc23/eng/20240514
LC record available at https://lccn.loc.gov/2024017069
LC ebook record available at https://lccn.loc.gov/2024017070

ISBN 978-0-06-337140-8

24 25 26 27 28 LBC 5 4 3 2 1

To Megan, Henry, and Isla

To be first—that is the idea. To do something, say something, see something, before anybody else—these are the things that confer a pleasure compared with which other pleasures are tame and commonplace, other ecstasies cheap and trivial. . . . These are the men who have really lived—who have actually comprehended what pleasure is—who have crowded long lifetimes of ecstasy into a single moment.

—MARK TWAIN, *The Innocents Abroad*

Contents

Route of the First Flight Around the World

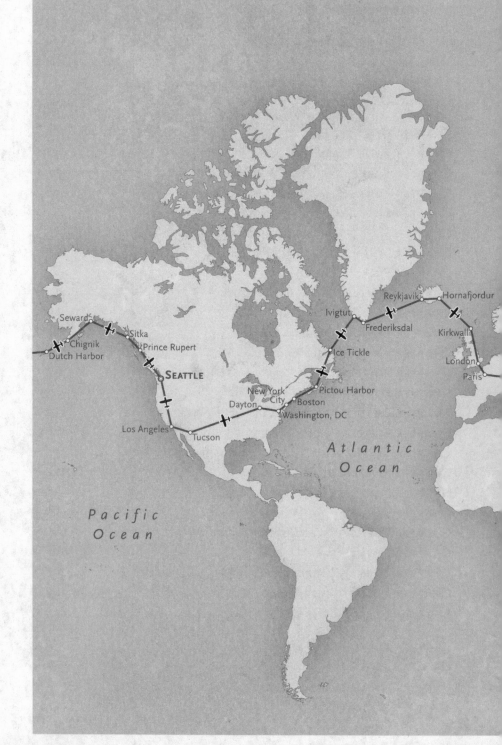

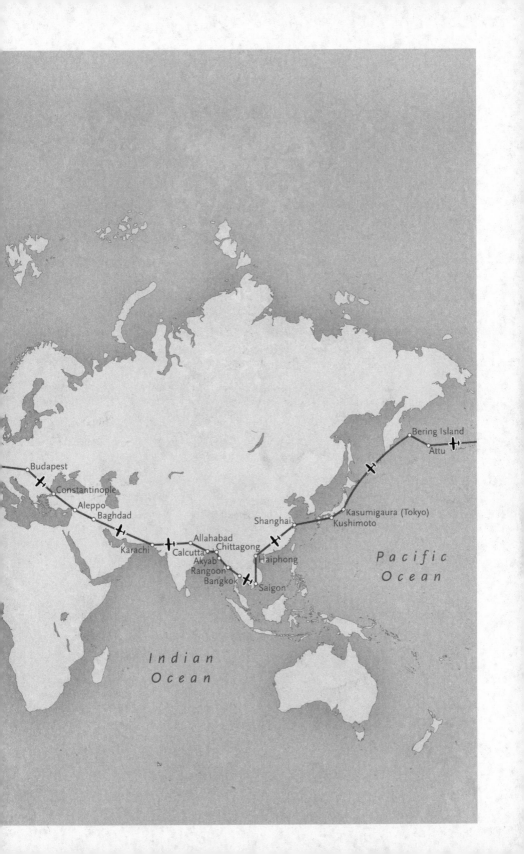

Budapest

Constantinople

Aleppo

Baghdad

Karachi

Allahabad

Calcutta Chittagong

Akyab

Rangoon

Bangkok

Haiphong

Saigon

Shanghai

Kasumigaura (Tokyo)

Kushimoto

Bering Island

Attu

Indian Ocean

Pacific Ocean

PREFACE

One Year

O N MY DESK I have a copy of the Riverside, California, *Daily Press* from the summer of 1924. I would like to say that this particular newspaper on this particular day was particularly special, but that would not be altogether true. It was but one of hundreds that arrived each morning in America during a time when booming literacy rates created a nation of readers, whose hunger for news bound the country together like never before. I'm choosing to highlight it mainly because it is my hometown paper, and I enjoy seeing familiar names alongside forgotten events from long ago.

In this issue, more than half the stories on the front page of the *Daily Press* share the same focus. It was not a war that gripped the nation's attention, or a scandal out of Hollywood, or even the Olympic Games then underway in Paris. The biggest news story of them all was a race that seemed to defy the imagination. It had no official starting point or finish line. Its contenders had been unknown until newsreels made them famous from Iowa to Australia. The machines they climbed into were unproven, though recent history suggested death was as likely an outcome as survival. Still, the world could not look away from the pursuit of an audacious goal: to fly an airplane around the globe.

It can be difficult to conceive of just how revolutionary the idea of long-distance flight once was. Airplanes were loud, unreliable machines, built of wood and canvas and held together with glue. Pilots died in alarming numbers, done in by everything from rainy weather to malfunctioning engines to losing their way in a cloud. At the start of 1924, most people assumed, with good reason, that they would never step foot in an airplane in their lifetimes, no matter how long those might be.

One summer changed all that. With a fervor that would not be equaled until the race to the moon four decades later, the world aimed its best pilots and engineers at a dream. By the time the race finished, a new era had begun, one in which airplanes appeared to be the thread that would connect distant cultures, even as the shadows of another world war grew larger.

This book tells the story of one incredible year during which a handful of pilots and engineers pushed themselves to conquer the Earth in a way no one had thought possible. Though all of it is true, its elements—white-knuckle flights over fog-covered iceberg fields; treks through tiger-infested jungles to rescue a lost pilot; an airplane designer so poor he ate potatoes he grew in his backyard but who remained convinced that the world would soon know his name—feel like fantasy. That seems fitting. Even as the race began, flying around the globe was the stuff of make-believe. Each mile flown closed the gap between reality and imagination and set the world on a course that led directly to our current age, when commercial space travel feels tantalizingly near.

It is a tale of triumphs and failures, heroes and skeptics. It stretches from the coldest reaches of Alaska to the hottest deserts in Iraq and connects a cast of characters ranging from schoolchildren in Japan to the king of England to a failed Broadway actor just hoping to get away from his hometown in Connecticut. Through its dozens of stops, at some of Europe's first airports to places that had never seen airplanes, the race forced a change of perspective. For the first time, the power of flight allowed the people of the world to see themselves as part of a collective whole rather than as members of scattered nations and suggested that a lasting peace built on human connection was at hand. We know now, of course, that this optimism was fleeting, a bright light wedged between the darkness of two world wars. Yet as we look toward the next era of space travel, the promise of technology and ingenuity to bring us together remains.

This is a story with the globe as its stage. And it all starts with a man, banished far from his home, who was cursed to see what the future would bring.

INTO UNKNOWN SKIES

CHAPTER ONE

The Prophet

WHEN HE CLOSED his eyes, he could still see the flames.

A steady breeze murmured through the curtains of his bungalow, letting in the soft Hawaiian sun. Unpacked luggage crowded the living room, leaving the impression that he was building a barricade. Somewhere nearby seabirds trilled above the rustle of palm fronds, drowning out the low sounds of the busy harbor. Yet at that moment, Billy Mitchell was far away, lost again in anger.

No matter what he did, he came back to the same image in his mind: hundreds of airplanes burning on a field in France. They had been set aflame intentionally, though none were so damaged that destruction was the only course left. Their sin was being seen as no longer necessary. When Mitchell protested, his superiors in the army told him that the aircraft were surplus now that the Allied Powers had won the World War.

And so they torched them.

Over twenty-three hundred airplanes were eventually incinerated, their apparent use in the modern world nothing more than kindling. Planes had played a pivotal role in this Great War, but that would be the end of aircraft as far as the US military was concerned. Airpower was not the future of warfare; life would go back to how it had been and always would be, no matter what Mitchell thought. As the smoke over France fizzled, he sensed the future slipping away. He had come so far, but it was still not enough.

He opened his eyes and paced his bungalow as the faint rhythm of crashing waves hummed in the background, providing a metronome for his rage. Lean, with sharp cheekbones and a cleft chin, he presented a regal picture, falling naturally into the center of attention. At the age of forty-four, Mitchell had done all that was asked of him, and his grateful nation had given him numerous medals for his service. His father had been a US senator; his paternal grandfather, a railroad baron, was once the wealthiest person in the state of Wisconsin. Yet when Billy Mitchell opened his mouth, all of that refinement evaporated. His temper was legendary, his willingness to humiliate those who disagreed with him unmatched. In the world of business in which his grandfather operated, those traits might have been virtues. But in the regimented world of the US military, where hierarchy and tradition mattered above all, Mitchell might as well have painted a target on his own back. He had only to look at the ever-present sun of Honolulu—where he had been shipped months earlier in a less than subtle maneuver to get him as far away from his beloved town house in Washington, DC, as possible—to see the consequences of insulting the wrong person. After a lifetime of trying to climb higher, Mitchell had effectively fallen off the ladder.

The reason that he was here, exiled in paradise, was simple: the airplane. Though it was the birthplace of flight, America had turned its back on its most revolutionary invention. The country had few pilots and fewer planes and almost no one in power who cared to change that. "For the time being at least the United States is lagging behind the march of aviation progress," a newspaper columnist complained in 1922. "The European Nations, particularly those of them like Great Britain and France that have attained the utmost degree of efficiency in the flying art on the military as well as the commercial side, are spending much more money in the development of aviation, are developing superior types of machines and in general [are] quite a few steps in advance of the United States."

Mitchell was the loudest—often the lone—voice advocating for change. It came naturally to him. Despite enjoying the benefits of his family's privileged past, he could not help but keep his attention on the future. He was stuck with a restless mind, and all the freedoms that wealth could offer did not distract him from what was coming over the horizon. In time, he would predict that commercial airliners would cross the Atlantic in as little as six hours, though no one had ever flown across the ocean before; that Japan would launch a sneak attack on Pearl Harbor, eighteen years before it actually happened; and that a strike by a single airplane near the New York Stock Exchange would one day paralyze "the financial center of the Western Hemisphere." That his prophecies were largely ignored did nothing to dim his conviction. Born and raised to be sure of himself, Mitchell was the rare officer who had no fear of his superiors. He enjoyed total faith in his own senses and searched for the biggest megaphone to broadcast his ideas, uninterested in the potential fallout.

Those who accepted him loved him. But it was a realistic love, one that recognized that the full Billy Mitchell experience was a roller coaster whose tracks had not yet been completed. He drank too much, ran out of money often, and had a habit of bending the truth for his own ends. Mitchell was "very likable and has ability; his ego is highly developed and he has an undoubted love for the limelight; a desire to be in the public eye. He is forceful, aggressive, spectacular," one of his superiors whom he often clashed with later wrote. "I think I understood quite well his characteristics, the good in him—and there was much of it—and his faults."

The future had been his obsession since he was a nineteen-year-old undergoing military training in Florida in hopes of seeing action in the Spanish-American War. It was there that he was assigned to the US Army Signal Corps, which at that time was attempting to determine how the emerging technologies of the automobile, the dirigible, and the camera would shake the bounds of tradition. No longer, Mitchell understood, would history be shaped by guns, horses, and cannons. Instead, information, technology, and the coming age of speed would transform ideas and ingenuity into the most powerful weapons of the next century. He was young at a moment when the world felt like it had been reborn, and he wanted to grow along with it.

He arrived in Cuba in December 1898 just in time to witness Spain's formal surrender. He spent the next eight months supervising the construction of 137 miles of telegraph line through dense jungle, proving that he was more than just a senator's son. Not long after, he led a signal company through mosquito-filled swamps in the Philippines to hang telegraph wire there, and in 1901 he traveled by dogsled during the bleak Alaskan winter to build a telegraph system for the territory. "Mitchell's realization that Nome could henceforth communicate with New York at the speed of light was the first in a series of his Signal Corps experiences which shrunk the world for him," a biographer later wrote. He slowly moved up the chain of command, impressing his superiors with requests to tour battlefields during the Russo-Japanese War and his command of tactics used during the Civil War. At the age of thirty-two, he had earned a spot on the general staff in Washington, the youngest person ever appointed to the army's most elite rung.

His interest in developing the tools of the new century naturally led him to the airplane, a machine waiting to be embraced by the country that invented it. Whether from doubt that safe long-distance flight was possible or from a lack of demand due to having more miles of railroad track than any other country on Earth, Americans showed little interest in the air. Aviation became an arena full of charlatans and daredevils, each one willing to push the limits in hopes of money or attention. Gustave Albin Whitehead, a German immigrant living in Bridgeport, Connecticut, briefly became famous when he claimed he had flown a motorized aircraft for more than seven miles in 1902. Yet when twenty thousand people gathered in Morris Park in the Bronx for a demonstration of flying machines in 1908, his aircraft was nowhere to be found, cementing the impression that even the most celebrated designers were frauds. "If [Whitehead] had made such spectacular flights, he had apparently forgotten the secret, for he failed to fly at Morris Park or anywhere else people were watching," noted one historian.

The Wright brothers' success did not translate into the birth of a bustling aviation industry in America. The two former bicycle mechanics had used the impression that they were on the margins of society to their advantage. Even after their initial demonstration at Kitty Hawk, North Carolina, a local newspaper editor in Ohio didn't find their test flights worthy of coverage, which gave them the freedom to hone the Wright Flyer without pressure from crowds or investors. One or the other of the two men could often be found soaring above the treetops outside of Dayton, tracing wide figure eights above the uncaring farmland. Driven more by the challenge of invention than by its potential commercial benefits, the Wrights were initially unable to come up with a price when the War Department asked to buy their machine. They eventually asked for $100,000—roughly $3.1 million today—but agreed to take $25,000.

What the Wrights did care about were their ideas. They initially refused to license their patents, prompting their most prominent competitor, Glenn L. Martin, to follow suit, creating a blizzard of competing lawsuits that all but froze the American aviation industry before it had a chance to sprout. In 1914, eleven years after the Wright brothers completed the first powered flight of a heavier-than-air aircraft at Kitty Hawk, a total of forty-nine American-made airplanes were sold in the United States. Of those, thirty-four were exported elsewhere. The demand from foreign buyers, however slight, was considered a good sign, given that

American planes were seen as poor substitutes for those designed and manufactured in Europe. Sensing the inevitability of conflict in which airpower could turn the balance, France and Germany had emerged at the turn of the twentieth century as the leaders in the field of aircraft engineering, with France holding nearly all world records for flight and Germany dominating the field of airships. "Everything aeronautical coming out of America is always taken with a grain of salt here," the London-based secretary of the Royal Aero Club told the *New York Times*.

The US military saw little distinction between airplanes and balloons, the latter a technology that had been used on battlefields since the Civil War. A balloonist was seen as a giant periscope, useful for directing artillery fire and communicating enemy troop movements through a series of relayed messages. There was little reason to think that airplanes— uncomfortable, unreliable, and slow—would be capable of providing much more than that.

Mitchell had once been among the doubters. "Now the offensive value of this thing has yet to be proved," he said in testimony before Congress in 1915. "It is being experimented with—bomb dropping and machines carrying guns are being experimented with but there is nothing to it so far except in an experimental way." Nor was there a pressing need to try. The country, after all, was protected on both sides by oceans, making the navy the natural point of military emphasis. Congress appropriated just $1.8 million for all forms of military aviation in 1916, less than half of 1 percent of its budget for the navy. Even if Washington had wanted to, there were few manufacturers in the country that it could turn to. At the start of World War I, just five American companies had proven that they were capable of producing more than ten airplanes in a given year.

The path toward irrelevancy would have continued if not for Billy Mitchell deciding to climb into a cockpit himself. He took his first ride as a passenger in 1916 after he had been promoted to major and placed in temporary command of the army's aviation section. Suddenly, after more than a decade of searching for the future, Mitchell saw it was already here. An instant convert, he began taking flying lessons, and when the army refused to pay for them, given that he was too old and too married to qualify for pilot training—the army restricted eligibility to young bachelors, given the high death rates—he spent nearly $1,500 of his own money for twenty-five hours of flight time. Flipping his plane onto its back after one rough landing did not deter him in the least. "What did

I do wrong?" he asked his instructor as soon as he climbed out of his upside-down seat. He took to the skies again, ready to lead a division consisting of 46 officers, 243 enlisted men, and 23 aircraft. These were the aerial capabilities of an army so bound to tradition that it still required its pilots to wear spurs.

When the United States formally entered the Great War on April 6, 1917, Mitchell was among the first to reach the front lines. He accompanied French soldiers to the battlefields and sat in trenches, watching planes duel in combat as bullets whizzed over his head. Soon he was flying as a passenger in French observation planes, and before long he had his own two-seat French-built SPAD airplane that he paid his mechanic to decorate with his personal insignia, a silver eagle he'd copied from the dollar bill against a red field. Mitchell sent constant messages up the chain of command demanding more American airplanes and more decision-making power for the pilots rather than the "non-flying officers [who] should not be entrusted with work they cannot possibly know anything or very little about," he wrote.

His commanders quickly tired of Mitchell's insistence that airpower was going to be crucial in a war fought with machine guns and poison gas. "We had no planes to fly, no organization to train them, and no facilities to sustain operations," wrote General Benjamin Foulois, an early army aviator who arrived in France in the fall of 1917 to take over air command from Mitchell, a man he loathed. To Foulois, Mitchell's total faith in aviation was at best a distraction, given that there were no American-made planes available in Europe, a humiliating reminder of the puny capability of American aviation that would not be remedied by the end of the war. "The expression on Mitchell's face was pathetic," Foulois later recalled of the moment he was told that he had been demoted. "He turned gray and his jaw sagged open in shock as if I had kicked him in the groin."

Mitchell was not one to back down even after he had lost. On his sleeves he wore a pair of mother-of-pearl cuff links he'd found in the bag of his younger brother, John, after he died during a botched landing attempt in France in spring 1918. Billy just had to look at them to remember the stakes as he helped plan what would become the largest attack by aircraft the world had ever seen. A multinational force of nearly fifteen hundred Allied aircraft was assembled in France to clear the way for the first major American ground offensive in the war, finally giving

Mitchell a chance to show his countrymen the capabilities of airpower on a grand scale.

The attack was set for September 12, 1918. At a time when few officers at his level of power remained near the front, Mitchell was frequently seen walking out of planning sessions and into the cockpit of his personal airplane, which he flew over the German lines for firsthand updates on enemy positions. On the morning of the assault, Mitchell's plane was among hundreds of Allied aircraft taking to the air despite low clouds that left some pilots disoriented and unable to find their way home. Bombers demolished German ammunition dumps and railways; fighters strafed retreating forces and horse-drawn wagons with machine-gun fire. Mitchell made repeated flights in his own plane, watching to see how closely aircraft in combat adhered to his theories. Within four days, the Battle of Saint-Mihiel was over, and Allied tank divisions led by George Patton advanced deep into the western front after years of stalemate. The war ended two months later.

Mitchell, his reputation as a military genius secured, received the Distinguished Service Cross, the nation's second-highest military decoration, and was promoted to brigadier general. He became the new face of American aviation, so renowned that French pilots celebrating in Paris after the armistice was signed jumped on the hood of his vehicle and cheered, *"Vive notre général américain!"* On his voyage home aboard a commercial ocean liner, Mitchell peacocked across the decks of the ship in full uniform each morning, confident that he was leading his country to its destiny. "No one ever had a better time being a general," noted a reporter who was a passenger on the ship.

He returned to Washington to find military bureaucrats attempting to stuff innovation back into its box, apparently desperate to maintain the old order. Within three days of the signing of the armistice, the US government canceled more than one hundred million dollars in aircraft contracts. Within three months, a booming industry that had churned out 14,020 aircraft in 1918—nearly seven times more than its output the year before—had shriveled to 10 percent of its wartime peak. The sudden turnaround briefly forced the Boeing Airplane Company in Seattle to pivot to building boats and furniture to keep the lights on. With each passing day, it seemed as if the army was attempting to erase the idea of the airplane from the collective mind by destroying the evidence. Nearly all American planes that remained in France at the end of the war were stripped of their parts and burned. Thousands of engines sat idle, with no machines to put them in, not far from warehouses that held more than thirty million feet of aircraft-grade lumber collecting dust.

The few planes in the United States had a diminishing pool of pilots available to fly them. Rapid demobilization in the months after the war's end slashed the number of officers in the US Army Air Service from twenty thousand in 1918 to thirteen hundred a year later. Those who remained stateside after the war had little to do and found ways to entertain themselves, prompting the army to send out a memo prohibiting "the shooting of wild fowl with machine guns from airplanes." After touring a military airfield in Virginia, one of Mitchell's aides noted, "The spirit de corps was very noticeable on account of its total absence."

Sitting in what Mitchell saw as his rightful seat leading the US Army Air Service was Major General Charles T. Menoher, once the star of the West Point choir and now the walking embodiment of military tradition. Whereas Mitchell saw airpower as key to winning the next great conflict, Menoher believed that success would depend largely on ground forces, with aircraft in, at best, a supporting role. Though not the head of the air service, Mitchell expanded his role as head of its training and operations group and attempted to sway it toward his aims. Mitchell had no intention of staying in the shadows, and he quickly let others know that. "The General Staff knows as much about the air as a hog does about skating," he told reporters, the first volley in what became an ongoing crusade to prod Washington to follow Britain's lead and create an air force separate from the army or navy.

The nation's rejection of aviation in the immediate wake of the Wright brothers had been forgivable at a time when the capabilities of aircraft were unproven. Now, however, airpower had shown its deadly capacity in battle, and Mitchell feared the country would be vulnerable if it kept ignoring this violent new reality. If he did not act, he realized, then America would be fighting its twentieth-century wars with nineteenth-century technology and tactics. "I cannot conceive of any use that the fleet will ever have for aircraft," proclaimed Admiral William S. Benson, the chief of naval operations who disbanded the navy's aviation division at the conclusion of the war. "The Navy doesn't need airplanes. Aviation is just a lot of noise."

While publicly confident, privately Mitchell felt his grip on reality loosening as his focus on airpower began to take on an air of mania.

Never one to control his drinking or spending in the best of times, he grew increasingly erratic. Menoher asked the secretary of war to fire him. His marriage disintegrated in spectacular fashion when his wife, Caroline, forced him out of the house in September 1920 after he accidentally shot her while drunk on moonshine. Months later, Mitchell was required to sit for a psychiatric evaluation at Walter Reed in order to remain in his position. Though he was on the edge of ruin, his focus was unbent, and he plotted ways to change the course of a dream that had become intertwined with his own life. He knew that only an eye-catching demonstration of the future he saw coming would save him.

He sponsored the first coast-to-coast air race, put on touring exhibitions featuring stunt flying, led squadrons of airplanes on mock bombing runs over New York City, and—in a pointed move—at the US Naval Academy at Annapolis, Maryland, did anything he could to get the public to engage with the airplane at a time when most aircraft were used to deliver the mail or spray crops. Nothing broke through. He needed to think bigger to get attention, and he found what he was looking for in the navy's greatest assets: battleships. "The air will prevail over the water in a very short space of time," Mitchell told reporters, arguing that aviation would make navies "almost useless." He insisted that planes could destroy moving targets by dropping bombs from above, and he goaded Josephus Daniels, the secretary of the navy, into agreeing to let him publicly attempt it using a captured German dreadnought. "I'm so confident that neither Army nor Navy aviators can hit [a battleship] when she is under way that I would be perfectly willing to be on board her when they bomb her!" Daniels reportedly told his contemporaries.

On the morning of July 21, 1921, eleven army bombers flew through bright and clear skies to the *Ostfriesland*, once one of Germany's most feared instruments of war, anchored fifty miles off Virginia's Cape Charles. Dozens of politicians, War Department officials, foreign military representatives, and reporters crammed onto the deck of the nearby USS *Henderson*, the photographers' cameras rolling. Mitchell circled high above in his personal plane, the *Osprey*. Just after 12:15 p.m., the attack squadron approached in formation and began dropping two-thousand-pound bombs. Each of the six explosives landed a few yards away from the 546-foot-long ship, the pilots following Mitchell's order to avoid scoring a direct hit. He instead expected concussion waves produced by the underwater blasts to tear the ship apart at its seams.

The first bomb came up short; the second rocked the ship; the third tore a hole in its forecastle; the fourth lifted the hull upward and threw a wall of water over the deck; the fifth pushed the nose of the ship skyward and sent the first of its big guns underwater as the stern began to sink; the sixth, which was later judged unnecessary, accelerated the *Ostfriesland*'s descent, exposing barnacles glistening on its belly as it sank into the deep. "It was as if the Washington Monument had been placed slantingly in the sea, with its base ploughing into the sand," the *New York Times* reported. Twenty-five minutes after the attack started, the great ship was underwater. "This shot will ring around the world. That's been said before, but it's true," said an officer of the British navy in attendance as he stared at the space where the *Ostfriesland* had recently floated.

Mitchell relished the praise raining down on him in the days immediately following the test. "The achievement was a great triumph for the intelligent, strong-willed, persistent Assistant Chief of the Army Air Service, a leader who asks no subordinate to take any greater risks than he is willing to face himself," the *New York Times* editorial page noted, adding, "It is pleasant to remember that Brig. Gen. William Mitchell won many decorations for his gallantry and daring in France." But as Billy Mitchell edged closer to finally achieving his goal, he could not help getting in his own way. Unable to contain himself, he wondered aloud whether a navy was truly necessary, displaying none of the political skills required to convince Congress to change how it spent the nation's money. Mitchell had believed that a demonstration of the future of airpower was all it would take to convince skeptics, and he could not understand why months and then years went by without any progress. The navy's position was that the method used to sink the *Ostfriesland* was fundamentally unrealistic and unlikely to be replicated in real-world scenarios. "I once saw a man kill a lion with a 30-30 caliber rifle; under certain conditions," said Theodore Roosevelt Jr., the assistant secretary of the navy. "That does not mean that a 30-30 rifle is a lion gun."

While Congress debated whether to increase spending on aviation and build the nation's first aircraft carriers, Mitchell was ordered to Europe and then the Far East, muting his influence. He vowed to make the most of his time away from Washington by learning more about the aviation capabilities of other nations. These statements did little to conceal his frustration. After grabbing the spotlight and demonstrating to the nation that airpower was the future, he had essentially been thrown off the stage. He had proved that he was right; he realized now that it didn't matter.

Two years after what he thought would be his signature victory over his doubters, he filled the long hours in Honolulu reading newspapers and writing letters, attempting to remain influential despite the thousands of miles separating him from all the things he thought mattered. He had already done everything he thought possible: demonstrated that an airplane could fly across the United States; shown that the nation's largest cities were vulnerable to air attack; sunk a battleship. There was only one option left that would prove to America the need to control the skies. He dialed a number in Washington and waited for his chance to convince the person at the other end that the time had come for his last, best idea.

CHAPTER TWO

A Reverend's Son

I

T SHOULD HAVE been him.

Death draped over the life of Lowell Smith, its presence as familiar as a blanket. As a child, he had spent his Sundays in a hard pew listening to his father preach about the coming Day of Judgment. Other days of the week gave no respite. The hours of a minister were filled with funerals, and Lowell, the second of the family's four children and the eldest boy, turned into his father's shadow. He learned from a young age to be quiet and fade into the background, the goal to make as little an impression as possible. His father's ministry took him from Santa Barbara to Spokane, Washington, and back down to the Los Angeles suburb of San Fernando, but Lowell's proximity to death remained the same.

Now, as a lean thirty-two-year-old with startlingly blue eyes, heavy eyebrows, and a soft chin that made him look timid, Smith listened as the familiar wail of an ambulance signaled the end of another young pilot's life just a few weeks before families across the nation would sit down to Thanksgiving. Though he was in no position to change the outcome, Smith felt responsible all the same. For the past month, Smith had been a temporary flight instructor at Kelly Field in San Antonio. There, he taught students how to curtail their fears and use them in the cockpit, to rely on cold logic to save them when their emotions ran hot. A cadet who attempted anything too daring was gently reminded of Lieutenant George E. M. Kelly, the namesake of Kelly Field, an Irish immigrant who in 1911 was thrown from his plane after one of its wings clipped the ground. To fully relax in the cockpit, Smith told his charges, meant accepting that your life could be taken away in an instant, no matter what you did up there. A pilot "may figure every [thing] right and kill himself in [a] crash," an early aviation writer noted. "He may break every rule in the science of aviation and live to brag about it. There are graves near an American training school in France which never should have been there, according to the same rules."

Five months earlier, Smith had been the first pilot in the world to successfully refuel while in the air, and he saw it as his duty to pass on his knowledge to those willing to learn. Though officially based in Oregon, he traveled to army airfields from San Diego to New York, instructing others how to fly like him. Few pilots, however, had as instinctive a feel for their aircraft as he did, and they struggled to replicate his technical skill. Smith often consoled them that it simply took practice and patience, two resources that were within the reach of anyone who wanted them.

On this November morning in 1923, he stared up at a dark sky. More than fifteen thousand people were packed into temporary grandstands at Kelly Field, all drawn by the promise of an air show. The Wright brothers pioneered such spectacles of stunt flying by forming what was known as the Wright Exhibition Team in June 1910 in order to supplement their income and demonstrate the capabilities of their machines. Yet the deaths of several pilots while performing prompted the Wrights to quit the practice by November 1911, pushing aviation further to the margins. By the start of the 1920s, most Americans had never seen an airplane in real life, much less flown in one. As part of Billy Mitchell's plan to promote aviation, air bases across the country often opened their doors and put on shows featuring pilots doing everything from flying in loops to racing laps around the field.

The weather for today's show could not have been worse. Rain soaked the wooden grandstands and dirt runways of the field. Given the rudimentary technology of the time, flying in even fair weather was considered dicey; flying during a rainstorm was done only out of necessity. Pilots would normally never think of taking to the air in these conditions. Yet, because of the audience, they felt compelled to go on.

Smith watched as his former students banked and turned their squadrons of planes in formation, as synchronized as a flock of birds. One soared as high as his aircraft could take him, becoming a faint speck against the gray sky. Finally, the audience's attention turned to Paul Wagner, who at the relatively advanced age of thirty-three was among Smith's oldest pupils. Smith saw him fly a long oval around the field in order to get a feel for the wind and then lift skyward. Another plane joined his and settled into position for refueling, a daring maneuver that before today had never been attempted in the rain or at low altitude. But Wagner, forced to choose between showmanship and safety, had decided to give the people what they wanted. He leveled off just a few hundred feet above the ground, a volatile space for an aircraft due to the strong gusts caused by friction between the air and the ground. If Wagner had flown higher, the crowd might not have been able to see him through the rain.

Wagner, the pilot of the fueling plane, flew just a few feet above his partner and dropped a hose down for him to catch. The other pilot grabbed it and secured it to his own tank. The two aircraft, now joined by the taut line running between them, passed in front of the grandstands to applause. A sudden blast of wind rocked Wagner's plane and pushed it lower. With the planes nearly on top of each other, the hose line grew slack and hung limp in the air, threatening to become tangled in a propeller. Wagner pulled back on the control stick to create some separation. As he did, the hose line caught the right wing of the other aircraft and pulled it hard into the underside of Wagner's right wing. In an instant, Wagner's wing sheared away. He had no time to react. Seconds later, his plane slammed into the Texas field and caught fire.

Smith had had no idea that Wagner was going to attempt such a complicated maneuver under such harsh conditions. He was neither Wagner's superior nor his close friend and he had been in no position to stop him. Yet he felt the burden of guilt just the same. Perhaps he hadn't explained things well enough, he thought. Perhaps he'd let Wagner feel too confident in his abilities. Perhaps. Perhaps. Perhaps.

As with every accident he witnessed, Smith wondered why it hadn't been him. Certainly he was due. For some pilots, the ever-present closeness of death in a cockpit fueled nihilistic abandon, all but compelling them to drink as much as they could from life's cup because it could be snatched from them tomorrow. Yet for Lowell Smith, who had always felt death walking nearby, the inevitability of the grave instilled in him an unwavering morality, grounded in the sense that judgment was imminent.

Where others might wear their righteousness on their sleeves, Smith from an early age took the opposite approach. His mother would later say that he was "never inclined to be boisterous in his play," a family trait of moderation that she traced back to one of her great-great-uncles, the frontiersman Daniel Boone. Smith's reserve, however, masked his compulsion to do what he saw as right. As a child, he had pulled up all the flowers in the family garden and replanted them in an order he thought was better. Later, a few years after he finished high school, he worked as a mechanic in an automobile repair shop in Los Angeles until he laid down his tools and crossed the Mexican border to join the revolutionary army of Pancho Villa. No matter that the United States had sent some five thousand soldiers into Mexico to capture the rebel leader—Smith saw Villa as a modern Abraham Lincoln fighting to free Mexican peasants from bondage. He soon became the engineering officer in charge of the three planes that constituted the revolutionary army's air force. When two of the planes crashed and the third was so riddled with bullets that it could not take off, he gave up and returned to the United States, still looking more like a librarian than a revolutionary. "Lowell to many people is an enigma," a friend later said. "They don't quite know how to take him because he usually wears a poker face."

In all ways but one, Smith never allowed his inner passions to reach the surface. The only glimpse he gave the world into the fires that raged within him was through the power of the engine. Speed, he found, soothed him. No other experience unified the parts of his brain that loved the solitude of tinkering with machines with the parts that sensed death was always near. In his view, going fast compelled someone to do the right thing, both mechanically and morally, in order to survive. When he was behind the wheel of a car or in the seat of an airplane, life was a problem finally fixed.

That a powerful engine let a quiet person get away from the burden of talking with others sealed his love for them. As a twenty-one-year-old, he had raced a Model T Ford from Los Angeles to San Diego to Phoenix along unpaved desert trails that the local press called a "death-defying run." As a twenty-five-year-old, he had taken his first flying lessons as a US Army Air Service recruit and was such a natural that the military wouldn't let him go to France and instead kept him stateside in Texas to work as an instructor. And as a twenty-seven-year-old, he soared above various cities from Chicago to Boise, taking part in mock air battles in a drive to sell war bonds. The deafening roar of his plane's propellers made it difficult for him to speak with anyone for nearly an hour after he landed, a problem that for Smith was no problem at all.

Nothing, it seemed, could shake his cool exterior. While he was flying in an air show over Portland, Oregon, his plane's propeller splintered in midair (authorities were never sure if it was an accident or if someone in the crowd had fired a shotgun). Smith's plane came down hard in a field at Twenty-Sixth and Gladstone Streets and somersaulted in the muddy earth. When a local man raced up to see if he was okay, Smith responded by calmly asking for a cigarette.

His superiors realized what they had on their hands. Here was a man who craved the freedom of speed and movement yet was bound by a deep sense of morality and fairness—an ethos, it appeared, that remained constant even in the cockpit. Whereas others would allow excitement to turn into carelessness, Smith remained as vigilant in the air as he was on the ground. For him, flying faster, soaring higher, and banking sharper than anyone ever had were acts without emotion, a controlled chain of reason that somehow added up to audacity.

The reverend's son was a natural racer. Less than a month after the air-show circuit ended, the US Air Service had Smith in a Packard-Lepère, a French-designed fighter plane built in the United States that was the army's preferred experimental aircraft during the Great War. On his first test run, Smith flew from DeMille Airfield in Los Angeles—built by prominent movie director Cecil DeMille—to San Diego's Rockwell Field in forty-seven minutes, covering the one hundred and twenty-five miles six minutes faster than anyone ever had before. A month later, he shattered the record time from San Francisco to Los Angeles, prompting the local press to call him "a demigod off for a new conquest of the heavens." Not long after, he set a new national record for the highest speed ever achieved in an aircraft. "Science has passed another milestone in the annihilation of time and space," the *San Francisco Examiner* crowed. The attention was the one thing he hadn't counted on. When asked by a reporter what record he would topple next, Smith mumbled, "I may make better time back to San Francisco, but I want to get there before doing any more talking."

In the fall of 1919, Smith was one of more than sixty military pilots who entered what General Billy Mitchell dubbed the first Transcontinental Reliability and Endurance Test. To win, a pilot had to fly across the country and back again, showing the American people that such a thing could be done. Two groups of pilots—one starting in New York, the other starting in San Francisco—raced over a 5,400-mile loop, their paths following the railroad tracks below.

Smith was among the first to take off from the Presidio in San Francisco, and he completed the first leg to Sacramento ten minutes faster than his closest competitor. He kept his lead as the race pushed eastward, landing in Salt Lake City before anyone else. He was there drinking coffee when a de Havilland plane piloted by Major Dana Crissy went into a tailspin seventy-five feet above the ground and crashed into the airfield, killing him and his mechanic, Sergeant Virgil Thomas. The tragedy did not stop the race. Flying was interwoven with casualty, and the question facing the remaining contestants was not whether there would be another death, but who it would be. The next day, as Smith flew through a blizzard to Cheyenne, his controls froze. Snow stung his eyes and ice accumulated on his hands, but his thoughts were on those who might not have the skill to survive. "It was impossible to see more than a few hundred feet ahead of us and it was necessary to fly at an elevation of about fifty feet to do this," he told reporters that night. "I was very much worried about the safety of the pilots following me through the storm."

After several stops and a total of twenty-four hours and thirty minutes in the air, Smith reached New York before anyone else in his group and readied himself for the return trip. "We expect to be the first ones to reach the Golden Gate," he told reporters. While Smith grabbed a meal in Buffalo, he left his plane in the care of mechanics who, due to their unfamiliarity with the type of aircraft or possibly simple error, accidentally replaced kerosene with gasoline when flushing the plane's oil tank. Within seconds the aircraft burst into flames. Smith returned to find himself without a plane. Unwilling to concede, he approached a competitor who was near the rear of the pack and, with the quiet skill of persuasion learned at his father's knee, convinced him to drop out and let Smith take his aircraft. "I wanted to fly bad, and he was simply good enough to give me the ship and his chance," Smith told reporters. Six days later Smith reached San Francisco, the first pilot from the West Coast to complete the round trip.

The race back and forth across the country did not have the galvanizing effect on aviation that Mitchell had hoped for. Aircraft and those who flew them remained on the margins of American society. That was where Smith felt the most comfortable. He notched more records—the longest endurance flight and the fastest flight from Mexico to Canada, among others—before the US Air Service decided to use Smith's prowess in the air for more than glory-hunting. Aircraft rescue patrols were relatively new and untested, given that the pilots themselves were often the ones who needed rescuing. Smith was placed in command of a squadron based in Eugene, Oregon, that would fly over dense green forests searching for fires before they grew deadly. Each pilot would battle clouds, elevation, and wind, well aware that the lack of flat, open spaces to land provided little recourse when something inevitably went wrong.

Smith was unfazed by the assignment and took over as captain in charge of the US Air Service's Ninety-First Aero Squadron. Over the next three years, he and the men under his command flew thousands of miles without a fatality, a streak unmatched in a field where death was the one constant. There were several near-misses, such as the time when a disabled camshaft forced Smith to land in the dark near Roseburg, Oregon, a city that its mayor proclaimed "is taking no interest in a landing field." As he waited for new parts to reach him, Smith passed the time by fishing for rainbow trout in the fork of a river.

For him, accidents were not a reason to panic but another paragraph in a story whose ending was unknown. Unmarried at a time when many of his peers had families of their own, Smith looked to the air as a way to give his life meaning. He had flown back and forth across the country; pushed machines to their fastest limits; kept the men under his command alive far longer than even they thought possible. Built to chase the horizon, Smith searched for the next thing that would combine his quiet spirituality with the thrill of speed.

It came in the form of a rumor. Word spread through the US Army Air Service in the fall of 1923 that Billy Mitchell was planning something big, a flight so audacious that its record could never be broken. Soon, a group in Washington began accepting applications from pilots and mechanics who wanted to volunteer for a mission that many in the military thought had no chance of success. No matter. Mitchell had accomplished the impossible before by sinking a battleship, and there was no reason to think he couldn't do it again. A total of one hundred and ten officers applied, roughly one out of every eight eligible men in the US Air Service.

Smith was among those who put their hats in the ring. Though he had an unimpeachable résumé, he did not expect to be chosen. The sense among pilots was that Washington would not select anyone who had already participated in a record-breaking flight, instead searching for fresher, younger faces to use in advertisements. Left unsaid was that the potential talent pool was restricted to white Christian men, tossing aside aviators like Eugene Jacques Bullard, the first and only African American pilot in the Great War. When his own country would not let him fly, he enlisted in the French Foreign Legion, in whose service he downed several enemy aircraft while in the cockpit of a plane on which he had painted a heart and a dagger and the words *All Blood Runs Red*. Female pilots were roundly ignored. Bessie Coleman, the first Black woman to earn a pilot's license, had to move to France to find an instructor willing to train her, and upon her return to Chicago began a career performing in front of desegregated crowds at air shows. Bessica Raiche, a white woman, made the first recognized solo flight by a woman in the United States, lifting into the air in a plane that she designed and built with her husband. She later founded and led a company that produced airplanes on Long Island before becoming one of the nation's first female gynecologists.

Smith could list the negatives against the military choosing him as easily as he could his achievements: he had flown too many high-profile missions; he was not gregarious in an organization that rewarded the feeling of brotherhood; he was too far away, serving in the deep forest, for anyone to remember him; he was too quiet to matter. Yet a few days before Christmas 1923, Smith received a terse order to report to Langley Field in Virginia, an air base that was little different than the farmland surrounding it. He was given no information other than the time and date he was expected to appear.

For nearly two decades, Smith had relied on the power of speed to fill the holes dug by his worries. It had taken him far away from his father's church and across the country and turned his boyhood fantasies into reality as he soared above the weight of his concerns. Flight had long offered clarity, but now, for the first time, he did not know where it would lead.

CHAPTER THREE
The Whole World Round

IN THE FALL of 1923, making a complete circuit around the Earth was, although not easy, certainly doable if you had enough time and money. Ocean liners would bring you across the blue parts of the globe; trains could take you through most of the green and brown sections. Horses—or, in the worst case, your own feet—would fill in any remaining gaps. American journalist Nellie Bly had used all of the above to circle the globe in seventy-two days in 1889, cutting short a lunch outside of Paris with Jules Verne, whose novel *Around the World in Eighty Days* had inspired Bly's attempt, in order to catch a train. "I looked at the watch on my wrist and saw that my time was getting short," Bly wrote. "There was only one train that I could take from here to Calais, and if I missed it I might just as well return to New York by the way I came, for the loss of that train meant one week's delay."

As more trains and ships dotted the Earth's surface, time replaced distance as the measure of travel. A New York theatrical producer and lyricist by the name of John Henry Mears circled the globe in a record thirty-five days in 1913, traveling 21,066 miles from Manhattan and back again. "We affirm that the beauty of the world has been enriched by a new form of beauty: the beauty of speed," Italian poet and future Fascist leader Filippo Tommaso Marinetti wrote in a manifesto celebrating what he saw as a coming utopian era built on the output of engines. In terms of land and sea, the planet had been mastered; the only spaces left to explore lay at the extremes of ice and heat.

No one, however, had ever fully circled the Earth from above. Breaking the tether of gravity for that distance required developing technology that allowed an aircraft to withstand all the planet could throw at it. The list of potential obstacles was endless. What would you do about fuel? Food? Supplies? Just considering the big questions was enough to make flying around the world seem more like a theoretical exercise than something that could happen in real life.

Yet the temptation was too great. If mankind harnessed the air, it would effectively shrink the planet, making crossing an ocean as inconsequential as walking over a bridge. No longer would distance get in the way of human desire. Perhaps due to this lure, early attempts at flight drifted toward a voyage around the world. And no wonder—attempts to circumnavigate the globe are "the longest tradition of human activity done on a planetary scale," historian Joyce E. Chaplin wrote. "Around-the-world travelers make a grand gesture, as big as the physical world itself, even though they are individually so small that the huge global stage on which they act makes them hard to find."

In 1783, Joseph-Michel and Jacques-Étienne Montgolfier, sons of a wealthy paper manufacturer in southern France, invented what is now known as the hot-air balloon. They demonstrated it with a twenty-five-minute trip over Paris, the first exhibition of piloted flight in history. Not to be outdone, in 1804 Belgian aristocrat Guillaume-Eugene Robertson proposed the first world-circling flight aboard a yet-unbuilt airship to be named the *Minerve*. He envisioned it as a huge balloon with a cabin capable of holding sixty scientists who would make geographical, astronomical, and meteorological observations en route. The ship would be large enough for a laundry, a kitchen, and, ambitiously, a music hall. Its exterior would be crafted of raw silk and take the shape of a rooster. That Robertson's proposals were roundly ignored by potential investors affirmed his belief that he was on to something. "The opinion of certain savants who have never discovered anything and who, seated at the fireside with their compasses, never seek the unknown except in the known, need not alarm the genius," he wrote in a pamphlet seeking sponsorship in Vienna. "Time is with him, maturing everything, disclosing sooner or later new levers to human power in the arts, in chemistry and mechanics." The *Minerve* was never built, and Robertson turned his attention to building robots instead.

Blimps—variously known as dirigibles, zeppelins, and airships—are essentially steerable balloons with engines, and for some time they appeared to be the most likely vessel for an around-the-world flight. The first known airship design, which was never tried, was created by Italian naturalist and Jesuit priest Francesco Lana in the late 1600s and based on fellow Italian physicist Evangelista Torricelli's 1640 discovery that air

had weight. Airships and balloons work by taking air out of a hollow
sphere and replacing it with a gas that weighs less than the air surrounding it, causing it to float. Until the Wright brothers, no one had proved
that heavier-than-air machines could become airborne. Both methods of
human flight—airplane and airship—seemed deeply flawed, and well
into the twentieth century, it was not at all clear which technology would
prevail. "I always fancied the dirigible against the airplane for the overhead haulage in the years to come," English novelist Rudyard Kipling
wrote in 1920.

The first attempt to cross the Atlantic by air came in 1910, when the
America, a 228-foot-long airship originally designed to fly over the North
Pole, launched from Atlantic City, New Jersey, with a crew of six. No
one thought they could do it. "We will make those blooming critics eat
their own words," Murray Simon, the ship's British navigator, wrote in
his logbook. Their strategy for crossing the ocean was not much more
detailed than flying eastward until they spotted land. "While the plan is
to follow the steamer tracker the best we can, we do not aim to make a
landing at any particular place, nor even in any particular country . . .
any spot between Gibraltar and the North Cape will look good to us,"
said Walter Wellman, an American journalist and adventurer who led
the expedition.

Minutes after takeoff, Kiddo, a stray cat that one of the airmen had
brought aboard for luck, began darting around the airship "like a squir-
rel in a cage," Simon wrote in his logbook. The crew took a vote and decided to expel Kiddo from the ship by means of a canvas bag lowered to
a group of journalists who were following below the airship in a motor-
boat. In what may have been the first air-to-ground voice transmission
in history, the *America*'s radio operator yelled, "Roy, come and get this
goddamn cat!" to his counterpart in Atlantic City. Dropping a cat onto a
small boat from a moving airship proved too difficult, and the *America*,
Kiddo still aboard, elevated once again into the dense fog. Within twenty-
four hours, heavy winds forced the airship to descend so low that sea
spray splashed its lifeboats. The crew began planning to abandon ship
as their gasoline level plummeted, resulting in another groundbreak-
ing moment for the *America*'s radio operator, who had the distinction of
making history's first aerial distress call. A passing mail steamship, the
Trent, rescued the crew of the *America* northwest of Bermuda, ending a
voyage of just over a thousand miles and seventy-two hours in the air.

"We sacrificed the airship but we saved our lives, and above all, we have gathered a vast amount of useful knowledge which will help largely in the solution of big problems relating to the navigation of the air," Simon, the navigator, wrote. "And we also saved the cat!"

Crossing an ocean by airplane hardly seemed easier. Unlike airships, planes required constant refueling and designated places to land, making the great span of sea a daunting obstacle. "Such an attempt would be the height of folly," Orville Wright wrote in 1914, noting it would be impossible for a craft to hold enough fuel to carry it the distance required, even at the lowest known energy consumption. "The Atlantic flight is out of the question."

That did not stop people from trying. The organizers of the 1915 world's fair in San Francisco, the Panama-Pacific International Exposition, offered one million dollars (roughly thirty million dollars today) to anyone who completed a round-the-world flight in any form, as long as it started and ended on the exposition grounds. Hoping to stir interest, the organizers published an itinerary of twenty-eight stops that would theoretically complete a circuit of the world in ninety days. Refueling in Iceland and Greenland would solve the range problem. "The English, who were at first prepared to scoff, now admit the race is entirely feasible and genuine," the *New York Times* reported. "The detail with which the projected flight was worked out had convinced them that it was genuine and no mere American bluff." Guglielmo Marconi, the inventor of the radio, pledged that his entire organization of radio operators would be at the service of any round-the-world aviators.

Yet the hurdles—chiefly, constructing a craft that was both durable enough and light enough to fly great distances—had not been overcome as the competition's start date drew near. No one proved willing to attempt a world flight, leaving hometown hero Lincoln Beachey, perhaps the world's most famous stunt flier, as the fair's main aerial attraction. Beachey's wizardry in the air—which included tricks such as flying loops and recovering from intentional tailspins—had led the press to dub him "the Man Who Owns the Sky." "An airplane in the hands of Lincoln Beachey is poetry," Orville Wright said. "His mastery is a thing of beauty to watch." His brilliance inspired other pilots to attempt his feats, often killing themselves in the process. The death toll weighed on Beachey, who in 1913 announced that he was quitting flying so that no other imitators would get hurt.

Two years later, fifty thousand spectators crowded near the water as the thirty-one-year-old Beachey once again climbed into the cockpit and flew a series of somersaults over San Francisco Bay in a monoplane with his last name painted in big black block letters on the undersides of its wings. On his second flight of that day, March 14, 1915, Beachey flew low above the water while attempting to straighten out after completing a giant loop. His plane's wings suddenly crumpled, forcing the aircraft into an uncontrolled spin. It plunged into the cold Pacific near Alcatraz Island. Dozens of pleasure boats raced to the crash site, their passengers hoping to free Beachey before the craft took him under. No one was successful. Two hours later, navy divers located the plane, and it was hauled up from forty feet deep. Beachey was still strapped in the cockpit's seat. The words "Hats off to Beachey" ran through the stunned crowd, and soon "almost every man in the great packed mass of humanity bared his head," the *New York Times* reported in a front-page story the next day.

And so it went. Around-the-world flight in an airplane seemed doomed to end in failure, death, or both. But despite the odds, dreamers kept coming up with new approaches to an apparently impossible task. In the spring of 1917, Glenn Curtiss—whom Alexander Graham Bell considered "the greatest motor expert in the country" and who had been locked in patent disputes with the Wright brothers for years—built what was essentially a flying boat at the request of US Navy officials, who thought it would be useful in patrolling for submarines. None of the planned ships, known as NCs, were finished by the end of the war. Hoping to demonstrate its command of the seas to a Congress looking for places to cut military funding, the navy assembled crews of six sailors to pilot each of the three NCs across the Atlantic. The aircraft, which could fly as high as three thousand feet, was designed to land with its hull directly on the surface of the water, unlike seaplanes, which landed on pontoons sitting underneath their bodies like skis. The navy positioned forty-four of its vessels along a planned flight path that stretched from New York to Newfoundland to the Azores to Lisbon, Portugal, and equipped each one with backup engines, replacement parts, and lights to guide the planes at night across the dark ocean.

In May of 1919, not long after a propeller accident that took the hand of the chief machinist of the flight, the planes rose from Naval Air Station Rockaway in Queens, New York. Things went downhill quickly. One plane became lost in the fog and landed far off course. Twelve-foot-high waves rocked the ship and prevented it from taking off again. The crew of the stricken plane refused to give up and, cementing the idea that their machine was more boat than airplane, sailed the downed craft over two hundred miles through high seas to the Azores. A passing Greek freighter rescued the crew, who watched their craft sink not long after. Another plane landed near Newfoundland and had to jettison one of its crew members and all of its radio equipment because the aircraft proved too heavy to take off again. The third plane, NC-4, lost power in its engine and had to land in the open sea near Cape Cod, where it was outfitted with a new motor and propellers.

Its crew pressed on. After twenty-three days and numerous stops, the repaired NC-4 arrived in Plymouth, England, completing the first aerial crossing of any ocean. Two weeks later, two amateur English pilots, John Alcock and Arthur Brown, completed the first nonstop crossing of the Atlantic, flying through a snowstorm from Newfoundland to Ireland without the use of their radio after it shorted out in the freezing air. They landed twenty miles off target, surprising the locals in the small village of Clifden. "I rushed outside to investigate," Harry Sullivan, a local boy who was seven years old at the time and home with the measles, later recalled. "I was just in time to see this greyish-colored machine swopping over the main street. Its two propellers were whizzing around and its huge wings nearly touched the top of the church. I was amazed. I had heard of flying planes but I had never seen one before . . . where had the machine come from, and where was it going?" Staff members at the local wireless station initially refused to believe the pilots' tale, despite Alcock repeatedly telling them, "Yesterday we were in America." Only when he produced a sealed mailbag from St. John's, Newfoundland, did the locals start to accept what had happened. Alcock and Brown won prize money offered by the *Daily Mail* equivalent to $1.1 million today, though few pilots appeared willing to follow their lead.

With one ocean now conquered, engineers studied ways to cross the more daunting Pacific. In Chicago, early aviation writer Henry Woodhouse passed on rumors of a design for an electric plane with a 6,000-horsepower engine that could hold seventy-five passengers and would be capable of circling the world. Nothing came of it. (The first electric plane did not fly until 1973, and as late as 2023 the record distance for a battery-powered flight was 155 miles.) A straight shot across the width of the Pacific was impossible, given the more than five thousand miles separating San Francisco and Japan. A plane would instead have to land along the frozen coasts of Alaska and Siberia, putting its pilots in conditions that seemed inhospitable to flight.

The first serious attempt at a round-the-world flight via airplane took place in 1922. Sir Ross Smith, who a year earlier had become the first to fly from England to Australia, prepared to soar over France, Egypt, India, Japan, Alaska, and Iceland before returning to the United Kingdom via Scotland. Smith, however, died in a crash less than three weeks before his planned world flight. Major W. T. Blake of the Royal Air Force took his place at the last minute. He had trouble from the start. His first crash-landing came near Marseilles, France, where he shredded his propeller and running gear. His second came two months later in Sibi, modern-day Pakistan, where the undercarriage of his plane smashed into the ground. The third came near what is now known as Chittagong, Bangladesh, after he ran out of gasoline. Unable to continue due to illness, Blake was replaced by two captains in the Royal Air Force, who attempted to press on along his planned path. They did not have an easier time. Within hours of taking off from southern India en route to what is now known as Myanmar, their seaplane developed engine trouble. They made a forced landing in the Indian Ocean and drifted for fifty hours without food or water before they were rescued. "The attempt of Major Blake around the world has been beset with difficulties and mishaps," the *New York Times* wrote in what proved to be the eulogy for the mission.

Blake's troubles did not deter others from trying. In early 1923, British and French pilots separately announced their intention to complete a world flight. The British were led by the Legion of Frontiersmen, a group founded by writer Roger Pocock made up largely of members of the upper class who were bored with city life after the thrill of war. "Roger decided to achieve something spectacular or die in the attempt," a biographer later wrote. For pilots, Pocock chose Norman Macmillan, a former Royal Air Force officer, and British film director Geoffrey Malins. After studying Blake's attempt the previous year, Pocock sent sixteen yachts crewed by men who called themselves "gentlemen adventurers" to points around the world to act as a supply line.

The flight made it as far as India before the plane broke down over the Bay of Bengal, a loss that Macmillan blamed on the work of a local mechanic who had never seen an airplane before. Their fate was slightly better than that of the thirty-nine gentlemen adventurers aboard the *Frontiersman*, which was stuck in Los Angeles Harbor. "Their yacht has been seized by Federal officers for violation of the liquor law and libeled by commercial firms twice for alleged debts and their ship's surgeon has been stricken with malarial fever," the *New York Times* reported. "Their bank roll admittedly is short, and fears were expressed that their supply of food would be exhausted today. Many of the men aboard the ship are World War heroes and they have never worked as longshoremen, but they are said to consider that work as a probability."

The French attempt consisted of five former military pilots flying in five planes painted in the national colors. To pay for it all, the pilots announced that they would participate in exhibitions and competitions along the way. Their ambitious route would take them east across Egypt, India, and Korea before crossing the Pacific. Once that was done, they planned to fly down the western coasts of North and South America as far as Chile, pass over the Andes to Argentina, finally cross the Atlantic on a flight from Brazil to Dakar, then head to French West Africa.

The squadron took off on April 1, 1923, a decision that their captain had made "in spite of the fact that it is All Fools' Day," a reporter noted. Two planes immediately developed engine trouble and crash-landed while attempting to turn back. A third crashed an hour later. Of the five originally expected to circle the globe, only two made it across Europe. But once again, India proved too hazardous for an airplane to handle, and the French effort ended before either plane reached the Pacific. Chile remained an item on their list of dreams and nothing more.

Billy Mitchell knew the history, but it did not scare him away. In fact, the implausibility of a world flight just made him want it more. Until now, Mitchell had maintained the reputation of American aviation mainly through stunts. American pilots were the first to fly a distance as great as New York to San Francisco nonstop; the first to sink ships; the first to fly higher than twenty thousand feet. Records were something to brag about when there was little else to point to, keeping up the spirits of pilots and engineers who feared that the United States would never spend the same amount of money on planes as it did on ships. "We hold every airplane record that was ever known, if there is one around that we don't know of, and if someone will tell us of it, we'll proceed to take it," Mitchell said, as if running up the score would replace funding from Congress. (Other countries found the American focus on records silly, given the nation's paltry fleet of planes and engineers; one French official scoffed, "There is nothing behind it.")

The failure of English and French pilots to fly around the world in 1923 left Mitchell hungry to show that Americans could do it first. He was not alone. Circumnavigation, once the province of dreamers and outsiders, emerged as the culmination of a quest stretching back to the Renaissance to find the rules of flight. There was no organization putting on a race, no set boundaries for starting points or finish lines. Instead, the idea seemed to be the logical end in a field that made the once impossible achievable. Flying around the globe became the ultimate proving ground that would demonstrate the skills of a nation's pilots and engineers. England announced that its pilots would again attempt to fly around the world in 1924. France soon followed. Not to be outdone, pilots in Portugal, Italy, and Argentina decided that they, too, would compete. (Germany, which had had a proud history of airships prior to the World War, was forced to end nearly all of its aviation industry under the conditions of the Treaty of Versailles and for nearly two decades trained its pilots in secret.)

For the first time in history, a race to fly around the world was on. Mitchell clamored for the United States to launch a flight of its own, if only to inspire the country to keep doing big things in the air. One problem was obvious: If Europe, with its more advanced planes and pilots, couldn't produce a craft capable of circling the globe, then how could the comparative backwater of America meet the challenge? During the war, American pilots had flown in European-designed and -manufactured aircraft, and it remained rare for an American air show to consist solely of domestically made and designed planes.

In addition to the question of whether the nation could do it, Mitchell grasped that if he truly wanted to put his country on a different course, he had to face another problem: himself. Any plan that was seen as his pet project would run into instant friction in Washington simply because his name was attached. If America was going to win, it would have to do so without the fingerprints of a prophet who understood the importance of aviation better than anyone else in the country. Mitchell felt most at ease in the spotlight, willing through his force of personality to bend the production his way. Now, however, he needed to remain offstage, his influence felt but not seen.

Throughout 1923, Mitchell worked in the shadows, sending US Air Service lieutenants on pathfinding trips through Greenland, Alaska, the Aleutian Islands, and the Faroe Islands that doubled as scouting trips for a world-flight route. Unlike the proposed plans laid out by Europeans, Mitchell envisioned a flight that headed west in the spring, into the prevailing winds. This would theoretically avoid the extremes of the seasons by crossing the North Pacific after the worst of winter and reaching India before its summer monsoons. What's more, no one had ever flown across the Pacific before, making it possible for America to claim a record even if its attempt to circle the globe failed. Flying westward, however, meant a daily battle with the wind, which would run up the cost of fuel and increase the probability of the unplanned. Mitchell added more stops to the proposed route. At each stop, he wanted to have a military cargo ship waiting with food, fuel, and shelter, providing the supply chain required for a pilot to circle the globe and offering the hope of rescue if something went wrong.

It was a plan that might be adopted as long as no one knew that it came from him. Fighting the inclinations that had driven him since childhood, Mitchell stepped to the side and allowed Major General Mason M. Patrick, the chief of the US Army Air Service, to act as the catalyst for the flight. The son of a surgeon who had served in the Confederate army, Patrick became perhaps the nation's oldest pilot when he took his first flying lessons at the age of sixty. He was placed in charge of the air service before he knew how to fly. Quickly, however, he learned that Mitchell, for all of his faults, saw clearly where the world was headed. "Undoubtedly the next war will be decided in the air," Patrick said in a speech not long after returning from Europe that earned him no friends in the navy.

With Mitchell as his confidant, Patrick officially announced in late November 1923 that the United States would launch an attempt at a world flight in 1924. "The Air Service has endeavored during the last few years to foster the development of aviation in spite of the limited funds available, and though we still lag behind the world powers in the size of our air force and in the commercial use of aircraft, the Army Air Service has brought to this country many aeronautical records of importance and has done much to place America in the lead in airplane performance and development," Patrick wrote in a long opinion piece in the *New York Times*, hoping to build public support for an American entry into the unofficial race to circumnavigate the globe. "The successful completion of the proposed flight will further stimulate interest in commercial aviation and will likewise demonstrate the importance of aircraft in national defense."

Patrick knew that his support in Washington was tenuous at best. The same month that he announced the plan, navy officials bickered among themselves about whether to supply the ships along the route that would be necessary if the American aviators were to have any chance of survival. In memos sent back and forth, navy brass debated staging their own attempt at a world flight without the input of the air service and trying to squelch Patrick's proposal before it went any further. "The disadvantages, at this time, seem to have more weight," Rear Admiral William R. Shoemaker wrote. "When funds are available, and the ships can be diverted from other duties, the Pacific part of this flight would be valuable. I do not think the publicity argument—'beating the world to it'—is of much weight," he added.

Rear Admiral William A. Moffett, who often clashed with General Billy Mitchell over whether airpower should become a separate force in the military, unexpectedly came to his rival's aid. "A flight 'round the world is the surest, quickest, and cheapest test of the capabilities and limitations of aircraft," he wrote in a long memo outlining his support for the plan Patrick announced. "We think we shall be able to operate aircraft with the fleet anywhere in the world by the time the next war comes along, but we haven't proved it. It's high time we started to prove it before we are too far along in placing reliance on aircraft. Maybe we're placing too much faith in aircraft. Maybe we aren't placing enough."

Still, Moffett could not stand by while the US Army Air Service upstaged the navy. As Patrick readied the world flight, Moffett drew up plans to send the airship *Shenandoah* from Seattle to the North Pole in February, beating the Army Air Service to a long-desired prize. It would then cruise over all of America's chief cities and fly around the world to the South Pole. (President Coolidge eventually canceled Moffett's plan, viewing it as not worth the cost.)

America entered the race to fly around the world as a distinct underdog. Little about its aviation industry—its engineers, its manufacturers, or its pilots—suggested that the nation possessed enough raw skill to overcome the towering disadvantages of being underfunded, underappreciated, and ignored. Its best hope was that an unsuccessful attempt would spur the innovations necessary to keep it from falling further behind. With the nation's pride on the line, Patrick—with Mitchell in his ear—assembled what became known as the World Flight Committee, a group of the nation's military and civilian aviation experts who worked largely in secret.

If American aviation was to remain relevant, it needed to make a good showing on the global stage. And for that to happen, the country needed to build a plane capable of doing the impossible.

CHAPTER FOUR

"An All-American Airplane"

THE COUNTRY THAT was the birthplace of flight was not very good at building airplanes. This was the first uncomfortable fact in what proved to be a long stream of them that America had to face if it wanted to make a round-the-world flight a reality. With the windfall of war spending behind them, the US Army Air Service relied heavily on European-designed aircraft for nearly every task. An American circum-navigation powered by European know-how would undercut its accomplishments, signaling that it relied on the engineering genius of other nations to provide what it could not do alone.

"The best airplanes to be used for such a flight are at present undoubtedly DH-4Bs . . . although this airplane, as it stands today, is practically an American product with an American engine, nevertheless, its basic design is that of the British de Havilland, together with Handley-Page wheels [which] makes this airplane essentially a British product," the staff of the US Army Air Service engineering division wrote in a report on possible aircraft for the world flight. "It would be highly desirable to make a flight of this nature in a thoroughly American airplane." Given "the structural changes we have made in the de Havilland airplane, it might be feasible to give it an American name," the authors added. Yet, perhaps recognizing that this sham would quickly unravel, they ultimately recommended devoting what little money was available to "[make] this flight within two years with an all-American airplane."

Patrick didn't have two years. Already, America was far behind its European rivals and would be lucky to launch any entry—European-designed plane or not—in the world race in the coming year. With time getting away from them, Patrick and the World Flight Committee began a desperate search for an existing American-made plane that could do what no other aircraft in the world had done before.

This hopeless task fell to Lieutenant Erik H. Nelson, a man who, at the age of thirty-six, had a lifetime of experience turning far-fetched ideas into reality. As a child in Stockholm, Sweden, he grew bored with elementary school and talked his engineer father into enrolling him in night courses on mechanics. When he was sixteen, wanderlust propelled him to sign up as a crew member on a ship that took him across the Atlantic for the first time. By the age of twenty, he had sailed around the world twice and taught himself English with the help of magazines. While on leave in Hamburg, Germany, he heard that wealthy Americans were paying good money for sailors to race their yachts. He arrived in Hoboken, New Jersey, in the spring of 1909, a few months shy of his twenty-first birthday. By the start of summer he was aboard the ship of a New York millionaire, basking in the sun and spray of the Long Island Sound.

From there he sampled a bit of everything his new country had to offer. He worked as a masseur and a swim instructor at Fleischman's famous three-story Turkish bathhouse just east of Times Square; played a Roman centurion in Oscar Hammerstein's Manhattan Opera House production of *Salome*; and ran a small automobile-repair shop in Miami. It was there that he encountered aircraft for the first time when a stunt pilot came in looking for someone to fix his engine. The customer never paid him and Nelson soon had to close his shop and bum rides back to New York City with only twenty-two cents in his pocket, but he was hooked.

Flying became the center of his peripatetic life. When war broke out in Europe, he tried to enlist in the Lafayette Escadrille—a French air force combat unit made up largely of American volunteers—but was rejected. He then moved to Buffalo and worked at the Curtiss Aeroplane Company, where his talents for building and testing engines were quickly recognized. Yet he longed to enlist as a pilot. An attempt to join the Royal Air Force after crossing the border into Canada failed because he was, at the age of twenty-five, considered too old for training; further efforts to join the Army Air Service in New York were also denied. Finally, in October 1917, he was accepted into a training program at Cornell University, where for the first time in his life he received formal instruction in the machines that had become his obsession. He quickly became more adept than his instructor. When asked where he'd learned to do such work on aircraft, he replied that he'd gone to the College of Gasoline and Oil.

In April 1918 he was in Texas, finally in a cockpit of a bomber in service to his adopted country. The war ended before he reached Europe, but his love of being in the air was just getting started. He flew more than seven thousand miles across the country on recruiting trips for the army; became the first person to fly over the Grand Canyon and photograph it from above; worked as the chief engineering officer of an expedition that flew from Long Island to Nome, Alaska, and back without a single engine failure. "Erik is one of those individuals who can dream and make his dreams come true," a friend later said.

The ability to manifest hope into action gave him a sense that anything he put his mind to was not just possible but probable. As soon as he heard rumors of an American world flight attempt, he volunteered, even though at the time the plan for the expedition consisted of little more than pencil marks on paper. All he knew was that General Patrick and the World Flight Committee expected to outfit a squadron of four planes, each of them with a pilot and a mechanic. (A plan to send six planes, with two teams of three flying around the world in opposite directions, was scuttled because of the fear that the Americans would start racing each other.) The Americans' approach differed from that of all other countries, which were ready to place their confidence in a single aircraft and crew, as if designating a knight to joust for honor. "The Army Air Service believes in the maxim that there is safety in numbers," Patrick later said.

Though he was praised for his technical abilities, Nelson was considered by some members of the World Flight Committee to be too old for the task. Given that some other pilots under consideration to command the squadron were older, concerns about Nelson's age were a convenient cover for the nation's prejudice. Though Nelson was blond-haired and blue-eyed, he was an immigrant at a time when a wave of xenophobia was surging through the United States, tainting anyone not born in the country as suspect. Instead of a seat on the crew as a pilot, Nelson joined the World Flight Committee as its equipment and engineering officer.

Forced to sit with the knowledge that his background meant more to Americans than his skills, Nelson spent the spring of 1923 trying to find a domestic machine that had at least a chance of circling the globe. It was not easy. There were few manufacturers to choose from, and the aircraft they built were held in low regard, prompting some overseas competitors to dub American-made planes "flying coffins." At the time, the longest nonstop flight in US history—from New York to San Diego in May 1923—was accomplished in a German-made monoplane designed by Dutch engineer Anton Herman Gerard Fokker. His machines were considered perhaps the best in the world, a reputation reinforced by the armistice agreement's demands that Germany immediately surrender all its Fokker planes. Fokker's most recent design, the Fokker F-5, was specially made for long-distance flight, with a wide cockpit that increased the comfort and visibility of pilots, larger fuel tanks, and an alignment that enabled a pilot or mechanic to easily access the engine and make minor adjustments while the plane was in the air.

The United States had nothing that could compare. With little government funding and few commercial uses for its products, the American aviation industry limped along without a clear purpose. Its fate appeared to be, at best, supplying the workforce to build foreign designs. American genius, when it appeared, seemed in a hurry to get off the stage. The Wrights had no interest in developing a line of planes once they had established that heavier-than-air flight was possible. They went into business mainly to protect their patents and soon sold their company to investors. After a short-lived wartime merger with competitor Glenn L. Martin, the newly established Wright Aeronautical focused on building aircraft engines in its plant in Paterson, New Jersey, leaving others to take up the mantle of invention. Martin, who'd built his first plane in a rented church in Los Angeles with the help of his mother, turned his attention to bidding for the dwindling number of government contracts, often manufacturing the designs of rivals at costs far lower than what they could manage themselves.

Glenn Curtiss, who had battled the Wrights over patents, felt the sting of canceled orders in the aftermath of the war, and in 1920 he decided to cash out his $32 million in company stock (equivalent to roughly $503 million today) and move to Miami. There, living in a large two-story Pueblo mansion that his wife named Dar-Err-Aha (which she said meant "House of Happiness"), Curtiss bought up hundreds of acres of real estate and began developing what became the cities of Miami Springs and Opa-locka during the first Florida land boom. In Seattle, Yale dropout William Boeing was keeping his struggling company alive with Army Air Service contracts to modernize British-built de Havilland fighter planes.

The demands of a world flight seemed beyond the capabilities of any aircraft, no matter who made it. The basics of getting a heavier-than-air machine airborne were by then well established: Speed created a difference in pressure between the air on top of a wing and the air below it, which resulted in a force that lifted the wing upward. Keeping an aircraft aloft was a balance between speed and weight. Engines capable of producing faster speeds were often heavier, negating their benefits, and aircraft that were exceedingly light often struggled to retain enough forward thrust not to be tossed about like a kite. Biplanes, which had two sets of wings, usually stacked one on top of the other, offered one solution to this dilemma: They increased the total surface area of the wings without adding as much weight as the one set of longer, heavier wings of monoplanes did. The drawback, however, came in the interference caused by the pressure difference between the two sets of wings, which created drag and required more fuel consumption.

An aircraft capable of flying around the world would need to solve the problem of range and be sturdy enough to withstand arctic winds, ice-strewn bays, broiling deserts, and torrential rains. Nelson toured manufacturing plants across the country and spoke with each of the nation's leading designers, hoping to find someone with an answer. Despite Washington's insistence on using an all-American aircraft, he drew up a proposal recommending the selection of the Fokker F-5. Before he filed it, however, he made one last stop at a company housed in a former movie studio in Santa Monica, California, and run by an unfailingly serious twenty-eight-year-old who personally disliked flying.

The youngest son of a bank cashier in Brooklyn, Donald Douglas grew up listening to his father tell tales of the sea, all the while dreaming that he would one day have his own adventures to share. Yet his life path changed in 1908, when he was on hand for one of the first public demonstrations of the Wright Flyer at Fort Myer, an army base near Arlington National Cemetery outside of Washington, DC. He watched as Orville Wright and army lieutenant Thomas Selfridge took the Wright Flyer skyward, to the delight of a crowd. Within minutes, the plane's propeller snapped, and the craft plummeted to the ground. Orville Wright was knocked unconscious and broke his leg and several ribs. Selfridge's skull was fractured. He was taken to the hospital but later died of his injuries, making him the world's first fatality in a powered aircraft.

Despite the horror he had seen, Douglas was drawn to the possibilities of flight. In 1909, he followed his older brother into the Naval Academy in Annapolis, expecting to finally live his own stories. No matter how much time he spent on the water, he could not ignore the lure of aviation, and he often made rubber-band-powered model airplanes in his dorm room at Annapolis. When his older brother died from appendicitis while aboard a naval ship, Douglas resigned from the academy and followed his passion by transferring to the Massachusetts Institute of Technology. There, he earned the first degree in aeronautical engineering offered by the university, completing the four-year program in just two years, and designed one of the first airplane wind tunnels in the United States.

Douglas felt no desire to sit in the cockpits of his creations, making him the rare airplane designer who preferred to remain on land. His days were ordered by precise routines. He woke up every morning at seven thirty without the need of an alarm clock, ate the same breakfast (one egg, one piece of white toast, and one cup of black coffee) every day at eight, and sat down in the same spot in his office by nine, his Scottish family's coat of arms and motto *Jamais arrière* (Latin for "Never behind") prominently displayed on his desk. "Donald Wills Douglas is a tall, good-looking, brown-eyed, brown-haired, brown-tweedy sort of man," a reporter for *Time* magazine wrote in 1943. He "is a precision instrument himself, a man of almost fantastically unvarying habit, and of a simple efficiency that is metronomic in its ticktock exactitude."

Douglas toiled in solitude in part because he had little patience for others. In Los Angeles, he worked for Glenn Martin, who was dismayed to find that his new chief engineer looked much younger than his age of twenty-three. Douglas abruptly quit when he discovered that Martin's approach to innovation was based on trial and error rather than theory, a method that he considered shockingly dangerous. "There was practically no engineering, it was all done by good judgement," Douglas later said. "When I got there, they made no detailed drawings of anything. So when I told the people I was going to give Martin detailed drawings, they all said, 'The boy is crazy—it can't be done.'"

A short stint as the chief civilian aeronautical engineer of the US Signal Corps followed, but he could not stand the bureaucracy. Douglas returned to working for Martin, who had relocated the company to Cleveland, Ohio. There he directed the design and construction of the Martin GMB bomber, the first American warplane that could compare with anything built in Europe. Its first flight took place on August 17, 1918, and by the time it was ready for production, the armistice had been signed.

Only ten were ever built. The cancellation of war contracts brought out Martin's less attractive personality traits—he was prim, socially clumsy, constantly adrift between the shores of vanity and insecurity—and Douglas made plans to go into business for himself building civilian aircraft. When Douglas told Martin this, Martin laughed in his face and said there was "no better way of going broke than building commercial planes in Southern California," Douglas recalled.

Douglas returned to Los Angeles with his wife, two sons, and six hundred dollars in cash hoping to go into business for himself. With money tight, he rented the back room of a barbershop on Pico Boulevard and sat at a drafting table designing planes while waiting for investors to materialize. When they did not come as quickly as he'd hoped, he resorted to washing cars and planting potatoes in his yard to support his family. Finally David R. Davis, a wealthy businessman, asked if it was possible to build a plane that could fly nonstop across the country. Douglas said he could do it with the right resources. With a $40,000 investment (equivalent to roughly $625,000 today), the Davis-Douglas Company was formed and began operations in a loft above a lumber mill.

Construction on its first product, a biplane called the Davis-Douglas Cloudster, started in July of 1920. In February, it became the first aircraft in history to carry a load that exceeded its own weight, which caught the attention of the military. In March, it set an altitude record of 19,160 feet. In June, however, its maiden attempt at a transcontinental flight ended on the runway due to an engine failure. Davis suddenly lost interest in the aviation business and looked for a way out. He agreed to maintain ownership of the prototype plane and received two thousand dollars in cash from Douglas in exchange for all the company's assets, from its blueprints to its wrenches.

Douglas renamed the business, and the Douglas Aircraft Company was born. Douglas borrowed money from his father-in-law, took out a bank loan guaranteed by Harry Chandler, the powerful publisher of the Los Angeles Times, and got to work. A few months later, Douglas signed a contract with the US Navy to build what became known as the DT-2, a two-seat, aluminum-clad biplane that was among the navy's first bulk purchases of domestic bombers (the D stood for Douglas, the T for torpedo). Within the span of two years, Douglas had gone from the backroom of a barbershop to signing a contract to produce forty-one planes for the navy. His future finally looked secure.

The success of the DT-2 brought Lieutenant Erik H. Nelson to Douglas. There, in the company's factory at 3000 Ocean Boulevard, which was so close to the Pacific that you could feel the sea breezes coming through its open windows, Nelson inspected both the aircraft and its maker. Douglas, for all of his genius, had a reputation for an inability to work well with others. That alone could have been enough for Nelson to move on. A designer who agreed to build an aircraft for the world flight would have to submit to the demands of a committee and a squadron of pilots, a task requiring a well of patience that Douglas never possessed. His contract to build the DT-2 had relied on his vision alone, freeing him to pitch it to the military instead of trying to adhere to a set of demands.

A world flight, however, would be different. Douglas had lost the chance to build the first plane to fly across the country, a feat that would no doubt have brought in more business. Here was an opportunity to make his company's name relevant to a global audience and prove the superiority of his designs. He was not so far away from washing cars and sought a measure of vindication to make up for the hours lost to doubt and desperation. Taking on the task, however, could upset the security that he had finally found. The rivalry between the navy and the army often extended to their suppliers. Building an experimental aircraft for the US Army Air Service without the guarantee that a world flight would happen might upset his most important customer.

For the first time, Douglas had to choose between the two sides of himself. The engineer craved the chance to solve the largest puzzle; the businessman wanted the predictability that permitted him to provide for his family. In what would prove to be the largest gamble Douglas, a man known for his conservative approach in all things, ever made, he agreed to work with Nelson to modify the DT-2 into a machine suitable for a world flight and to do it within six months.

It was a pairing that allowed each man to fill in what the other was missing. Douglas, who rarely flew, provided the theoretical basis for pushing the aircraft to its limits; Nelson, who never formally studied engineering, pushed back with practical insights gained from hours in the air. Together, they began experimenting with the craft, with Douglas adding or changing a component and Nelson testing it by soaring above the palm trees of Santa Monica.

Their first problem to solve was range. The existing DT-2 could fly about 275 miles before it needed to refuel, a figure that was low even among bombers. Douglas added fuel tanks wherever he could, wedging them in the upper wing, the firewall that separated the engine from the cockpit, and under the pilot's seat. He managed to up the gas capacity from 115 gallons to 644, empowering the aircraft to fly nearly two thousand miles but also drastically increasing the likelihood that a fire on board would quickly turn catastrophic. The range issues settled, Nelson and Douglas turned to fine-tuning the aircraft to make it both durable and responsive. The changes came one after another, like dominoes falling in a line. They enlarged the radiator, redesigned the cover of the engine, expanded the rudder to improve pilot control, cut out a portion of the upper wing to boost visibility, strengthened the pontoons, replaced the wooden rear fuselage with steel, and finally moved the back seat, known as the observer's seat, forward to make it easier for the pilot and mechanic to communicate with each other over the thrum of the engine and propellers. In one nod to comfort, Nelson convinced Douglas to increase the padding in the seats to a luxurious three inches instead of one.

The new aircraft began to reveal itself with each modification, emerging like a sculpture from a block of marble. It was fifty feet long across its wings; thirty-eight feet from its propeller to its rudder; thirteen feet and seven inches tall from the wheels to the tip of its top wing. When completely empty, it weighed three tons; when loaded and with a pilot and mechanic, it weighed over four. Power was supplied by a Liberty engine, which had been developed by the US government at the start of the war and mass-produced by the nation's early automobile manufacturers. (The design, with its distinctive hum and attractive weight-to-output ratio, became the standard for American machines for the next two decades, appearing in automobiles, speedboats, airplanes, and tanks through World War II.)

Its speed topped out at 103 miles per hour. Its ceiling, or the maximum height at which it could fly safely, was a relatively low five thousand feet, dictating that it stayed clear of mountains. A wheel in the cockpit and rudder bar at foot level allowed a pilot to steer left or right, while a yoke operated the hinged horizontal sections of the wings known as ailerons that moved the craft up or down. The same controls were also found in the rear cockpit, so either member of the crew could fly at any time. A baggage and tool compartment sat behind and beneath the back seat, not far from a hand-operated wobble pump that could power the engine in emergencies. Small glass windshields were placed at the front of each seat, though they offered little defense against the elements. Fliers still needed goggles and leather helmets that acted as both protection and insulation from temperatures that dropped severely with increasing altitude. When the need arose, funnels known as relief tubes permitted a man to urinate while still seated in the cockpit, the waste sprayed out behind the aircraft into the atmosphere.

For instruments, the pilots had a tachometer, which displayed the revolutions per minute of the propeller; an air-speed indicator; oil-pressure and gasoline-pressure gauges; an altimeter, which told them how high they were flying; meters for the plane's electrical system; and controls that let them change the amount of gasoline fed into the engine based on altitude. Navigation depended on the newly invented earth inductor compass, which used a wind-driven generator to create a current that interacted with the Earth's magnetic field. Once a pilot set a course, he simply had to keep the compass dial pointing to zero to ensure he was on the correct path. (Charles Lindbergh depended on an earth inductor compass in his solo flight from New York to Paris in 1927, although it stopped working as he neared Ireland.) Two small gyroscopes functioned as a bank and turn indicator, ensuring that a pilot could keep the wings steady when flying in fog.

If all other navigation instruments failed, a small compartment held a sextant so that crew members could chart their location by the position of the sun or moon. There was nothing else to help if they became stranded or lost. Though radio transmission was available, the plane contained no such technology. Forced to choose between the added weight of a bulky system and the performance of the aircraft, Douglas and Nelson opted to bet on the skills of pilots to get themselves out of any jam.

Forty-five days after they started, Douglas and Nelson stood before the first prototype of what was christened the Douglas World Cruiser. Nelson put it through a final set of preliminary tests in Santa Monica and then flew it across the country to Dayton, Ohio, where it was inspected by other members of the World Flight Committee. Among them was General Patrick, who flew the airplane over the Ohio farmland where the Wright brothers had perfected their craft. When he landed, his first comment was that he wished he were "young enough to go on this great undertaking."

The prototype was taken to Virginia and outfitted with pontoons. A lieutenant named Ernest Dichman put the Douglas World Cruiser through a series of tests in Chesapeake Bay, loading the plane with more and more weight to determine its limits. It passed. In September 1923, Washington approved the purchase of four Douglas World Cruisers. Each plane cost $22,221, slightly more than $401,000 today. Each was expected to be completed within three months, a nearly impossible deadline given the constraints of the small Douglas workforce.

America, against all odds, finally had its plane. Now it had to find pilots capable of flying the country into a new era.

CHAPTER FIVE

The Proving Ground

A
s LOWELL SMITH passed through the front gate at Langley Field on a cold December morning, he had the sense that he was entering a cemetery. Four ruined hangars and the skeletal frame of a bomber slumped ahead of him, the charred remains left by a fire less than a year before. Not far away, empty steel sheds that had housed nearly two thousand men during the war sat rotting in the low winter sun. The structures that remained in use—a hospital, a mess hall, and a handful of hangars—were little more than garages, impossible to heat in winter or cool in summer. Nearly half the buildings on the air base, the largest in the country, were temporary constructions, a polite term meaning they could fall down at any moment. A wet, bitter wind blew in from the adjacent bay, threatening to hasten the process.

The profound sense of desolation was unnerving. For some, it was a few short steps to desperation. Ten months before Smith arrived, two corporals stationed at the base kidnapped its chief finance officer and two of his assistants in an attempt to steal the payroll of $43,000 (nearly $780,000 today). At the men's arraignment, one of them told the board of inquiry that "life was not worth living the way things were going with us, and we decided to get some money and have one real fling or get killed in the attempt." The barren streets and buildings exaggerated the loneliness of those who endured.

Despite a postwar economic depression that left many men looking for work, the US Army Air Service struggled to fill positions, so the wide runways of Langley were quiet for much of the day. Few young Americans, it seemed, were willing to sign up for a job that appeared so closely linked to death. In its three years as a formal combat arm of the army, the air service had accounted for nearly half of all military casualties, despite its minuscule number of personnel. Four of the streets on the base—Thornell, Mabry, Harris, and Hillard—memorialized crew members killed in February 1922 when the *Roma*, a hydrogen airship the American government had purchased from Italy, crashed after taking off from Langley with thirty-four aboard. The newly named Roma Road ran parallel to the site of the now-empty airship hangar, which was nicknamed Roma by men on the base.

Yet what Langley lacked in people, it made up for in purpose. The base was "undoubtedly the finest airplane landing field on the entire Atlantic Coast," said Thomas Dewitt Milling, an early pilot who received the first US military badge awarded to an aviator. No other place in the country had such a wide variety of aircraft and people willing to test them. Five bomber squadrons flew planes ranging from newly built Martin bombers to leftovers from the war; service squadrons took off in flying boats; photo sections buzzed through the air in biplanes and tiny Sperry Messengers. Anything went, as long as your goal was getting airborne. Failure—in design or in execution—was expected, given the might-as-well-try ethos of a service that knew it was starting from nothing. In one unused corner of grass sat the remains of the Johns Multiplane, a seven-winged experimental bomber designed by a New Yorker named Herbert Johns who had attempted to use the extra lifting surface area of triple-stacked wings to improve handling. The top-heavy aircraft never flew more than a few feet before landing nose-down due to excessive weight. It still fit right into an environment that rewarded effort and was willing to look past unfortunate results.

If nothing mattered to you other than flying, Langley was your heaven; if you cared about anything else, it quickly became your hell. It was a place perfect for Smith. Though he was by no means a misanthrope, building relationships with others had always felt like a chore for him. He wanted to fly and leave the heavy weight of emotion behind. Here, finally, was a place that cared little for all that. He had felt like this once before, in Mexico, where the idealism of revolution bound men together and made conversation unnecessary.

As Smith neared the main building on the base, he knew that his future lay inside. His spot on the world flight was not guaranteed. To be able to stay here, among other men who understood the joy and freedom of flying, he had to prove that he belonged. He could only hope that his pure skill as a pilot would compensate for his quiet and withdrawn nature. If the army was looking for someone to connect with and inspire others—the qualities of a natural leader often found in those in the cock-pit—he would be lucky to last one day. The alternative to being chosen, of course, was returning to Oregon and flying missions over empty forests for as long as he could stand it. His days of chasing dreams would be over. If he was ever going to make the life that he wanted, he had to begin now. Before Smith was escorted into the air base, he could not take his eyes off the planes parked outside. One of them would soon be his, and he wanted his chance to start.

Fourteen men crammed into the briefing room, the heat of their bodies the sole bulwark against the bracing cold. Each had been selected by General Patrick out of hundreds of applicants who wanted to represent their country in the race to fly around the world. They had shown themselves worthy of the assignment, the general explained. Now they had to prove themselves in action. The air service was scrappy, still young enough that there were no legacies who would have an unseen advantage. Nothing other than merit would dictate their path forward.

Each man knew the outlines of the mission, but Patrick began filling in the details. The American attempt at a world flight would consist of four planes, each carrying a pilot and a mechanic. The term *mechanic* was a misnomer, given that both men on the aircraft were expected to be able to fly the plane and repair any problems they encountered. Yet it functioned as a form of hierarchy; even if two men were of the same rank, the pilot would serve as the plane's leader, ultimately responsible for every decision necessary to keep them safe over a course of more than twenty thousand miles.

Just one man out of the fourteen gathered in the frigid Virginia countryside knew that he would be among the final eight: Major Frederick L. Martin, a forty-one-year-old Purdue University graduate who had been tapped to serve as the commanding officer of the squadron. The eldest of the men and the only one who was married, Martin was a relative latecomer to aviation. He had served on the ground during the war in France, fulfilling the prophecy of school classmates who had said he was obsessed with the idea of becoming a soldier. After a stint in the army of occupation in Germany, he returned to the United States and earned his wings at Kelly Field in Texas. He then became the commanding officer at the Air Service Technical School in Rantoul, Illinois, training nearly all air service mechanics under the base's motto: Keep 'Em Flying.

In a squadron made up of the best pilots in the country, Martin saw it as his duty to keep each man happy and ready. For now, that meant standing to the side and waiting for them to reveal their personalities. In the confined world of training exercises at Langley, Martin fell into the group as an equal, following expectations handed down from the chain of command as best he could. Yet once the mission started, Martin would ultimately decide its fate. Each morning, he would have the final say on when the men would lift off; each evening, it would be his call whether to press on or stop if something seemed wrong. His power over the other seven aviators on the world flight would swell the farther they traveled away from home, building an unspoken barrier of leadership.

Until then, finding any cracks in the assembled men vying for a spot on the squadron was the job of General Patrick and the World Flight Committee. For six weeks, tests both in the air and on the ground would try each person's abilities and prod at their weaknesses. At the end of that time, three additional pilots would be chosen. Those who were selected would then pick their own mechanics from the assembled group, forming partnerships that were expected to keep both men alive through unparalleled challenges.

So began the most grueling experiment in Smith's life. No one had ever flown around the world, so no one knew what to plan for. Initially, the World Flight Committee had expected to train its crew members in a twenty-five-week program consisting of "practicing great circle courses, night flights, flights over clouds in daytime, and a few flights over Lake Erie, testing the sextant on the horizon," according to an early planning document. But now there was no time. The British and French fliers appeared ready to take off at the first hint of spring. Others would soon follow. If America was to win the race around the world, its aviators had to be willing to fly before they were ready. The plan called for the planes to take off on their round-the-world trip by mid-March at the latest. Even then, they would most likely be starting behind.

Faced with a blank page and a ticking clock, the air service officials filled the hours with everything they could. One morning, Smith and the other twelve men competing for seats were woken up before dawn and sent on a six-mile run, after which they attended a lecture on the subject of weather forecasting. Another morning, the pilots and mechanics were tested to see how long it took them to assemble the scattered parts of a Liberty engine. They took quizzes on navigation, marine law, and the types of foods to avoid in the tropics, their grease-streaked hands struggling to hold their pencils without smearing the page. Games of tennis and basketball and sessions of tossing medicine balls appeared on their daily schedules, leaving one man to joke that he suspected they were secretly training for the Olympics. When not in the classroom or the gymnasium, the crew members were in the air, taking the prototype Douglas World Cruiser out over the Chesapeake Bay to learn the plane's quirks and suggest any improvements.

Slowly, Smith began to find out more about the men vying for the role he wanted. Like him, LeClair D. Schulze was thirty-two and from California, but the similarities ended there. Whereas Smith had had little use for the classroom and began working to supplement his family's income as early as he could, Schulze held a law degree from Stanford University. He had enlisted in the army when the war started and received his flight training in France. He stayed following the signing of the armistice, and his life seemed to lift into a higher orbit: monoplane-pursuit training in Italy; test pilot and instructor in France; an eventual return stateside to compete in air races. While he had fewer total hours in the air than Smith, his experience and education were more refined, holding out few branches between the men that Smith could cling to for connection.

The man whose life most closely mirrored Smith's own was also the youngest man there: Lieutenant Leigh Wade, a twenty-seven-year-old from Cassopolis, Michigan. In a quirk of fate, Wade had served in the National Guard in Texas during the search for Pancho Villa while Smith was on the other side of the border in Mexico keeping rebel aircraft running. Lean, with a handsome face and a mischievous smile, Wade could trace his family's presence in America to ancestors who came over on the *Mayflower,* and he appeared intent on fulfilling the family tradition of aiming for the horizon. He had left his parents' farm in Michigan as a teenager to work on a Dakota ranch, thinking that it would impress a girl back home, and he enjoyed the freedom of the frontier so much that he never went back.

He learned to fly after volunteering for the Royal Air Force in Toronto, hoping that it would be his chance to see fighting during the war. His rebelliousness on the ground translated into deftness in the air. Without trepidation, he was soon putting his plane into tailspins, nosedives, and long, elegant loops. Once he reached Europe, he was instructed to teach other pilots the maneuvers that came naturally to him as part of dogfighting training. He remained in France after the armistice was signed and began flying surplus French and German aircraft back to the main Allied depot near Tours, France, eventually sitting in the cockpit of most European machines that had wings. "Leigh has flown nearly every contrivance, both safe and unsafe, that was ever designed to leave the ground," a reporter noted. He became a test pilot after he returned to America and kept a running list of all the times he had crash-landed. Over drinks, he often told the story of when his engine caught fire while he was flying at two thousand feet, and he landed on a farm just as the flames licked at his cockpit. When he jumped out of the aircraft, his skin was so covered in soot that the farmers thought he was Black. They stood by in silent amazement when his skin color changed as he rinsed himself off with soap and water from a nearby bucket.

Besides Martin, the squadron leader, there was one man older than Smith: Erik Nelson. He had been passed over by the committee members once based on his age yet had been given a second chance because he knew the Douglas World Cruiser better than anyone other than Douglas himself. With fifteen hundred hours of total flying time, Nelson also had impressive experience in the air. Smith consoled himself with the thought that he had flown more hours and through more trying conditions, though he did not know how much that would matter in the eyes of the committee. The more he learned about his rivals, the less certain he felt that he would be among the final eight men. Not only was he out-educated and out-experienced by them, but his main qualification was as a pilot, not a mechanic. Instead of the seven possible slots on the squadron, Smith realized there were three that he could hope to fill.

Over the weeks of training, Smith recognized that one man appeared to be his opposite in every way: Leslie Arnold, a thirty-year-old who in body and spirit still resembled the teenager who had prayed his good looks, athletic build, and gregarious personality would pick every lock that threatened to keep him in his hometown of New London, Connecticut. Arnold had always been loud and happy and not afraid to let others know it. In high school, Arnold was constantly on the edge of expulsion, and when he graduated, his principal told him, "Arnold, my hand just itches to get at you." Whereas Smith often did his best to blend into the background, Arnold searched for something that could meet the passion he felt inside of him. The summer before he graduated high school, he toured New England as an actor in a summer-stock company, playing small roles in productions of *Brewster's Millions* and *The House of a Thousand Candles*. Once free from the classroom, he used his charm to sell pianos as a traveling salesman. A stint as a tobacco salesman followed, then four years building and testing submarines. When the United States entered the war, he took classes in aviation at Princeton, then refused the shackles of flight instructor once he qualified as a pilot. He "made himself such a general nuisance that his superior officers sent him to France to get rid of him," a reporter later wrote. He arrived just as the armistice was signed and spent the next several months flying recovered German aircraft. Once back home, he worked as a stunt pilot, bouncing from one excitement to another. His personal life was no more stable—an early marriage quickly ended in divorce once it became clear that Arnold had no intention of toning down his charisma because he had a ring on his finger.

Arnold, like Wade and Nelson, had flown in General Mitchell's mission to sink the *Ostfriesland* two years earlier, which helped win the confidence of the man behind the scenes of the world flight. The question of whether those three men's spots were already secure, and Gen. Patrick's competition was simply a show, ate at the confidence of those who did not have a personal connection with the men on the World Flight Committee. Smith understood that he had no recourse if the worst was true, but the belief that had led him here, so far away from the hard pulpits in Santa Barbara, still applied: the solution to most problems was simply to work harder.

The army continued to put the assembled men through rigorous exercises, their discomfort matched only by what their plane was going through. The prototype Douglas World Cruiser was taken up in fog, in wind, and in rain, conditions that it had never experienced in the sun-kissed valleys of Southern California. It was intentionally pushed past its stated capacities, as if provoking it into a tantrum. Each time it passed a test, the army came up with another. Different types of pontoons were installed. Loads up to 8,300 pounds were piled on, giving the aviators a sense of how the aircraft would handle under stress. Each tweak that the men hoping to be chosen for the flight asked for was sent via Nelson to Douglas in Santa Monica, where he was rushing to finish the four aircraft he believed would make his reputation.

The strength and maneuverability of the plane in the air was undisputed. Its fragility in the water, however, remained a concern. The world flight path would take the craft over thousands of miles of coastline, from Alaska to Japan to India, making its ability to withstand the punishment of the sea nearly as important as its ability to soar through the air. "No boats of any kind, or of any size, should come so near that they could by any chance touch any part of the plane," one army engineer involved in the planning of the mission warned in a letter to General Patrick.

At the end of February, the World Flight Committee announced the four pilots who would represent the United States in a race so grueling, so implausible, that no one was sure the pilots could finish it, much less win. Martin, of course, was the squadron leader. Nelson, whose understanding of the machine in the end outweighed his age and nationality, would join him. The third was Wade, the test pilot who had proved that he was not afraid of anything. And finally there was Smith, a man who was as much a mystery to the assembled aviators after they had been together for six weeks in Virginia as he had been on the very first day. Still, he had made it. His dream, as always, was to be given the chance to keep flying. Now he had the whole world as his proving ground.

First he had to pick the mechanic who would be his partner, responsible for every revolution of the engine and every drop of oil and fuel that would keep them both alive. Smith initially chose Sergeant Arthur Turner, a twenty-six-year-old he had once flown with in San Francisco. He did not feel any special affinity for him nor did he see in him any special skills, but Smith valued familiarity. But over the following days he noticed that Turner had a lingering cough. Though the man seemed otherwise healthy, it was enough to create doubt in Smith's mind over whether Turner was up for the challenge. After all, if Turner's body could not handle Virginia in January, what would happen to it in Alaska or Baghdad? It pained Smith to take another person's dream away, but he felt he had no option but to rescind his offer.

He then turned to the person who seemed built from an entirely different blueprint than he was. Smith found Leslie Arnold working alone on the base and asked if he had a second to talk. Unused to Smith having any interest in conversation, much less one that lasted longer than a few words, Arnold listened but didn't pay much attention. Without preamble, Smith asked if he would be willing to fly with him as his mechanic.

"I'll fly to Mars if you say so," Arnold replied, thinking Smith was joking.

Smith kept probing, unsure whether Arnold understood the demands that lay ahead. "Will you work like the devil?" he asked.

"I'll work like a whole flock of devils," Arnold said, still in jest. He then looked up and realized that Smith was serious. "What's the matter with Turner?" Arnold asked.

"I've decided that he is not going," Smith said, and then he turned and left. Arnold sat for long moments in a daze, unsure if the past few minutes had truly happened.

When Smith had his choice of the best mechanics in the air service, he decided to hitch his fate to a person who appeared to orbit a different star than he did. For as long as he had been in a cockpit, he had played it smart, focusing on the small details so thoroughly that he had an unmatched record of safety. Yet here, on the doorstep of the biggest challenge that the world could throw at him, Smith had chosen a man who took a ready-fire-aim approach to life. He would never explain what compelled him to pick Arnold out of all the options. Perhaps it was Arnold's love of being on stage, a prospect that terrified Smith more than anything that could happen in an airplane. Or perhaps it was his malleability, which allowed him to maintain his cheer and optimism regardless of circumstance. Whatever the reason, the futures of Smith and Arnold were now intertwined, and they would have to find a way to work together if they wanted to survive what would come next.

CHAPTER SIX

"God Willing We'll Be in Los Angeles in September"

THE PUBLIC LOVED it.

When pitching the idea of a world flight, General Mitchell had emphasized that it would allow the military to prepare itself for future conflict and likely rekindle American excitement in an industry that appeared to be headed nowhere. He did not realize how right he was. On January 1, 1924, the World Flight Committee announced the names of the men who would be flying for the honor of their nation. Smith woke up to find a picture of himself plastered on the front page of a Virginia paper, the squint on his face making him look very much like a man who would take to the air to get out of having to make conversation. For the first time, he realized that his seat on the mission had come at the cost of the anonymity he cherished.

In the early weeks of 1924, it was close to impossible to open a newspaper in America without finding at least one mention of the flight, which turned the eight men stationed at a dreary air base into unlikely national celebrities. Newspapers introduced America to each man by detailing everything they could about him, from his wartime record to his favorite foods. Nothing was too small to report. A Santa Barbara newspaper ran a front-page picture of Smith accompanied by a one-sentence story reporting the last time he had been in town. The thrill of Americans attempting a world flight gripped the public mind so tightly that soon newspaper cartoonists were referring to it in their daily work, confident that their readers would get the joke. One strip in the *Oakland Tribune*, for instance, showed the pilots scared that they had been blown off course and lost in the Arctic because all they saw below them was white, then realizing that it was just California's blossoming trees.

The race came at a golden time when newspapers were the main source of both information and entertainment for most Americans, bringing the world into homes filled with hungry new readers. Illiteracy rates fell by nearly half between 1900 and 1920, and the number of newspapers, magazines, and books sold exploded. Magazines such as *Time, Reader's Digest,* and the *New Yorker* debuted during the first half of the 1920s, connecting a nation stretched over thousands of miles. Reading each day's news united someone living by a swamp in Mississippi with a person riding the subways in New York and a farmer tending his fields in Minnesota. Newspaper sales rose by a fifth over the decade; New York City alone supported twelve daily papers. Tabloids, such as the upstart *Daily News,* pioneered a new photo-heavy format, focusing on the public's love of sports, entertainment, and crime. Soon, that paper was selling more than a million copies a day, more than double the circulation of the staid *New York Times,* making it the bestselling newspaper in the country.

A group of attractive young pilots who were daring to take their planes on a global adventure could not have been more perfect for public consumption. That they would be competing in a race against the best of Europe turned an interesting story into a sensation. The nation instantly fell in love with them, their status as underdogs only adding to their charm. "The men who are courageous enough and willing to risk their lives in the effort to achieve this further distinction for their country will be backed up in every way, and if failure should result it will be due to causes unforeseen and that could not have been guarded against," the *Mendocino Coast Beacon,* a small paper on the Northern California coast, wrote in an editorial. In Washington, the air service received dozens of requests from civic groups across the country asking if they could host the aviators before their journey. The chief complaint came from the city of Dayton, Ohio, which felt slighted when it learned that the world fliers would not be making a stop in the hometown of the Wright brothers before they departed.

The fervent interest in eight everyday Americans traveling around the world ran contrary to the mood of a nation that appeared to want nothing more than to stay home. Since its entry into the World War, the country had turned increasingly inward, uninterested in other cultures and determined to root out any perceived foreign influence. Scandals revealing the outsize profits of arms manufacturers and suppliers during the war seemed to prove that internationalism was intertwined with moral rot. At a time when technology such as flight, telephones, and radio opened up the world more than ever before, America seemed determined to close itself off and attack anything that questioned the image of a white, Christian nation steeped in Anglo-Saxon tradition. Less than two months before General Patrick officially proposed the world flight, a crowd of more than thirty-six thousand people attended a Ku Klux Klan rally held in Whitewater, Indiana, that vilified immigrants, Catholics, Jews, and African Americans. In Tulsa, Oklahoma, an affluent neighborhood known as Black Wall Street that was once home to more than ten thousand wealthy Black families was in tatters after an attack two years earlier by white supremacists who killed more than three hundred people. The last thirty-six prisoners sitting in federal prison for protesting the country's involvement in the World War would not be released until June of 1924, ending seven years in which at least one American sat behind bars for expressing a political belief.

Hanging over it all was the idea that cultures—and, more specifically, variations of the human race—were locked in perpetual conflict. A 1911 commission led by William Dillingham, a Republican senator from Vermont, spent four years and one million dollars of taxpayer money on a forty-one-volume study, known as *The Dictionary of Races or Peoples*, that attempted to classify world ethnicities by supposedly fixed traits such as intelligence. Bohemians, it proclaimed, had a "weight of brain [that is] said to be greater than that of any other people in Europe," while "Ruthenians are still more broad-headed than the Great Russians." By the time Smith and the other aviators were preparing to travel around the world, Dillingham had spearheaded restrictive US immigration laws that made it difficult for anyone not from Northern Europe to come into the country. Federal policy targeted nearly all Asians, instituted literacy tests for those arriving from Southern Europe, and established quotas that set the number of visas available for each nationality at 3 percent of their total in the 1910 census, an attempt to keep the country from becoming more diverse.

A world flight—which by definition required landing in other countries and conversing with those who spoke foreign tongues—would challenge the nation's growing sense of xenophobia by exposing its pilots to the unfamiliar, even if the intent was to prove American superiority. The eight men who were finishing their training at Langley Field would act as the representatives of a country that had largely turned its back on the world in order to foster its isolation. "They must deal with many nationalities, and overcome innumerable obstacles," the *Los Angeles Evening Express* warned as the race date drew closer. "American pluck and ingenuity will, indeed, be necessarily in evidence."

Like many in America, the aviators who would be representing the nation had little personal experience overseas outside of their time in France and Germany during the war. Nelson, the lone immigrant, had sailed to America as a teenager and if not for his slight accent could easily have passed as the son of farmers from Minnesota. Alva Harvey, Martin's handpicked mechanic, joined the military in 1919, too late to serve anywhere far away from his home in the flatlands of Bono, Texas. Henry Ogden, who was chosen by Wade, had never left the South. Raised on a cotton plantation between Baton Rouge and Natchez, Louisiana, Ogden spoke with a drawl that was nearly unintelligible to the Northerners he referred to as Yankees. The youngest of the crew at twenty-three, Ogden had not met the army's minimum age requirement until 1919 and had never seen an airplane before he was assigned to the repair depot in Montgomery, Alabama. There he displayed an aptitude for mechanics that he had not known he possessed. He was soon tapped as an instructor and spent his leisure time experimenting with engines or, for extra excitement, jumping between airplanes in midair. When he arrived at Langley, Ogden was skeptical that a world flight was feasible, but told himself that at least it offered the chance to inspect a new Douglas aircraft. He felt out of place competing against men who had seen combat or broken records, and was shocked to learn that he had been chosen as a mechanic. "'Hank' declares emphatically that there is nothing interesting or romantic about himself, or anything that he ever did, up to the time when he was picked to fly around the world by Lieutenant Wade," a reporter wrote, noting that Ogden called it "the happiest moment of my life."

Another mechanic on the crew, Jack Harding, was also from the South, though his experience was closer to the remnants of the Southern aristocracy than Ogden's isolated and self-taught existence. Harding grew up on the family plantation, Belle Meade, outside of Nashville and attended boarding school at the Webb Preparatory School in Tennessee, widely known as the most conservative of its kind. From there, he studied engineering at Vanderbilt University and the University of Tennessee, groomed to take his place in a society that cherished the past and often feared the future. His attempt to broaden his horizons by enlisting in the army during the war fizzled before it started after he lost his temper at training camp when a superior officer teased him about the fact that he had one brown eye and one blue eye. Harding punched him, which led to months digging ditches in Texas as punishment. When given another chance, he entered a training program for mechanics and made a name for himself by repairing a Martin bomber that no one else at the air base could. He had never left the country, though he had seen all ten thousand miles of its borders in 1919 as a mechanic on one of General Billy Mitchell's public relations stunts, the Around the Rim Flight. Harding was part of a crew of three pilots and two mechanics who flew along the Canadian border, the Pacific Coast, the Mexican border, the Florida peninsula, and the Eastern Seaboard to Washington, DC, over the course of four months.

When officials planned for the world flight, American insularity touched everything from the creation of the Douglas World Cruiser to the route that its pilots would take. Securing permission to land and store stocks of oil, fuel, extra parts, and food across a ribbon of the twenty-two countries fell to the army. Officers were sent to capitals worldwide to explain that mission and avoid a conflict. Each of them was entrusted with the duty to "make clear that we have no military motive in making this round-the-world flight other than the training of personnel, testing of equipment, and such incidental motives," according to a memo from Washington.

The route would take them over thirty thousand miles in dozens of stages. From the Douglas plant in Santa Monica, they would fly the Cruisers up the West Coast to Seattle, where the planes would be refitted with pontoons to allow water landings. From there, they would fly north to Alaska, then hug the shoreline as they made their way westward to the Aleutian Islands and the edge of Asia. In each planned stop along the coast, an American destroyer would be waiting with food, supplies, and shelter. Because the United States did not recognize the Soviet Union, established two years earlier, the pilots would face a stretch of over five hundred miles, from isolated Attu Island, the westernmost part of Alaska, to their next landing stop in northern Japan, without any ships or radio transmission that could warn them about adverse weather ahead. Japanese resentment over the treatment of Asian immigrants in the United States left it unclear in the weeks leading up to the flight whether the country would allow the foreigners to land at all. "Just bear in mind the importance of getting the flight through Japan in as few days as possible," a memo from the World Flight Committee noted.

Should they successfully pass Japan, the American crew needed to race across South Asia and India before the monsoon season began, bringing rain that would make it impossible to go on. After that, they had to cross the deserts of modern-day Pakistan and the Middle East. If they made it that far, they would head northwest through Europe toward Scotland, then cross the frigid, iceberg-strewn waters of the North Atlantic via Iceland and Greenland, finally reaching North America again nearly two months after they started. On paper, it was possible; in reality, it was a prospect that seemed more daunting as the days went by.

The final embers of February began to fade and still the planes were not ready. Each day's delay increased the chances of running into bad weather in the weeks ahead that would make a flight impossible. The World Flight Committee circled March 17 as the start date. Servicemen at Clover Field in Los Angeles built a clubhouse on the airfield especially for the world fliers, signifying their new exalted status. Organizers put the finishing touches on plans for a spectacular send-off. Red, white, and blue bunting was ordered for grandstands that could fit the more than five hundred dignitaries expected to be on hand, and before anyone forgot, they ordered the grandstands too. The Automobile Association of Southern California announced that it would create makeshift parking lots for the anticipated fifty thousand spectators who would be there to see the world fliers take off.

Donald Douglas felt the time slipping away from him. He knew better than anyone that the flight would be lucky to leave in March or even April. Any flight before May would give the pilots at least a chance to cross Asia before the monsoons and make a potentially deadly flight above the North Atlantic before icebergs choked the small coves designated as their landing stops. But first they had to take off. Any prolonged delays, he feared, would metastasize into doubts that his machines— and, by extension, his ideas—were capable. As he crossed out the final days of February on his calendar, the weight of what he was trying to do felt crushing.

Less than three weeks before the American world flight attempt was scheduled to begin, over a hundred men working in round-the-clock shifts raced to put the four World Cruisers together in the Douglas factory. Each of the eight aviators who made up the world flight crew walked the production floor, watching the aircraft that would take them into the unknown come together, strut by strut. Ocean breezes swept in through the open windows. The aviators studied the construction and blueprints, perhaps hoping they could learn something about their machines that might later save their lives. Nelson often took the prototype on test flights over Santa Monica Bay and the Hollywood Hills. Even at this late date he was still finding faults, prompting Douglas to make tweaks, such as repositioning its horizontal stabilizers so that the tail no longer felt heavy in the air.

Nothing seemed to be going right. One day, the engine nearly failed while Nelson took one of the newly built World Cruisers on a test flight to San Diego, forcing him to fly all one hundred twenty-five miles at low altitude so he could continually look for possible places to crash. As soon as he arrived, he popped open the machine and discovered that a valve had malfunctioned. The thirty-five Liberty engines that the World Flight Committee had secured as backups and were preparing to load onto navy supply ships and send to supply depots around the world were immediately inspected and overhauled. Another day, the aviators woke up to the news that Tuffy, the white-haired terrier owned by Clover Field base commander C. C. Mosley that the crew had chosen as its mascot, was missing. "Fortunately aviators are not superstitious [or] his disappearance might be considered by some a bad omen," the Los Angeles Times noted. "The officers are confident that Tuffy has either felt the call of spring or has been picked up by a motorist and will find his way back before the time of the flight." Washington, meanwhile, appeared to be getting cold feet as the flight date got closer. "Unless the flight moves throughout the entire route with a regularity which will allow it to pass through the danger zone at a given period its eventual success is doubtful," officials at the War Department said in their first official statement on the world flight. Details of European flight plans leaked in, adding to the pressure the American crew members felt to leave while there remained a chance that they could be first.

During the empty hours of waiting for the planes to be ready, Les Arnold enjoyed himself. The fact that the city of Los Angeles provided the fliers with two luxury Wills Sainte Claires and one Rickenbacker—advertised as the fastest four-passenger automobile on sale in the United States—turned his life into a roving party. He led his fellow crew members through a tour of the city's bars and up into the mansions of movie stars in the Hollywood Hills, all of them celebrating like they had already returned from their mission. Martin, the squadron leader, and Smith remained in their rooms, each man puzzling over the possible troubles in the flight ahead. The friendly press turned its eyes away from the increasingly ribald tales of the crew's carousing, though the rumors grew so loud that Martin felt the need to address them. "Every effort has been made to limit the amount of entertainment," he said in a news conference. Being in the atmosphere of Hollywood, they had had some rather unusual experiences forced upon them, he said, "some of which have been rather embarrassing at times [that] . . . savored of a lack of appreciation of the dignity of the service." He did not specify whether it was the movie stars or Arnold who fell short of grace.

On Friday, March 14, three days before they were to leave for Seattle, the fliers were the guests of honor at the newly opened Biltmore Hotel, a sprawling half-block of Spanish-inspired luxury that was the largest hotel west of the Mississippi. There, studio heads, actors, prominent bankers, and military officials toasted the men in a spectacle that was "almost as epochal as the round-the-world flight itself," the *Evening Post-Record* reported. One man approached the crew and gave them each five-dollar bills with the promise to pay them fifty more if they returned the cash to him at the conclusion of their flight. Toward the end of the night, Martin rose and addressed the audience. "A British expedition starts this month, going eastward, and will probably meet us in Japan. They are using one ship. We'll beat them," he said to rousing applause. "God willing we'll be in Los Angeles in September."

On the eve of the flight, the city of Santa Monica held what it called the largest air carnival in the history of the West Coast. The idea that the flight would usher in a new utopian era was so widely held that it seemed a given. The eight aviators were about to embark on a journey that would "establish perhaps the last material and physical bond of peace in the form of an around the world airway," an advertisement for the show boasted. A newspaper called it "man's greatest conquest of the air since aviation became more than a fanciful dream." More than fifty thousand spectators jammed Clover Field while another fifty thousand watched from the nearby beach as dozens of pilots entertained the crowd with flips, spins, and other aerial acrobatics. The four Douglas World Cruisers sat in the middle of the infield in a spot of honor, three-foot-wide insignias of an eagle flying across the globe painted on their sides. Few other than Douglas and the fliers knew that only three of the planes were fully functional. The last, which would be piloted by Nelson, needed several hours of fine-tuning. The work was not completed by the evening. Rather than miss the planned send-off date and get the mission off on a bad note, the World Flight Committee instructed Nelson to stay behind and catch up to the squadron when his plane was ready.

Finally, on March 17, six of the eight aviators climbed into their planes before dawn. Each man wore a gold wristwatch, a gift from Donald Douglas's mother. A small crowd of spectators huddled in the cold wind as torn programs and litter left over from the air show swirled around them. Low, heavy fog kept them grounded past 7:00 a.m. In the days before radar and accurate weather forecasting, reports from the field were often all that aviators had to go on. A scout plane was sent ahead to gauge the conditions. It returned and reported that fog remained heavy through the nearby Tehachapi Mountains, potentially grounding them for the day. The men huddled in the cold, unsure what would happen next. Smith took Martin aside and assured him that he had flown up and down the state so often that he knew every curve in the mountains, fog or not. Martin, in his first decision as commander, gave the go-ahead, choosing to trust the skills of his pilots over the safer course of waiting, which might lead to embarrassment. Though he would never admit to being superstitious, Martin often trusted gut feelings, even if they were not his own. A few days earlier, his wife had told him that he would be safe while on the world flight, and that was all he needed to feel protected. "All her life she has been governed by an intuitive sense in making decisions, and when I was considered for the world flight she urged me to undertake the big adventure," he told a reporter. "So my mind is at peace, and all of us feel that her hunch may be followed with absolute confidence."

Martin gave one final wave to his wife and his eight-year-old son, John Robert. He then shouted "Contact," the signal for the other pilots to pull away. He took the lead and lifted off at 9:32 a.m., followed by Smith one minute later and Wade a minute after him. Each plane traced a sweeping lap of Clover Field and then nestled into a V formation, and the squadron headed north. An escort of ten planes took off a few minutes later and trailed behind the three World Cruisers. Smith, as promised, moved into the lead and deftly led the squadron through the mountains, flying so low that they could see the walls of the narrow canyons. An escort plane that attempted the same maneuver a few moments later became lost in the fog and made an emergency landing in the first flat field that the pilot could find.

The world flight was less than one hour into what would be hundreds of them, and already one plane had been left behind due to engine trouble, and another pilot flying with them had nearly crashed within minutes of takeoff. Tuffy, their adopted mascot, had never been found. As they flew north toward Sacramento, the six men sitting in the seats of the Douglas planes hoped that the mounting number of bad omens would not turn into something more deadly.

CHAPTER SEVEN

A Shining Light of England

F IVE THOUSAND MILES away from the beaches of Santa Monica, a well-dressed man hurried through the London fog.

Tall and lean with a long, rectangular face and deep-set eyes that made him look unforgiving, Archibald Stuart-MacLaren was, at the age of thirty-two, unmistakably a product of the British Empire. His posture was crisp; his diction excellent. When he spoke, his words fell in the slow, distinctive meter of the upper class, signaling to all Britons his elevated social status. Though he was not yet famous, his reputation was growing. He was "one of the shining lights of England," in the words of one reporter. Since childhood he had been groomed to become one of the countless hands on the tiller that maintained the glory of a small island nation that ruled continents. He received his education under the Gothic spires of the Charterhouse School, one of the most prestigious boarding schools in England, where all the boys wore ties in the colors of their competing houses. The school's immaculate grounds "proclaim complete confidence that Charterhouse educates men who are destined to rule the universe," a politician would one day say of the school. "Academically and pastorally, it is near beyond criticism." Whether students were learning geometry, history, or literature, the underlying lesson imparted by the school was always the same: For a Briton, failure in any regard was unthinkable.

MacLaren could have been anything. In the early days of the twentieth century, Britain controlled the largest empire the world had ever seen. Some four hundred million people—roughly a quarter of the planet's population—were ruled by a small cohort of Britons, many of whom had attended Charterhouse or one of its rivals. Law, business, medicine—all were easily within MacLaren's grasp. Instead, he chose the path of adventure. Shortly after graduation, he sailed to Canada and started a farm in the wilderness. Next, MacLaren traveled to the Far East and tried his luck at running a rubber plantation on the Malay Peninsula. When war looked likely, he returned home and accepted a commission in the King's Own Scottish Borderers in India before transferring to the Royal Flying Corps. He was not a natural flier. At six feet, two inches tall, he struggled to fold his body into small cockpits, and once he was in the air, his misery compounded with the miles. He would have given up and tried something else if not for Sir Hugh Trenchard, his commander, who made the act of flying seem like the highest calling a British subject could undertake on behalf of the empire.

With a towering height and loud voice that could be heard over the roar of airplane engines—giving him the nickname "Boom"—Trenchard was the first and most insistent advocate for Britain to pursue a policy of relentless aggression in the air. It was a remarkable turnaround for a man who was virtually unable to spell, rarely read a book, and boasted that his quiver of languages consisted solely of English and Louder English. "Overbearing, tactless, obstinate to the point of insubordination, impatient with all orders except his own, he lacked almost all the social and diplomatic skills required to aspire to high office in the military, yet he rose to the highest rank in the Royal Air Force," a biographer marveled. Though a critic once said that his loud voice compensated for "a permanently vacant mind," Trenchard was among the first to realize that airpower would forever change land warfare, in part by making it impossible for armies to move in secret. After enrolling in flight school in 1912 at the advanced age of thirty-nine as an antidote to an unremarkable career in the service, he began teaching other aspiring aviators how to read maps, fix engines, and maneuver while in the air despite being what a colleague called an "indifferent" pilot himself.

Within five years of stepping into a cockpit for the first time, he had become chief of the air staff and was working alongside Winston Churchill—whom he had met while playing polo in South Africa—to establish the world's first independent air force. It was while leading Britain's airpower during the World War that he met General Billy Mitchell. He took him on a tour of his operations, calling the American "a man after my own heart." In the final months of the war, Trenchard directed crews flying Handley Page bombers (at the time, the largest aircraft ever built) conducting waves of bombing runs in Germany, prompting Churchill to say that his nickname should have been Bomb instead of Boom.

"My job was to prod, cajole, help, comfort, and will the pilots on, sometimes to their death," Trenchard later said.

MacLaren was among the men who fell under his spell. Though Trenchard would later admit that he had but two close friends and never felt comfortable enough with another person to call him by a nickname, he shepherded young MacLaren through the ranks of the military aristocracy by giving him opportunities to make himself known. MacLaren responded with unwavering loyalty and asked Trenchard to serve as his son's godfather, cementing his bond with the figure pulling Britain into a new age. "Many of those who worked closely with him would unhesitantly claim he was not just the greatest man they had ever met, but one of the greatest leaders of the twentieth century," a biographer wrote of Trenchard.

In the summer of 1918, MacLaren was chosen to pilot the first flight from England to Egypt, connecting two distant dots of the empire. A month after the armistice was signed, ending the war, he was the commanding officer of the first flight from England to India, the populous jewel of the British crown. MacLaren completed the feat in a modified Handley Page bomber that he named *Old Carthusian* in honor of Charterhouse. Bringing India within a traveling distance of days rather than weeks helped assuage British anxiety over the imbalance of its imperialist presence in a country where three hundred million Indians were ruled by one hundred fifty thousand Britons. Faraway lands were now within reach, solidifying London's grip on its possessions. "You will see what is possible with the aeroplane," said Frederick Handley Page, one of Britain's foremost aviation pioneers, in a speech celebrating MacLaren's flight. "Nobody will be more than four days away from us, so that instead of writing letters and waiting for replies, it will be possible to visit distant friends by aeroplane, and have the pleasure of a personal conversation."

The next logical step was to attempt a voyage as grand as the empire itself. In 1922, shortly before his thirtieth birthday, MacLaren lobbied the Air Ministry—the government agency that both oversaw the Royal Air Force and inspected the design and construction of all British aircraft—to support a flight around the world. Perhaps because Major William Blake was deep into preparations, the Air Ministry demurred, responding that it had no capacity to assist in making "complicated and expensive arrangements all over the world for which we get no financial return." That Blake's attempt devolved into a fiasco that ended with two

British pilots drifting in a damaged plane across the Indian Ocean for fifty hours without food or water hardened the Air Ministry's position. "A world flight in which the Air Ministry is in any way involved must succeed, or a tremendous loss of prestige will result," MacLaren was told when he again presented his plan following Blake's return to England. "Bearing this in mind, it seems to me that we cannot anticipate success without a very much better organization than that suggested by you . . . the recent attempt of Blake did immense harm to the cause of aviation in India and the East, and we cannot risk another failure."

MacLaren kept trying. While stationed at a dust-choked airfield in Aden (a former British colony that today is the southern portion of Yemen), he wrote a letter to Trenchard seeking assistance. Mindful of his audience, he suggested that his crew include William Noble Plenderleith, who was stationed with him in Aden, as a pilot, and W. H. Andrews, who once lied about his age so that he could enroll early in the aircraft engineering school of the Royal Air Force, as the flight engineer. "I should like to make it an all RAF show," MacLaren wrote to the man widely known as "the Father of the Royal Air Force." He reminded Trenchard that Plenderleith, whom Trenchard knew from his service defending London from attacks by German airships during the war, was a "very gallant little fellow, and an extremely good pilot."

Trenchard, unsurprisingly, agreed. Here was a chance to show the world that Britain's pilots and planes were indeed the best in the world, destined to dominate the air just as its ships dominated the seas. He offered MacLaren the full support of the Royal Air Force in facilitating the route and its assistance should something go wrong. In return, he asked that MacLaren find private companies to furnish his aircraft, fuel, and supplies. Had he been in America, the lack of government funding would have ended MacLaren's ambitions. Instead, he turned to Britain's robust talent. "The striking thing about the structure of the British aircraft industry . . . was the number of firms willing to manufacture aircraft," noted one historian of the era. The dozen or so prominent aerospace designers in the United Kingdom had nearly thirty major domestic firms to choose from when turning their blueprints into production lines. Demand from some of the world's first commercial airlines, which ran hops over the twenty-one miles of ocean separating England from France, kept money flowing into the industry. By the time the year was over, MacLaren had turned the support of Trenchard into commitments from the cream of British engineering. Smiths and Sons—a firm known for building the first British speedometer, which it sold to King Edward VII when he asked for a way to measure how fast his car was going—agreed to provide instruments for the aircraft. Reid and Sigrist offered the use of one of its first turn-and-slip indicators, a now-standard piece of equipment that allows pilots to gauge their movements during bad weather or at night when they cannot see the horizon. Shell-Mex, at the time the largest oil producer in the world, donated fuel and oil.

With the support of British companies assured, Trenchard pulled the many strings available to him to ensure MacLaren's success. "Air Chief Marshal Sir Hugh Trenchard is personally interesting himself in the organisation" of the mission, the *Grimsby Evening Telegraph*, a newspaper in central England, reported. "The Chief of the Air Staff is convinced that a girdle can be put round the earth by airplane, and is looking to the RAF to do it." He prodded Canada into sending the HMCS *Thiepval*, a battle-class armed trawler, to deposit supplies of fuel and food in inlets along the coast of Japan and the North Pacific where no commercial fleets would dare to go. He asked Vickers, one of Britain's largest aircraft manufacturers, to modify its Vickers Vulture seaplane in order to expand its range and increase the comfort of its crew of three. Engineers added long-range radio communications, a modified compass, and new instruments meant to help a pilot find his way through fog.

When finished, the new aircraft was renamed the Vickers Viking, and MacLaren was given the first one produced. "Many modifications and improvements have been made, and the Viking—an excellent name for such a craft—that is to be used is now being built in secret," the *Daily Telegraph* wrote. By the time it was finished, the new Viking—composed of mahogany wood covered by fabric and secured by copper nails—had a range of sixteen hundred miles and could cruise at eighty-five miles an hour.

It looked curious, due largely to the fact that its propeller hung near its upper wing rather than its nose. Yet what it lacked in charisma it made up for in power. Drawing a route through the British Empire and the Soviet Union, MacLaren proposed pushing the Vickers Viking on a pace that would require only 240 hours of flying time. The audacious pace drew attention from around the world. "What, then, would Jules Verne and his amused countrymen have thought of a proposal which considers seventy days out of the eighty as so much wasted time?" a reporter in Nashville, Tennessee, wrote.

MacLaren's success seemed inevitable. He would no doubt become the first person to circle the globe by air "unless exceptionally bad fortune attends the flight," a London newspaper announced. Reporters began appearing everywhere he went, intent on documenting every moment of a life now destined for greatness. In July 1923, one of the first of many newspaper photos of him that would be published over that year and the next appeared in the *Birmingham Gazette*. He can be seen staring into the lens of the camera, his dark hair parted to the side, looking every bit the sort of gentleman flier who might step out of a cockpit and ask for a game of tennis or a cup of tea.

As the last days of 1923 ticked by, everything appeared to line up for MacLaren to begin his attempt in mid-April of the new year. Though other European nations had announced that they, too, would seek the prestige of completing the first world flight, he felt untroubled by the competition, confident that British greatness would be proven once again. His flight appeared ready to serve as the capstone of what was projected to be a year in which the United Kingdom reminded the world of its authority. In Wembley Park in London, the final preparations were then underway for the British Empire Exhibition, which planned to highlight the sweep of the fifty-eight territories of the Empire at a time of rising anti-colonist sentiment. In time, more than twenty-five million visitors would attend, drawn by exhibitions including elephants from India, metalwork from Nigeria, and a dollhouse made for Queen Mary. Explorers George Mallory and Andrew Irvine, meanwhile, readied themselves for their second attempt at ascending Mount Everest, the highest mountain on Earth and one that had never been scaled. It was entirely possible to assume that, by the end of the year, the country at the heart of the world's largest empire would have reached the globe's tallest point and been the first to fly an airplane around the planet's circumference, demonstrating that it had fully conquered all that stood before it.

Then America announced it, too, would join the race. Something about the upstarts throwing their lot in with nations that were well ahead of them in the global-aviation pecking order gnawed at him, offending his sense of position. He scanned each day's newspapers for word on the progress and plans of the American effort and asked the Royal Air Force for any updates that were not yet public. France, Italy, Portugal, and even Argentina were all widely considered capable of completing such a daunting task, but only America was desperate. It was at the bottom and had nowhere else to fall, making it unpredictable to the point of recklessness. Although its pilots were unproven and its machines untested, MacLaren could not fathom the idea of losing to an upstart, much less one that had squandered its chance at aviation supremacy. "The British are pretty well worked up over our flight and are planning to beat us if possible, making a race of it," an American military memo reported in early March. "They intend to leave the same time we leave Seattle."

There was suddenly no time to waste. MacLaren, whose status had granted him the privilege of patience, rushed to get his plane, crew, and supplies ready to meet the accelerated timeline of his American competitors. True, he had but one aircraft in a race against a squadron of four, which left him little room for error. But MacLaren trusted his own ambition, taking to heart the wisdom of the Rudyard Kipling line that "he travels fastest who travels alone." He also knew he had a built-in advantage: his flight path went directly through the Soviet Union and its territories, so he would fly a shorter distance overall than the Americans, essentially giving him a head start of more than a thousand miles.

It still didn't feel like it was enough. He pushed himself and his small crew to prepare their aircraft, checking and rechecking each bolt before loading their emergency supplies of rations, fishing poles, and shotguns in case they crashed in the wilderness. Death, of course, was a distinct possibility. Yet losing face was a greater fear to a man who had been forged in the culture of empire, and he pushed aside all other concerns to focus on winning a race that he considered his due.

On the bright and sunny morning of March 25, 1924, Stuart MacLaren, Plenderleith, and Andrews emerged from a hangar in the village of Calshot, England. Each man wore a dark Burberry flying coat over a uniform of a jacket and tie. They shook hands with Lord Thomson, the British air minister, and a dozen other dignitaries assembled. The squat gray circle of Calshot Castle, built in 1539 to defend England from invasion, could be seen just beyond the boundary of the airfield. The aviators were presented with a wired message from the king that read "I shall watch your progress with the greatest interest and wish you luck." Though no one would say it, the ticking clock was on their minds. "Officially, it is merely a coincidence that a group of American planes happened to be trying to accomplish the same thing at the same time," an American reporter for the Associated Press wrote. "Unofficially, however, everyone in Great Britain who cares anything about flying looks upon the venture which began here today as a race against the American planes which left California flying in the opposite direction last week."

A team of mechanics hurried to finish painting the plane's wings, the final step before it was ready. MacLaren hoisted his wife into one of the passenger seats and flew one brief circuit around the airfield, putting the instruments through their last tests. Once back on the ground, he kissed his son, Wallace, and daughter, Lilian, goodbye and climbed back into the plane. He maneuvered into position, trailed by an escort of Royal Air Force fighters. At 12:10, they rose into the air, drew two large circles around the airfield, and turned south. If all went well, they would cross through the fog cloaking the English Channel and land at their planned destination in France, ready to trace a southeastern route through Europe. Behind them stood their families and homeland; ahead of them waited the world.

"We're not afraid," Mrs. MacLaren said, hugging her daughter as her husband's plane disappeared into the gathering clouds. "We know they'll get back safely."

CHAPTER EIGHT

"Your Sporting Proposal"

H E WISHED FOR a war.
Never mind that Britain was his country's closest ally or that America depended on British manufacturing for the bulk of its aircraft and supplies. Some things were not forgivable, and this was one of them. General Patrick sat fuming in his office in the nation's capital, a telegram from England in his hands. It had come from the desk of Lieutenant Colonel L. E. Broome of the Royal Air Force and asked in the sort of polite British way saturated with snobbery whether it would be possible for the four American planes to take off from Seattle on their world flight at once in order to create a proper race with MacLaren around the globe. Broome, Patrick knew, was the logistics officer in charge of the British flight and was altogether familiar with the reasons why his request was impossible. His merely suggesting it was a form of ridicule and poked at Patrick's building concern that Billy Mitchell had talked him into a foolish plan that would embarrass him and the country. Summoning all his tact, Patrick sighed and began writing his formal reply. "Date of departure our flight from starting point so involved with laying down of supplies and schedule of steamer sailings that it is impossible to accede to your sporting proposal," he wrote. "Our best wishes for the success of your daring undertaking."

Patrick had little to fall back on to raise his spirits. Just getting from Los Angeles to Seattle had proved to be a small disaster. Separated from the start, the squadron that was meant to conquer the globe made little headway against the persistent rain and wind and did not come together as a full team until Nelson joined them in Eugene, Oregon. After taking off from Portland to the cheers of hundreds of people gathered at the airfield, the men were forced to return within twenty minutes as the rain intensified, landing before some of the startled spectators had even reached their cars. The following day a US Army Air Service lieutenant acting as the official escort for the leg between Portland and Seattle crashed in a remote forest thirty miles west of the small city of Roseburg, wrecking his plane beyond repair.

It did not help that Martin, of all people, seemed to have developed a sudden love for the spotlight. He had been chosen as the squadron leader in large part because of his age and modesty, a coach whom one could trust not to play to the crowd. Instead, less than a week into the journey he was already talking about how easy it would be. "We have prepared a schedule of five and one-half months for the trip, but I am telling the people that we will be on American soil in four and one-half months," he told the Sacramento Chamber of Commerce at a dinner in his honor. "I know that the route we are taking will of course not be the more practicable airline for commercial aircraft of the future. It is a step in the advancement of such transportation, however, and in many years to come you and I, all of us will think nothing of going abroad by airplane."

For now, however, the American planes sat idle in a hangar at Sand Point airfield in Seattle, the waters of Lake Washington glistening nearby. The schedule had allotted twelve days for the pilots and mechanics to remove the landing gear and affix pontoons to each airplane, effectively turning them into seaplanes. If all went right, they would not need wheels again until they reached India, nearly eight thousand miles away. Each day the aviators were up at dawn, tending to their planes. "This is where the real work begins," Martin told reporters.

The planes began to take on the personalities of their pilots. Nelson spent two days building a new ignition to coax more muscle from his machine, unable to stop himself from tinkering. "The engine worked fine coming to Seattle, but I know it can pull harder and I want every pound of power there is," he said. When no one was looking, he pulled a picture of his girlfriend from his pocket and taped it on his instrument panel (the picture was printed on celluloid, which protected it from water and wind but was so highly flammable that the material is rarely used today). Wade swapped out his motor for an entirely new one that had slightly more torque, following the mantra of all test pilots that the next version would surely be the best one. "There was no lack of power in the old engine," he told a reporter. "That is for land flying, but I want all the power I can have after the pontoons have been substituted for runners." Smith alone did nothing. "The engine I have works perfectly," he mumbled, withdrawing before a reporter could force him to speak any longer.

Persistent rain kept the aviators grounded on their scheduled launch day, turning their journey around the world into a waiting game full of false starts. In their first introduction to the difficulty of what lay ahead, they found themselves at the mercy of distant weather reports. Their planes remained idle on a sunny day in Seattle that seemed perfect for flying because of a storm raging six hundred miles away at their destination of Prince Rupert, British Columbia. Another clear day was scrapped because of what a local report called "the worst storm in years" in Sitka, Alaska, their second planned stop.

Adding to the indignity of waiting were daily updates of MacLaren's progress, each account of his grit another dent to their pride. On March 25, while the Americans sat watching the rain fall on Lake Washington, MacLaren flew into thick fog in the English Channel. Within the span of ten minutes, visibility shrank from three hundred yards to fifty. "Cannot see anything," he wrote in his logbook, recording that his altimeter showed that he was just fifty feet above sea level. Noting that Andrews estimated that they would reach the cliffs of the French countryside within ten minutes, MacLaren directed Plenderleith to climb up to one hundred feet amid zero visibility. Suddenly the cliffs appeared out of the fog just fifty yards ahead. With what MacLaren would later call "magnificent presence of mind," Plenderleith opened up the throttle and made what was known as an Immelmann turn, a maneuver developed by German ace Max Immelmann. The plane climbed until it was just short of a stall, banked sharply, and accelerated in the opposite direction, missing the cliff face by a few feet. They landed ten minutes later, "all as white as sheets," MacLaren wrote. An hour after that, they taxied to the outskirts of Havre, France, "machine and engine splendid throughout," MacLaren told a waiting reporter.

He arrived in Lyon, France, the next day, and the following morning took off in front of a small crowd into a bright morning sky streaked with clouds. "The airboat is greatly admired here, but the opinion is expressed that it is very heavy and rises with difficulty," a reporter for London's *Guardian* wrote. The plane climbed above the red rooftops and gray Gothic cathedrals of the city and followed the path of the Rhone, its ribbon of dark blue water leading them toward the Mediterranean. They expected to reach Rome, some six hundred miles away, by nightfall.

Still the Americans waited. Days went by with no apparent progress, blending one afternoon into the next, as MacLaren's lead grew and grew. Each hour that passed was one more they would have to somehow make up if they were to win. The gulf between themselves and the British expanded in front of them like an afternoon shadow, allowing embarrassment to creep in. What came naturally in the rush of excitement, such as the Los Angeles Chamber of Commerce including photos of their takeoff from Santa Monica in a time capsule laid in the cornerstone of its new downtown headquarters, now felt mortifying. After all the fancy ballrooms and the cheering crowds, the eight aviators had nothing to point to as proof that the nation should believe in them or in the promise of flight.

With the sense of momentum stalling, the US Army Air Service announced a contest to choose the cities that the four Douglas planes would be named for. Soon after, the aircraft were christened the *Seattle*, the *Chicago*, the *Boston*, and the *New Orleans* in a ceremony complete with a marching band. Instead of reigniting public interest, the move seemed to imply that the world flight was just another one of Billy Mitchell's stunts. For the first time, some members of the press began to question the wisdom of such an expensive undertaking. "If the purpose of this world flight is what they say it is, then it is a rather silly waste of time and money," Harry Carr, an influential journalist for the *Los Angeles Times*, wrote in his daily column. "I have faith that our government has a more sensible and important object in seeing the flyers on this adventure than the melodramatic one of the 'honor of being the first nation to circle the globe.' . . . I think the real purpose of the flight is to map out an air route to Japan," he added, arguing that it was "up to us to find a way to get to the hidden naval bases of Japan by air flight." No one "wants a war with Japan or expects one, but wars have a way of happening, nevertheless."

It was as if the nation's press corps had woken out of a dream and was now alert about what a world flight meant for a country that had little appetite for internationalism and none for war. The trip would "certainly have the effect of arousing suspicions and causing new armament plans. It will do [nothing] as a peacemaker," an editorial in the *Des Moines Tribune* argued. Aside from the threat of war, the flight might spell the end to the nation's sense of itself, the paper continued. "It is a little strange, and no doubt will appear so to the nations visited, that this country, the apostle—at present—of isolation, should be the first to show how easily any nation is to be reached by airplane from another. . . . Even if it should fail, the world will know the defeat will be but temporary, and the conquest of distance inevitable. That meaning, rather than the military one, ought to be having the attention of our statesmen."

Getting the press back on the American racers' side would not be an easy task, especially when their planes suddenly seemed incapable of flight. For several days in a row, Martin took his aircraft, now dubbed the *Seattle*, onto the waters of Lake Washington and attempted to become airborne. One day he came back in because of a broken propeller, another because he could not get enough speed to pull his plane above the wave crests. Six times he tried, and six times he failed. Once again he returned, drenched, to an increasingly skeptical group of reporters waiting on the shoreline. The planes would leave in the next few days "unless weather conditions are adverse, any more mechanical imperfections are discovered, or the great god Jinx takes a hand again," the *Seattle Star* noted. In London, the *Sunday Pictorial* ran a photo of what it mockingly called America's "earth bound fliers."

The issue of weight continued to plague the planes, no matter what the pilots tried. A Douglas World Cruiser could not become airborne if it exceeded 8,200 pounds, forcing the air service to weigh every item to the ounce. Plane, engine, and crew alone nearly brought it to the limit. Each aircraft was loaded with survival gear, including a rifle, ammunition, signal pistol, flares, fishing lines and hooks, a first aid kit, spare engine parts, and canned food. Nelson, as the flight engineering officer, also carried a bridle sling for lifting a plane out of water, a gasoline hand pump, radiator fluid, a blow torch and soldering iron, waterproof glue, heavy canvas, sheets of aluminum and plywood for patching holes in the plane or pontoons, and countless bolts, nuts, and tape, a bazaar of materials that left the other aviators joking that he was ready for a shipwreck. Each member of the mission was limited to bringing what he could carry on his body: a fur-lined flight suit, cap, and gloves; a pair of boots; two wool shirts; a safety razor and toothbrush; two pairs of pants; and an automatic pistol. Parachutes remained in the hangar, deemed too heavy to include. Either the pilots and mechanics would best every challenge and land safely countless times around the world or they would crash and most likely die. There was no room for error.

As Nelson continued to tweak the engines to allow the fully loaded planes to achieve liftoff from the lake, Pedro Zanni, an Argentinean pilot who was perhaps the most heralded aviator in South America, announced that he was in London for the purpose of buying three planes that he planned to lead on a flight around the world for the honor of his country. Slim, with a broad nose, wide ears, and square jaw, Zanni carried himself with a sense of purpose, his energy oversaturating his small frame. He held nearly every flight record in South America and was highly regarded even among European pilots, who thought little of anyone else. "The Argentine has a good record as a flier, having crossed and recrossed the Andes as long ago as 1920," a reporter noted. His flight would begin in June, he said. If MacLaren stumbled, there was no reason to doubt that Zanni would be in a position to pass him by.

As March turned into April, the American attempt appeared closer to failure than success. Ever since they were chosen at Langley, the crew members had asked themselves whether they would be lucky enough to make it all the way around the globe. Now the question loomed as to whether they would take off at all. Smith, of the eight aviators, had the least to fall back on. This mission was the last thing between him and the acceptance that his racing days were finally over. Though his mechanical skills were not as adept as the others, Smith could be found every sunrise at Nelson's side, ready to put in any effort that would get the squadron moving.

Finally, Nelson coaxed the engines into achieving enough power to break free from the windswept lake, breathing life back into the mission. To celebrate, Martin flew the *Seattle* above more than ten thousand fans crowding the bleachers at an air carnival held in the University of Washington football stadium. Arnold participated in one of the air carnival's scheduled races, ignoring the potential for a crash or injury that would likely scuttle the entire world flight. Following Arnold's race, a plane climbed high into the sunny blue sky until it was only a speck, and a man with a parachute jumped out. The crowd cheered as he gracefully landed in the middle of the stadium, secure with more lifesaving equipment than the world fliers would don over their long journey.

President Calvin Coolidge sent a message to the American aviators two days before their anticipated departure date. "More than 400 years ago men first navigated the world. . . . You are going to demonstrate the practicality of making such a voyage by the air," he wrote. "Before another 400 years this may be the safest and most comfortable way. Your countrymen will watch your progress with hope and record your success with pride."

On the morning of April 4, a large crowd gathered on the banks of Lake Washington despite a steady rain to watch the fliers take off. The pilots' presence had been the talk of Seattle for nearly two weeks, and the moment had finally come to send them on their way and vault the city into history. Martin, in the lead plane, slowly taxied away from his mooring to steady cheers from the crowd. The other men sat in their vibrating planes awaiting their turn. Martin gathered speed as he raced down the lake, then stopped suddenly. The other men cut their engines as Martin began taxiing back toward the mooring. Nelson jumped out, inspected Martin's aircraft, and found a damaged propeller. Sensing another letdown, the crowd began to thin, and those that lingered were treated to the disappointing sight of Nelson removing the bolts that secured the propeller to the plane. A new one was installed that afternoon, too late for another attempt.

The following morning, they tried again. Gone were the crowds and the cheers, though the rain continued to show interest. Martin again took the lead and became airborne shortly before nine. Smith, in the *Chicago*, followed closely behind, tailed by Nelson in the *New Orleans*. When it was their turn, however, Wade and Ogden could not get the *Boston* to break free of the water. Wade taxied back to their mooring and began dumping items from the plane to reduce its weight. By the time they were done, a rifle, a small anchor, and all the clothing that was not at that moment on their bodies lay scattered on a dock. They maneuvered back into position and took off, an hour behind the three other planes in their squadron. Wade piloted the plane through the fog along the tree-shrouded coast, skimming just above the gray ocean. Twice, he almost collided with fishing boats. He later learned that the three planes ahead of him had almost hit the same floating hazards, leaving the pilots to wonder what the boat captains thought would be coming at them next.

A hundred miles ahead of Wade, Leslie Arnold sat in the rear cockpit and watched as the snow-covered cap of Mount Rainier slowly shrank in the distance. He was taking the first steps in an adventure that he had not expected to be a part of and did not know where it would lead. He pulled out a diary that he had stashed in the plane before takeoff, somehow evading the strict rules on weight that forced every other aviator to leave their personal effects behind. With Smith piloting the plane, he began to write in his looping, graceful cursive, a handsome script no doubt practiced during the dark nights when he dreamed of becoming an actor who would one day have countless fans asking for his autograph.

"I keep wondering what the people in the streets are thinking," he wrote as the hum of the engine propelled him toward the unknown. "I wonder how many of us will get all the way around."

CHAPTER NINE

A Useless Rabbit's Foot

ON A MISTY Friday morning in July 1774, a Spanish naval officer named Juan Josef Perez Hernandez spotted land after more than a month at sea. Perez, as he was known, had risen quietly through the ranks of Spain's administrative government in Mexico, maintaining a career that did not single him out for mention in surviving historical records until he was likely past his fortieth birthday. Whatever he had done, he had evidently done well. He was now in command of a frigate, the *Santiago*, and on a mission on behalf of the viceroy of New Spain to chart the coastline far north of Alto California and establish a Spanish presence in the vast unknown before Russia or England claimed it. Now, four weeks after he had left Monterey, the principal city of Spanish California, he inched toward rolling lush forests he saw laid out before him, rising and falling like notes on a measure.

Great rocks, some as large as his ship, pocked the narrow sound. He proceeded slowly, "not trusting the place," he wrote in his diary, ever mindful of the "danger of running aground on a foul coast." Above the cresting waves he glimpsed several canoes launched from a nearby Haida village, its occupants keeping their distance from the mysterious strangers. The Spaniards beckoned the party to come near but with no success. Without warning, the waters suddenly churned white with foam and the sun disappeared from the darkening sky. "It was frightening to see in so short a time the entire sea become angry, stirred up by the blowing wind," Perez wrote that night in what was the first European description of the province now known as British Columbia.

One hundred fifty years later, the region remained a beautiful and unpredictable place. Its magnificence often forced visitors to stop what they were doing and simply gaze. In his first visit, Winston Churchill was said to have finished giving a lecture and then abandoned all other plans to spend the remainder of the day painting the panorama before him from the top of Grouse Mountain. He discovered that no matter how long one stared, there was always more to find. The province, four times the size of Great Britain, remained shockingly devoid of human life in comparison to everything that Churchill had known. There were fourteen times as many people living in London alone in 1924 than in all of British Columbia, a vast green region that spread from Montana to Alaska.

The buffet of topography—graced by stalwart glaciers, tiny lakes, secluded islands, deep ravines, and gnarled forests—mirrored its ever-changing weather. "For the last ten days our climate has exhibited a most variable character, marked by sudden alternations of frost, thaw, snow, sleet, rain, hail, heavy gales of wind, mingled with some mild fine weather at short intervals," colonists noted in a Christmas Day report from the capital city of Victoria in 1858. Later, settlers learned to make peace with the capricious skies that controlled their fates. "We seldom tried to buck weather, to quarrel with it . . . instead, we tried to get along with it, to understand it, and if possible figure out its shifting moods in advance," an early British Columbian writer noted.

As the four American planes buzzed northward over the gray ocean on April 5, 1924, the comforts of home receded behind them. They followed a path typically taken by steamships, flying nearly six hundred fifty miles into increasingly brutal weather. The problems that had delayed their takeoff and put them far behind MacLaren were mechanical; now it was the earth itself they had to battle. Strong winds blew in from the west, shaking their aircraft with the fury of the open sea. Twenty-foot waves crashed below, making an emergency landing impossible even with their pontoons. Snow and sleet stung their reddening cheeks and clumped on their goggles. At one point, Nelson, on one side of the formation, could not see through the billowing snow to find Wade flying in the *Boston* opposite him.

The planes reached Prince Rupert, British Columbia, eight hours after they left Seattle, the pilots spotting the yellow buoys marking their landing zone in Seal Cove through the worsening snowstorm. Martin, in the lead position, began his descent from four hundred feet and glided down, expecting there would be ample room in the bay to stop before he reached the mountains towering above it. As his pontoons were about to touch the water, he realized that he was going too fast and his momentum would carry him onto a rocky beach.

He opened up the throttle to try to escape. On his right loomed a sawmill; on his left and rear were mountains that he knew his plane did not have the power to climb. In front of him threatened trees whose canopies he could not see due to the storm. With nowhere to go, he aimed the nose of his plane upward, forcing it into a stall. The maneuver slowed him and he porpoised above the waves, trying to strike a balance between running out of speed and running out of water below. He appeared to be close to completing a graceful landing until he slowed down so much that he lost all lift while still ten feet in the air. The four-ton plane slammed backward into the sea, destroying part of its wing struts and brace wires. When he reached the dock, Martin found that the left side of one of his upper wings was now sagging, rendering it useless.

Smith, following closely behind in the *Chicago*, barely missed snagging his pontoons on high-tension electrical wires that could have sliced through the plane. He simply did not see them stretched behind two poles as he landed. The near-miss unnerved his normally jubilant mechanic: "125 miles in fog, 275 in rain and snow, hell of a day," Arnold wrote in his diary that night.

One day in and the lead plane was busted and another had narrowly avoided demolition. As Nelson slipped the sling over the *Seattle* and began hauling it out of the water for repairs, Harvey, Martin's mechanic, pulled out a lucky rabbit's foot he had been given by a spectator in California and tossed it into the black ocean. The mayor of Prince Rupert appeared on the dock and greeted them with the words "Gentlemen, you have arrived on the worst day we've had in ten years!" That night, the aviators slept in a small hotel, not knowing whether Martin's plane could be fixed in the morning. "Went to bed early as possible, next to exhausted," Jack Harding later wrote. At sunrise, the eight men were battered by snow and freezing rain on the village dock as they rebuilt Martin's wings with spruce planks donated by the local lumber mill.

Perhaps it was to their benefit that they were secluded in a small hamlet. The same day, the *San Diego Union* ran a lengthy article quoting anonymous military sources predicting that their attempt to circle the world would fail. "Many aviators believe that the War Department would have achieved better results if orders had been issued for the world fliers to 'go on their own' after leaving Rockwell Field" in San Diego, the paper noted. "At least two of the fliers, it is believed, would have been well along the Aleutian Island airway by this time, whereas the present finds the squadron limping along with a 'lame duck' and the flight to the next step postponed indefinitely." What's more, the long delay in Seattle made it seem inevitable that the aviators would run into impassable storms in Greenland and Iceland if they were fortunate enough to make it that far, the paper warned. The army investigated and later determined that members of the navy were the article's sources.

Less easy to look past was a scathing report filed by LeClair D. Schulze, whom Patrick had sent to Seattle for a final update on the crew's aircraft and supplies. Among the vulnerabilities Schulze noted were the quality of the pontoons, which he warned were susceptible to leaks. The largest potential danger, however, were the backup engines: while Nelson had ordered all of them refurbished after his near-accident in San Diego, it was likely that some faulty machines had passed inspection, Schulze warned. An officer in Seattle performing a last-minute check had found a broken shaft assembly in an engine that was intended to be shipped to a supply station in Japan. There was simply no telling how many other bad engines were now on destroyers streaming across the globe, their problems unknown. The American pilots were now at the mercy of parts that were "certainly not of a quality demanded by a venture of this importance . . . to subject the safety of any of these planes to the dangers involved in a forced landing, even for a minor cause, is, in my opinion, inexcusable," Schulze wrote.

SNOW WAS THE furthest thing from MacLaren's mind. For the past five days, he and his two crew members had been sleeping in a tent nestled between sand dunes on a lake on the Greek island of Corfu. Their damaged plane lay beached in the blinding sun. It had come to this after they encountered what MacLaren called "filthy weather" while crossing over the Ionian Sea from Italy. There was a "terrific vibration" in the engine, forcing the British aviators to look for a landing spot. "Lucky to have a lake, as the sea was very rough," MacLaren wrote. The three men had waded ashore. MacLaren walked ten miles past ancient marble ruins and olive trees with white blossoms shimmering in the rain to a town, also called Corfu, and returned with boiled eggs, black bread, and wine.

After sleeping in the plane overnight, they inspected the engine and found one of its gears completely stripped. The only way forward was to get a replacement motor shipped from England, which would take at least ten days. MacLaren returned to town and asked the British consul to send an urgent message to London asking for parts. A new Napier Lion engine, the most powerful engine used by the Allies in the war, was loaded onto a truck bound for the Italian port city of Brindisi. With nothing to do but wait for the engine's arrival, MacLaren bought food and a tent and tried to accept his fate.

He no doubt knew the history of the island and its reputation for hospitality to the unfortunate. According to myth, Odysseus was shipwrecked on Corfu on his way back to Ithaca. The Phaeacians, master seafarers, discovered him and pointed him toward home. MacLaren had closely studied the Greek epics at Charterhouse, and he likely noted the irony of his predicament, stuck in a place known for its hospitality to a sailor on his return journey across the known world while MacLaren was still in the early days of his own quest. The plane "is in a very inaccessible position, but I shall endeavor to get it into the sea, and towed round to Corfu by a destroyer as soon as the weather is sufficiently calm. I have managed to obtain a small tent and so the housing problem has been solved," he wrote in a message back home. "Depression is gradually wearing off in the sunshine, and I hope to make up the lost time."

The race—unofficial by public measures, official by the private ones that counted—was at a standstill. MacLaren remained ahead, benefiting from having left earlier and taking a shorter route that hopscotched over British colonies. Yet his likely prolonged delay in Greece gave the Americans now marooned in British Columbia their first chance to narrow the gap—assuming that they could fix Martin's plane. If they crossed the Pacific, they would have overcome one of the principal challenges of the entire flight, giving them hope that any further mishaps would be temporary and that MacLaren would have to face the gauntlet of snow and wind that they now found themselves battling. Back home in the United States, the public followed each step of the race and longed for them to keep going. "Other accidents will in all probability occur during the flight but so long as there is one plane left to continue the citizenry of this country will not despair of the flight's being successful," reported Tennessee's *Johnson City Chronicle*. "The people believe implicitly in the courage and intelligence of their flyers and are behind them to a man."

Martin, who just a week earlier had been bragging about how quickly the flight would be finished, was shaken by the experience of reaching Prince Rupert and quietly began nursing a growing sense of doubt. The harsh landing had jolted his body, making him feel his age and long for his wife and children back home. At the same time, the growing number of mishaps—damaged propellers, faulty engines, and now these broken struts—left him with the sense that he was cursed. Publicly, he told reporters that he took full responsibility for his "error in judgement" that resulted in the damage to the *Seattle*. But privately he fumed that the army's weather reports had said nothing about the potential for fog, leaving him unprepared at best and setting him up for failure at worst. What's more, no one had told him that the cove was so shallow. If the advance officers couldn't give him accurate information about the first planned stop, how would he be able to land safely in places on the other side of the world? After receiving the promises of reporters traveling with the supply ship not to reveal him as their source, he admitted that he now believed that the British would beat the Americans "hands down" and that flying one aircraft rather than a squadron was an advantage "unless some mishap happened to it."

Though he initially said he would need to pull out of the race, Martin changed his mind the following morning and went back to work on his damaged plane. The men under his command never let on, even to each other, how they felt about their commander's shifting moods. They had known one another for about three months, with all of their interactions coming in the constrained confines of training or public events. This was the first time they were put under stress and had only themselves to fall back on, forcing them to reveal their true characters. For now, the squadron members put their heads down and followed orders, not willing to upset the harmony of their group at the earliest sign of trouble.

By midday it appeared that the squadron would be ready to resume the flight. That is, until Wade took off his plane's cowling—the hood covering its nose—laid it down on the wing of his moored aircraft to grab a piece of rope, reached for it again, and accidentally knocked it into the deep sea. "Now the cowling of an airplane is not one of the things you ever expect to lose," Arnold wrote in his diary. "Although we had spare parts for almost every emergency, we hadn't any new noses for airplanes." After several unsuccessful hours spent trying to bring it up with his fishing pole and line, Wade found a coppersmith in town and convinced him to pound out a substitute. He secured it in place that evening, but the ordeal was not over. For the rest of the journey, the *Boston* flew with a copper nose instead of a silver aluminum cover, and Wade—known for his fastidiousness and sense of fashion—was embarrassed each time they landed.

On the morning of April 10, the four planes pulled away from their moorings and formed a line in the cove. Martin, who had pledged in Seattle that he would give each man a turn at leading the way, took his place behind Smith in the *Chicago*. For the first time, the squadron took off in succession and remained in single file about fifty feet above the waves as humpback whales breached in the frigid water below. They flew past docks and canneries and could see the wooden streets and totem poles of tiny villages too small to be named on the pilots' maps. An hour into their flight they passed the village of Ketchikan, Alaska, where several hundred people waved at them from the shore, the forest behind them so deep and green that it looked like it stretched to the end of the world.

The rain increased as they neared Clarence Strait, about sixty miles from their destination of Sitka, and they flew into a thick haze hiding the mountaintops. Smith, in the lead, brought the group down to twenty feet above the heavy surf, close enough that they were all soon drenched by the freezing mist. Wade, following closely behind, briefly became stuck in the turbulence caused by the aircraft ahead of him. His plane shook violently, forcing him to veer wildly from side to side in search of calm air. "In your wildest imagination you will be unable to conjure up a picture of what it is like and of what a shiver it sends down your spine, especially if one is only a few feet above the ground" when stuck in the wake of another aircraft, Wade later said. A short time later the crews of two fishing boats fighting through the swells waved up at them. "Their friendly salutations were quickly returned, although the rain drops felt like lead shot being thrown into our faces and against our hands," Harding later wrote.

Shortly after 1:30, they broke through the haze and spotted the harbor of Sitka, once the capital of Russian Alaska. Thousands of seagulls soaring along the docks were spooked by the sounds of the plane engines, while snowcapped mountains towered in the distance like the backdrop of a stage. The green patina of the bell tower of St. Michael's Cathedral, the first Eastern Orthodox church built in North America, perched on a nearby hill. As the planes landed and cut their engines, the aviators could hear the sounds of the brass band and the large crowds that had assembled on the waterfront to greet them.

Rather than immediately joining the festivities, the crew members began preparing their planes for the day ahead, a move that would become their ritual at every new stop around the world. Over the next three hours, they refilled their oil and gas, washed down their engines with kerosene to remove oil and dirt before it froze to the metal in the cold, refilled their radiators, flushed and cleaned their gasoline strainers, covered the engine and cockpits, and finally selected what personal items, such as maps and thermoses, to bring with them from their small cockpits. "Every move on the plane or near the pontoons had to be done carefully for fear of falling into the water, or breaking something," Harding later wrote.

Once they were finished, small wooden rafts piloted by native Alaskans took the crew from their moored aircraft to the shore, where representatives of the territorial government led them to a small hotel. In each of their rooms they found huge bouquets of gladioli grown in a local greenhouse, their bright tropical colors seeming to glow against the snowy landscape outside the window. "More than ever, we seemed to have flown out of the fog into fairyland," Wade wrote.

Heavy rain the next morning prevented them from leaving for Seward at dawn as they had hoped. The wind continued to build until it reached the strength of a hurricane. Accepting that they would not fly that day, all of the crew except for Smith and Martin walked to a nearby photographer's shop to kill time. A native Alaskan entered, but none of the men looked up. Eventually, the shop owner asked the Alaskan if there was anything he was interested in. "Yes," he replied casually. "I just wanted to let these folks know that one of their planes is adrift."

They rushed outside to find the *Boston* torn loose from its moorings and heading straight for the *New Orleans*. Three of the men jumped into rowboats and began furiously working their way through the choppy water while the others raced along the docks, grabbing ropes and any anchors they could find. A forest ranger in a nearby boat reached the *New Orleans* when it was within two feet of the *Boston* and began dragging it away. "Without him we would have lost two planes right then," Arnold wrote in his diary that night. The following day, the *New Orleans* broke from its mooring again and started to drift toward the rocky shore. Harding, who was servicing the plane from the wing, climbed into the cockpit and gave it full power until a boat could reach it and attach another anchor. "Such circumstances as these kept all of us under a tremendous strain as to the safety of our planes, both day and night," Martin told the press.

Arnold, in private, was more blunt: "Everyone was soaking wet, cold, tired, and hungry, and in spite of Prohibition we cracked the medical supply and all had a good stiff drink," he wrote in his diary. "And we needed it, too."

He did not realize that his bad luck was just beginning.

CHAPTER TEN

Three-Inch Holes

THE WEATHER FINALLY looked like it was on their side.

The dawn broke clear and calm on April 13, suggesting that the barrage of storms was at its end. As the sunlight shimmered off the snow-capped mountains around them, the eight Americans finished loading supplies into their aircraft. Hoping to make up for lost time, Martin told each man to fill up with enough gas to fly the roughly five hundred fifty miles to Seward. The journey would stretch their planes near the limit of their range, given the strong winds pushing back against them, and they would bypass their planned stop at Cordova. Shortly before 8:45, radio reports came in from vessels in the Gulf of Alaska suggesting that the weather would remain fair. A few minutes later, the four planes were in the sky, hugging the rugged coastline, with Wade in the lead.

An hour later snow started falling. Within minutes, it was coming thick and fast, making it almost impossible to see from one plane to another. The squadron descended nearly to the water's edge and followed the beach to keep from getting lost. The clouds lifted as quickly as they had come in, revealing the eighteen-thousand-foot peak of Mount Saint Elias, the fourth-highest mountain in North America and perhaps the most desolate. Its first known summit came in 1897. An Italian nobleman, the Duke of Abruzzi, braved avalanches, blinding snow, and near starvation to conquer what he called "a most hostile mountain." It would not be climbed again until the 1960s.

The four planes were the sole signs of human life for hundreds of miles. The planet seemed to be consumed by the Malaspina Glacier, one of the largest in the world, which spread out in every direction below them, ultimately covering a larger area than the state of Rhode Island. Fissures of ice splintered into the sea with a thunderous boom that could be heard over the plane engines, startling the pilots with their similarity to cannon fire. The power of the glacier unnerved the men, who flew over the unbroken expanse for nearly forty miles. "There was something weird and terrifying about that apparently inert yet living creature of the Arctic, brooding there between the mountains and the sea," Nelson later wrote.

Another storm, more menacing than the last, suddenly grew around them. The squadron, following Wade, again descended until they were just ten feet above the shore. The ground, the air, the ocean—all appeared the same shade of white, eclipsing variation so thoroughly that the men felt like they were flying in darkness. Finally, they spotted a line along the beach that looked like a small black ribbon caused by the crashing waves melting the snow, and followed it forward. When the clouds briefly parted, the men looked down onto abandoned villages nearly buried by snow, the ghostly relics of boom towns from the gold rush a generation past.

At times the planes flew so low that their pontoons nearly touched the water, forcing them to quickly climb when they spotted shipwrecks or thick logs washed up by the sea. "Most of the time I flew standing up in the cockpit braced against the back of the seat with my feet on the rudder-bar so that I could look out over the front of the plane as well as over the side," Nelson wrote. "Neither Jack nor I dared sit down because if we did we couldn't see the beach." Every few minutes, melting snow dripping off Nelson's forehead would lodge behind his goggles and blur the lenses, compelling him to pull them off his face and alternate with a second pair he had on his seat. Nearly blind, he saw neither ground nor sky, keeping his wings level by the waterline on the shore. Without warning his plane would jerk and pitch, the only signal that he was in a field of turbulence caused by an unseen aircraft a few feet ahead.

Finally, after an hour, they emerged into sunshine. Nelson found the *Seattle* and *Boston* ahead of him and turned back just as the *Chicago* pulled away from a cloud. Smith, its pilot, appeared so overjoyed at his liberation from the blizzard that he darted through the air like a hummingbird, swooping low over shipwrecks out of curiosity and then climbing back into the sky. "We all felt so relieved that we certainly would have 'looped' if our Cruisers had been suitable" for stunt flying, Wade later said.

The lure of clear weather prompted the squadron to fly past Cordova, to the eternal disappointment of the residents of the small village, who had not been informed of the change and had decorated their harbor and main buildings with bunting ordered at great expense from the States. (Martin, embarrassed when he learned what the town had done to welcome them, radioed his apologies to the village mayor that evening.) After an easy landing at Seward, the men rested through a blizzard that consumed much of the following day. Harding, who had rarely encountered a cold winter in his native Tennessee, spent the morning measuring snowflakes and proclaiming that these were the biggest that he had ever seen. That afternoon, the aviators—to a man lean, clean-shaven, and with closely cropped hair, per army regulations—listened to the stories of wild, burly, shaggy-bearded fishermen fresh in from a halibut schooner who tried without success to teach Arnold how to tie a bowline knot.

The men woke up at five on the morning of April 15 to prepare the planes in darkness and warm the day's motor oil over a bonfire on the shore. At eleven, the planes left in the clearest weather they had seen since San Diego on a four-hundred-twenty-five-mile flight to Chignik. The hamlet in western Alaska was almost exactly twenty-three hundred miles due north of the warmth and sunshine of Honolulu, which felt much farther away than that.

The first three planes took off without a problem. Again, Martin in the *Seattle* struggled to keep up. Twice he attempted to take off without success while the other three pilots flew circles in the sky and spent the time taking pictures of each other. On his third attempt he was able to achieve lift, and the squadron flew for four uninterrupted hours through flawless skies over deep blue water and past snow-covered mountains. For the first time since California, they found flying enjoyable. The pressure of the race, the problems with the planes—all of that seemed to melt away under the persistent hum of the engines propelling them further into a world that felt glorious and strange. The landscape was "beyond description in beauty and splendor," Harding later wrote.

Martin, however, continued to battle with his machine. When the other three pilots opted to fly directly over a mountain peak, he discovered that he did not have enough power to crest it. Forced to take a half circle around it, he found himself lagging behind the squadron, which seemed to gradually disappear into the horizon. As he attempted to increase his speed, Harvey grabbed his shoulder from the rear cockpit and began yelling at him to check the oil-pressure gauge. Martin looked down and discovered that it had dropped to zero.

There was little time to act. The fact that the plane remained airborne was a miracle. Within minutes, maybe seconds, without oil, the engine would begin grinding metal on metal, seizing itself into a stall that Martin would not be able to recover from. Five hundred feet above Cape Igvak, where the sea was the roughest of any section of the Alaskan coast, he scanned the horizon for a place to land while he remained in control of the aircraft. He somehow coaxed enough power from his fading engine to reach a cove near Portage Bay and landed in its smooth water, not knowing who or what lurked nearby.

He brought the plane closer to the shore, craning his head over the side to see if there were any logs or rocks that would puncture their pontoons and sink the aircraft. When the plane slowed to a stop, Harvey carefully climbed out onto the wing and inched forward to examine the damage. He found a three-inch hole in the crankcase, the housing that contains all the parts of the engine. Punctures the size of a quarter had been known to cause fatal accidents in other aircraft.

There was nothing that he could do. The plane, which had somehow limped along with a catastrophic injury, was dead. Both men looked up, expecting to see the other members of the squadron circling back to check on them. Instead, they saw an empty sky. They were all alone in the wilderness, with no means of contact. As the sun began to set, they sat in the cockpit of their plane, rising and falling with each passing wave, focused on how they would survive the night ahead.

In their training in Virginia, the men had been drilled in what to do in this situation: the crews of any operational aircraft should immediately circle back to those who were in distress. The stricken aviators would then fire a pistol signal to indicate the seriousness of the trouble. Though they did not see or hear any other planes, Martin and Harvey trusted that the others were coming. As the minutes ticked by, Martin again tested the engine, and confirmed that it was useless. He knew he would soon have to make a decision. If they remained in the wounded aircraft, they ran the risk that it would snap free of its anchor and drift helplessly through the cold darkness. Their other option was wading ashore through the deep icy waters and hoping that they would find enough dry wood to start a bonfire before their clothes began to freeze. If they failed, they would be dead by the morning. As they sat there contemplating their fate, Martin thought of the race. Abandoning their plane meant that there would be no way they could complete the trip, assuming that they were somehow rescued. As darkness fell, Martin told Harvey that he was free to swim to shore but that he would remain in the aircraft. Without hesitation, Harvey responded, "I am going to stay with you."

The men ate a portion of their emergency rations and agreed to divide the night into four-hour watches so that each could rest. Sleep never came. The bitter cold seized their bodies as they shivered in their small cockpits, aching for warmth. A three-quarter-full moon bathed the landscape in an eerie glow, lighting the peaks that towered above them in the white wilderness. The only sound Martin heard came from six sablefish, known in Alaskan waters as "butterballs" for their rich taste, that he watched darting along the surface of the water as if playing a game. "I sort of resented that they were so happy, so isolated from mankind, and I was so lonesome," Martin wrote. He turned from one side to the other, trying to stretch his long legs in the confined cockpit. Around two in the morning, the wind began to pick up, followed by icy rain and then snow. Running out of hope, the men pulled the canvas cockpit cover over their heads for shelter from the elements. They sat there, bobbing blindly in the swells, and prayed that their rescue would soon come.

WHEN THEY LANDED in Chignik, the six members of the American squadron waited on the water for a few paralyzing minutes, unsure whether Martin's plane would appear out of the haze. Each moment felt heavy, as if torn between optimism and fear. Finally, Wade and Nelson left their aircraft in the hands of their mechanics and came ashore. They found a radio operator and sent a message to the US Navy requesting that the *Corey* and *Hull*, two destroyers in the region, race toward Martin's last known location. Both ships replied that they were twelve hours away and would reach the area by morning. Other ships joined in the search, including the fishing trawlers whose crews the men had joked around with just a few days before. The safety of the two world fliers consumed the Alaska Territory, prompting a superintendent of a Standard Oil drilling operation on Kodiak Island to jump on horseback and ride through a mountain pass, braving snow that sank eight feet deep in some places, to order the company's local ship to aid in the search.

Reports of Martin and Harvey's disappearance dominated the front page of dozens of newspapers in the United States, Canada, and England.

"Major Frederick L Martin, leader of the army round the world flight, is missing and may have drowned in Alaskan waters," the Associated Press reported in a widely published story. Smith, in a statement to the press, admitted that the squadron had not noticed Martin's absence until they were too low on fuel to turn back and search for him. He and the other five men remaining in the squadron slept little that night. Each second that passed without news of Martin and Harvey was another that weighed on their conscience. An engine failure and forced landing was excusable; abandoning two men to perish alone in the wilderness was not.

As the seconds ticked by, the race with MacLaren felt like a memory. At that moment, he was on the other side of the world soaring above the Ionian Islands, his new engine finally installed. He landed at Athens at 2:45 in the afternoon in ideal flying conditions and was greeted by the head of the Greek air force. When asked by a reporter to describe his flight, MacLaren said only that he and his men were eager to start again the next day to make up for lost time. The following morning he was airborne again. He circled once above the Acropolis and then turned toward the Mediterranean and Cairo. He landed that night just as the sun was setting behind the Pyramids. The three British crew members sat down for dinner in the mess hall of a British air base, where, in the words one of reporter, "they appeared remarkably fresh after their eight and a half hour's flight, though, naturally, they were somewhat deaf after the roar of the engines."

In the early dawn Martin saw smoke on the horizon. Unsure if it was the fog or a trick of his tired mind, he watched and waited. He soon saw the outlines of two ships passing in front of him. Following protocol, Harvey fired three shots from a flare gun, each one a minute apart. The ships stopped briefly but then appeared to resume their path. Harvey fired three more. One ship turned and began heading toward them. Too far away to see any distinguishing characteristics, Martin told Harvey to prepare for the ship to be Japanese. The rescue of Americans by Japanese sailors at a time when their countries seemed headed for war would surely put the two men at the center of an international incident and likely mean the end of their careers. A small launch soon appeared, heading straight toward them. On it sat the executive officer of the USS *Hull*. They had been saved.

Martin and Harvey were brought aboard the ship and given warm meals and dry clothes. The *Hull* radioed that the plane had been found but would need a new engine. Crew members attached the *Seattle* to the ship's towline and floated it ten miles to the nearest village, at one point carrying it across a narrow creek so that the plane could sit safely in a small pond. With no other accommodations available, Martin and Harvey slept that night on the floor of the village's only store.

Once rested, Martin reasserted his command over the mission. He radioed Smith in Chignik and ordered the squadron to head to Dutch Harbor, a port on the island of Unalaska, Alaska (while scholars do not know the exact provenance of the island's apparently oppositional name, it appears to come from an Aleut word meaning "near the mainland"). He then reminded the men of their duty to each other. The arrangements were "that the last ship will fly over the ship in distress until they get a . . . signal indicating the seriousness of the trouble," Martin wrote in a letter to General Patrick in Washington. "Why this was not done I have not had an opportunity to learn. The seriousness of this oversight will be impressed upon all."

While he nursed a grudge at being left behind, Martin was briefly a hero back home. "These flyers are proving themselves worthy of the uniforms they wear," proclaimed an editorial in the *Spokane Chronicle*. "They are facing desperate odds and are winning. The mere fact that Major Martin was forced to land because of engine trouble after a flight of about 300 miles is of little moment. The fact is that he saved his ship and will [be] ready in a few days to hop off again."

While the remainder of the squadron proceeded with an uneventful flight to Unalaska, Martin and Harvey removed their damaged engine and began to install its replacement. For the first time, they witnessed the violence of williwaws—sudden, fierce winds that blasted down from the mountains to the sea. As Martin and Harvey drifted to sleep one night in the general store, they heard the howling of a williwaw and raced to the window to see their plane lifted completely out of the water, its reinforced lines barely keeping it from being pulled into the tree-tops. "We labored under the constant dread that the *Seattle* might be destroyed at any time, night and day," Martin wrote.

Nearly six hundred miles away, the other members of the squadron were also struggling to contend with wind more powerful than anything they had experienced. As Smith and Arnold walked down a street near their moored planes, they heard a clanking and turned to see an oil drum bouncing on the road toward them. They jumped out of the way and then watched as the wind lifted boards of lumber like it was shuffling a deck of cards. That night, the williwaws pulled the planes from their anchors. The men jumped into icy water up to their necks and grabbed the lines in the dark. It was not until after midnight that they finally pulled the planes up onto the beach. "We were so cold that we couldn't even unbutton our coats," Smith later said.

When the wind calmed down, Martin and Harvey, along with sailors from the ship that had brought them a new engine, worked all night under the light of gasoline lanterns to finish installing it. At six in the morning on April 25, nearly a week after their plane had become separated from the rest of the squadron, the craft was once again ready to fly. Though the snow kept coming, Martin felt the burden of lost time and was uneasy at the prospect of more delays. At eleven in the morning, the *Seattle* took off from Portage Bay into darkening skies and followed the shoreline for nearly two and a half hours toward Chignik. They briefly dropped into a secluded harbor to wait out the storm and then reached Chignik by nightfall.

Snow propelled by powerful winds coated the landscape over the following three days, blocking them in. By the time the storm died down, more than four hundred pounds of ice clung to the *Seattle*'s wings and pontoons, making the plane look more like an iceberg than a machine. Martin and Harvey spent over two hours scraping off the plane, the ice falling in large chunks at their feet.

Before the sun came up on the morning of April 30, Martin told Harvey that they would be flying that day. A steady snow poured from the sky, but the wind was mild. The men loaded the plane with two hundred gallons of gasoline and oil, enough to reach Dutch Harbor. At the suggestion of the superintendent of a local cannery, Martin planned to take a shortcut over an extended section of land. While it was a risk, given that the plane had pontoons and was without wheels that it could use for an emergency landing, Martin was growing antsy and felt like it was worth it. "Not knowing how long we might have to wait for another halfway decent day, we shoved off," he said.

A few hundred miles away, in Unalaska, the remainder of the squadron listened to radio traffic as Martin took off into the clouds. Though the *Seattle* carried no communication systems itself, canneries along the route planned to broadcast its location as it passed by. By nightfall, the eight Americans would be reunited and ready to take on the daunting task of flying to Japan.

An hour passed without any reports of the *Seattle*. Then another. And another still. By nightfall, there was no way to escape a frightening new reality: Martin was again lost, and this time without leaving any hint as to where in the vast frozen wild he could be found.

CHAPTER ELEVEN

Presumed Dead

THE REALITY OF how large Alaska is can sneak up on even those who are there. It is not enough to say that it is roughly three times the size of Texas, the second-largest state. Nor is it enough to know that half of all the coastline held by the United States is along Alaskan waters. Perhaps the best way to fully convey its size is to place a map of Alaska over a map of what its residents call the Lower 48. Only then do you discover that the chain of islands dotting the immense Gulf of Alaska stretch across an area equivalent to the distance between Tennessee and California.

It was within this great open expanse that Martin and Harvey disappeared, two grains of sand on a windswept beach. Radio messages pinged from the communications room on the US Coast Guard ship *Algonquin* to all navy and Coast Guard ships within hundreds of miles. Private vessels, many of them fishing trawlers, joined in the hunt. By the end of the first day, the search party included two ships that were in the middle of conducting scientific surveys and a fleet of small motorboats owned by cannery companies. Boats threaded through coves and inlets looking for signs of the lost men. Near Chignik, where Martin and Harvey had last been seen, two dogsled teams were organized and sent in opposite directions to search over the jagged terrain.

Though few wanted to admit it, most felt a sense of hopelessness from the start. The area was so large and the clues to go by so few. No vessels had reported seeing the flailing *Seattle*, nor had any villagers along the harbor noticed anything—a section of a wing, downed trees, a bonfire on a lonely coast—that would suggest the presence of a plane or survivors. "Fear that Major Frederick L. Martin and Sergeant Alva Harvey may have given their lives in their efforts to make the Stars and Stripes the first flag to be carried around the world by air was growing today," the United Press reported less than thirty hours after the *Seattle* was last seen.

The USS *Hull*, which rescued Martin and Harvey when they had become separated from the squadron nearly two weeks earlier, arrived in San Francisco to learn that the two men they had plucked shivering from an uninhabited cove were again missing. The captain of the ship tried to put a brave face on the string of mishaps that had plagued Martin and the *Seattle* since California. "When we hauled him aboard the *Hull* he hadn't had anything to eat for twenty-four hours and was suffering terribly from cold and exhaustion," he said. "But the first thing he did was smile broadly and say 'Leave it to the US Navy; it's always around when wanted.'"

Rather than being reassuring, the captain's forced optimism had the strange effect of making it seem like the obituaries for the two men were already written. The tone of each day's press reports grew more ominous as the hours mounted. "Those most closely concerned with the flight admitted they were feeling 'grave anxiety' as to the commander's safety. No such intensive search of the Arctic waters has ever been made as that which was under way today," the *Riverside Daily Press* reported on May 2, two days after the plane's disappearance. "There is a general belief here that the terrific storm of the last few days, reaching at times a velocity of 100 miles an hour, may have driven the plane far out to sea, or wrecked it completely," the *Atlanta Constitution* reported the following day. The *Miami News* noted that the fishing pole the *Seattle* carried in its storage compartment represented the "faint ray of hope that the men may not die from starvation," and the *Des Moines Register* reported that "All hope that Maj. Frederick Martin is still alive has been practically abandoned."

Evan J. David, a reporter for the United Press wire service, briefly became one of the most-read journalists in the world for his daily dispatches chronicling the search for the *Seattle* while he was aboard the *Algonquin*. A part-time pulp novelist, he seized the moment by centering himself in the story and adding dialogue from private conversations he claimed to have had with Martin prior to his disappearance that to skeptics sounded like they were torn from one of his books. (In one article, David wrote that Martin had told him shortly before he was last seen alive, "Personally I don't believe in luck . . . but you can say this for me: I am confident that I will be able to lead this flight around the world to a successful conclusion.") Yet beyond the hyperbole, the fact remained that Martin and Harvey were lost in an unforgiving place, and David saw firsthand the lengths that search parties went to in hopes of saving them. The *Algonquin* "steamed into the dozens of unexplored coves and inlets and I often imagined that I saw a flashlight, signaling to us, only to find, when we ran in and explored the shore, nothing but barren rocks and no sign of life," he wrote.

Martin's wife, whom the press rarely referred to by her first name, Grace, unwillingly became a national fascination. Reporters found her living in a small house in San Diego with her sister and eight-year-old son, Robert, unable to sleep. She had not yet told her son that his father was missing. "I'm hoping for the best," she said in an article that ran on the front page of the *Atlanta Constitution* and dozens of other papers nationwide. "These are terrible hours for me and my boy. I am afraid I will never see my husband alive again."

The reporters invited themselves in and wouldn't leave, chronicling every movement of her hands or wrinkle of her brows in search of good copy. Her stray comments appeared on front pages. "It's been so long now, more than two whole days, since my husband and his young mechanic left to join the others. How could they be alive in all that snow and ice?" she wondered in an article that ran nationwide.

Under the pressure of constant observation, Grace Martin felt the ties holding her together begin to fray. A map of the world lay spread out on a living-room table. On it, she drew a line each day charting her husband's progress so that Robert, with a glance, could see where his father was. The last mark was an *X* near Chignik. "She hopes to make the line longer, to draw it all around the world and back home again," one reporter noted in the sort of breathless tone that conveyed a sense that her husband was a fallen hero. "But her intuition tells her the end of the line on her map may mark the approximate point where a brave man met his death."

Enterprising reporters tracked down Martin's sixty-two-year-old mother, Nancy, in the home of her daughter's farm in the flat fields outside of Connersville, Indiana. She had last seen her son a year earlier and now relied on newspaper and radio reports to learn whether he was alive or dead. "It is impossible for anyone to tell whether my boy fell in the sea or on land," she said. "He might be trapped in the snow . . . I realize that transmission of news concerning him is slow but it seems to me that word must come soon."

In small rooms in Alaska and Washington, DC, the question was not whether Martin would be saved but when the squadron should resume its attempt. Publicly, military officials expressed total confidence that Martin and Harvey were alive and unharmed. In private, however, they felt that the men's disappearance threatened to cast a shadow over the remainder of the flight, turning what had been a tale of a plucky underdog into a tragedy. President Coolidge, attuned to the public's fascination with the flight, asked for daily updates on the search. No matter what ultimately became of the crew of the *Seattle*, however, there seemed to be no option but to go on. If they halted now, before the squadron left North America, much less United States territory, it would seem to confirm skeptics' suspicions that the flight was an arrogant and foolhardy move by a nation that had gotten ahead of itself. If Alaska was the end of the line, then the world's judgment of American aviation would be short and cruel: its planes broke down and its pilots went missing.

The nation's reputation suffered all the more by comparison to Great Britain's efforts. At that moment, while Martin and Harvey were lost and reporters circled their relatives like vultures, MacLaren was resting in Karachi, India (now part of modern-day Pakistan). He had landed several days earlier in front of a large cheering crowd of Royal Air Force officers under perfect skies at exactly the scheduled time, a feat that led a local reporter to call him "dramatically punctual." Since leaving England, he had flown 4,890 miles. Over the next several days, he planned to rest and service his plane before beginning the next leg to Tokyo. "All the airmen [are] in excellent health, sun bronzed and dusty, but perhaps a little weary and deaf," the *Western Daily Press* wrote. Despite the previous delays in Greece, his progress was now so swift that it seemed entirely possible that he would reach Japan and cross over to Alaska before the American squadron had escaped from its icy confines. MacLaren had "made it a race between American and British aviators for the honor of being the first to cross the Pacific," the *Pittsburgh Post-Gazette* reported, noting that the advantages he enjoyed from flying with prevailing winds put him on pace to pass over the North Atlantic before the weather turned against him.

"If the British Expedition succeeds in completing the flight around the world with one ship and their comparatively meager preparations, it will greatly distract from the prestige of American aviation, even if the Air Service flight is successful," the head of the army's War Plans

Division wrote in a memo to General Patrick. Trying to get the four planes around the world as a group would make it nearly impossible for America to win the race and restore its self-pride, he argued. While he did not outright call for it, he strongly hinted that the three remaining pilots should be ready to go it alone. "It is recommended that every effort be made to get the American flight around the world first," he wrote. "If this recommendation is approved, it is further recommended that the following be sent to [the remaining crew]: 'Vital that further accident to any one plane does not delay progress of other planes.'"

MacLaren's success wasn't the sole threat to America's dreams of achieving the first world flight. The nation soon learned of a thirty-two-year-old Frenchman named Georges Pelletier d'Oisy. Short, joyful, and talkative on land, d'Oisy seemed to transform into another person in the air. During the World War, he quickly recognized the advantage of altitude when confronted with an enemy and soared during dogfights to freezing heights that other men would dare not attempt. Soon he had five confirmed victories, making him one of his nation's first flying aces. He was named a knight in the Legion of Honor, France's highest national award, then became one of its most prized flight instructors, always pushing his students to brace themselves to withstand the shock of higher altitudes. His insistence on flying high led his fellow airmen to nickname him Pivolo, after his habit of telling recruits, *Pie vole haut—* "Magpie flies high" in French.

With his skill and bravery, he seemed to be the embodiment of a nation that had been early to grasp the importance of aviation and was ready to prove that its men and machines were the best in the world. On the morning of April 23, d'Oisy took off before sunrise from a small airstrip in a suburb southwest of Paris in a plane designed by Louis-Charles Bréguet, a French aviation pioneer who had designed aircraft that held numerous distance records and who built one of the first forerunners of the modern helicopter. Unlike the American and British flights, the date of d'Oisy's entry into the world race was unannounced beforehand. He had neither a planned string of supply depots nor a reliable source of gasoline and oil. His spare parts were limited to what he carried in the plane along with a six-day supply of emergency rations. The sole form of assistance he could turn to was his mechanic, who sat in the rear cockpit.

If he succeeded in his attempt, he would confirm that his country was leading the way forward. His goal was "to show France's predominance in the air," the *Baltimore Evening Sun* noted in a front-page article detailing the flight. While he publicly said that he was not racing anyone, it was widely assumed that Gallic pride would not permit him to watch anyone succeed ahead of France. "It is believed that one reason he kept the secret of his project until the very eve of his departure was that he hopes to beat both the British and American airmen," London's *Daily Telegraph* reported.

On the first day he reached Bucharest, charting some twelve hundred miles over eleven hours. The next he flew almost a thousand miles to Aleppo (in modern-day Syria), one of the oldest continuously inhabited cities in the world, sustaining hours in icy temperatures as he crossed over the Taurus Mountains at an altitude of ten thousand feet. The following morning he was airborne again, soaring over a broiling desert that stretched as far as he could see. Newspapers hailed him as "the French hero of the hour" for his unrelenting pace. He landed that evening in the port city of Basra, in modern-day Iraq, after logging another seven hundred miles, and took off the following morning for Calcutta (now Kolkata). When he landed, he found himself in possession of a new record for the fastest flight from Europe to India, having taken four days to fly as far as MacLaren had in nearly six weeks. "That French aviator, d'Oisy, is hurrying along at a rate which violates all accepted customs in world flights," an editorial in the *Indianapolis Star* marveled.

There was still more for the Americans to worry about. A minor Portuguese nobleman, António Jacinto da Silva de Brito Pais, and two crew members took off in early April from Lisbon in a French-built plane that Pais had already crashed and repaired twice. They headed toward Asia on a flight meant to add another chapter to the annals of the legendary Portuguese voyages of discovery that had occurred some four hundred years earlier. Pais named his plane the *Patria*, "Motherland," in homage to a line in the Portuguese epic poem *Lusíadas* that translates to "This is my beloved and blissful motherland." Soon, he, too, was in India.

The race appeared open to any of them. MacLaren had the organization of an empire behind him; d'Oisy the skill and engineering of a country that felt the air was its birthright; Pais the fortitude of idealism as he attempted to follow in his ancestors' proud footsteps and voyage around the world.

There was only one country that seemed adrift. In a sense, the *Seattle*'s disappearance played into General Billy Mitchell's vision for the future.

Though he was far away from Washington, he knew that those in power would never quit a world race at a time when their rivals were all progressing. If anything, they would remain in competition not out of faith but out of pride. America's lack of a robust aviation industry and its disrespect for planes had long been Mitchell's embarrassment. Now the nation's refusal to admit defeat would ultimately save the world flight even though it seemed fruitless to go on. In the White House, aides to President Coolidge told reporters that "when the flight was started the dangers which would be encountered were realized fully, but unless the regrettable fact that one of the aviators has disappeared has disclosed some obstacle insurmountable to the attempt, it is the President's opinion that the remaining aviators should continue."

The newspapermen, who saw the potential of even more great copy ahead, did not want America to quit and bow out of what had become a national obsession. "It is the dauntless spirit of America that speaks in the official order to the three airplanes yet intact in the world flight to 'carry on'—to continue their flight, despite the ominous situation with reference to their leader and his mechanician," argued an editorial in the Long Beach, California, *Press-Telegram*. "There must be heroic daring, and mayhap tragedies, among intrepid pioneers in these epochal air adventures. But eventually flying around the world will become comparatively safe." Martin's presumed death was seen by some as justification for America's decision to launch a squadron as opposed to the lone planes of England and France, and more reason for its remaining members to go on. Martin's "second disappearance from view is a reminder of the grimmest of the reasons why the war department chose four airplanes to attempt the world flight," noted Illinois's *Rock Island Argus*. "It will be a sorry start for the expedition if it has lost its leader before it attempted its first crossing from continent to continent."

With Martin gone, the weight of command fell to Smith. He was known for his unmatched combination of safety and skill, yet few thought of him as an inspiring figure. Quiet, with a tendency to let others guess at what he was feeling, Smith often saw human connection as a chore, not an instinct. Had Washington chosen the same strategy as other nations in the world race, he would happily have flown as the sole entry braving the elements. At the head of a squadron, he was out of his element, the leader who wanted nothing more than to be alone. He never let on how the countless hours waiting on Martin during his earlier mechanical failures frustrated the racer in him who felt that he was falling far behind. For a man who had once been bold enough to ask for a rival's plane so that his adventure would not end, still hours felt like purgatory. Though he did not show it, the twin sides of his personality battled over how to respond to Martin's disappearance. The need to escape into the air and feel the sensation of speed clashed with his profound sense of duty, his reverence for other men's lives. As the head of a forest patrol unit, he had never lost a man under his watch. Now, far from the woods of Oregon, he sat in front of the radio deep into the night, canvassing each ship in the area for any new information on his missing commander while keeping tabs on the progress of the European pilots.

As the search for Martin and Harvey continued, the other crew members tended to their planes and prepared for the order from Washington to resume their flight. Though they had not yet seen anything that made them question Smith's ability in the air, he seemed too distant to trust. His thoughts, his sense of humor, his passions—all were a mystery waiting to be solved. Even his choices for food gave no windows into who he was as a person. In his first fateful decision as the head of the squadron, Smith prepared eggs Vienna for the crew for breakfast, lunch, and dinner. After two days of this, his men were so desperate for variety that they began to forage for alternatives themselves through a trader's hut, dodging the rats running between their feet.

One night the waiting aviators awoke to the wild ringing of church bells. The men walked toward the sound, a full moon illuminating the snowy streets. They found every white person in the village of Illiiliyook inside the church. Twenty-one men gathered on one side of the aisle across from six women on the other, all of them holding a candle in their hands. A bishop of the Russian Orthodox Church, whose long beard and flowing robes danced in shadows on the wall, led the congregation in songs and chants in a ceremony that lasted until sunrise. None of the worshippers sat down during the service, though benches were eventually brought over for the benefit of the puzzled aviators shivering in their flying suits. "It was so cold that we could see our breath congeal," Ogden later said.

For the first time, the men were confronted with a culture foreign to them. Little about their upbringing or experiences had prepared them for the human aspect of a world flight. What had until now been a series of spots on a map revealed themselves to be full of people as vibrant and alive as they were, with their own aspirations and traditions. The realization, common to all travelers, that one's own way of life is just one of many seemed to catch the American aviators off guard, and their responses to the scene playing out in front of them varied. Ogden, the youngest and most sheltered of the group, found it disturbing. "The wailing of these primitive people in their strange tongue, the priest's strange vestments, the incense, the icons, the flickering candles, the howling of the storm outside, made me realize how far I was from my home in Mississippi," he later said. He often ducked out of the church that night, each time walking down to the harbor to confirm that the planes were still safe.

Smith received his first command as the new squadron leader on May 2. "Don't delay longer waiting for Major Martin," General Patrick wrote. "See that everything possible done to find him. Planes two, three, and four to proceed to Japan at earliest possible moment." The men waited a day for a storm to pass and then were up before dawn completing the final checks of their aircraft. A large crowd of villagers helped the men float their planes into the high tide and get them in position. Around eleven that morning, a naval ship to their west radioed that the weather was clear. The squadron, now consisting of three planes, rose and flew in single file out of Unalaska Bay and over the Bering Sea. Heavy clouds kept the men flying low enough to the ground that they could see herds of reindeer grazing on the open tundra. Martin and Harvey remained at the center of their thoughts. It was not hard to imagine a similar fate. If they crashed in this unforgiving place, what was to stop them from ending up as the men in the *Seattle*, lost and perhaps never to be seen again?

Nearly twenty-eight hundred miles away, in San Diego, Grace Martin collapsed in tears when she learned that the three planes had resumed their flight without her husband leading them. She shared the letter she had received from him just days before, which recounted his rescue by the USS *Hull* and seemed optimistic about the flight ahead. "This is one of the windiest places in the world and I will heave a sigh of relief when we get away," he wrote. In a widely published story, a wire service reporter said that Mrs. Martin "asserted that an overwhelming conviction that her husband was dead had seized her," and her sister "felt an unaccountable conviction that Major Martin was dead at the same moment." She fled the house for the small apartment she shared with her husband

and son and busied herself with housework as a distraction from what she called a "psychic death message."

Such an outpouring of grief and emotion was unwelcome by the army, and local officials moved to quiet a woman who was known for her hunches and other unexplainable convictions. The following day, an article in the *Los Angeles Times*, a paper that had been among the most boisterous supporters of the world flight, given its deep connections to the local aviation industry, refuted the report. "It would be foolish, of course, to say that I am not concerned over the Major's welfare, because it is a strain, but I haven't the least doubt but that he will be heard from in due time," a stiffened Mrs. Martin said.

No matter her true feelings, there remained no signs of her husband or Harvey. Each hour that passed felt like the narrowing of a window, inch by inch, until there was no more space for hope to sneak in.

Chapter Twelve

Dead White

THE MOUNTAIN WASN'T supposed to be there.

Martin crouched in the cockpit of the *Seattle* on April 30 and tried without success to get the streams and lakes he could see below him to match up with those on the map resting in his lap. He looked up and saw a rocky peak looming ahead. *That can't be right,* he thought. Assuming he had banked too sharply when departing Chignik an hour earlier, he turned and flew back in the opposite direction in hopes of re-orienting himself. Winds lashed at his wings, pushing him so far adrift from his intended path that an attempt to find the plane's position by means of dead reckoning—a practice used by sailors at least as far back as the days of Columbus in which location was estimated by evaluating the distance and course previously traveled—felt fruitless. Retracing his steps seemed the more conservative choice.

He thought he saw a familiar shape in the hills below and turned north. With Harvey sitting in its rear cockpit, the *Seattle* glided over what appeared to be a barren island, devoid of even trees. A dial on the instrument panel indicated that they were about two hundred feet above the ground. Flying over land rather than water made both men anxious, given that their pontoons would be useless until they found the open sea. They caught a glimpse of blue ocean a short distance to the west. Martin angled the plane toward it.

Later, in the quiet of the wilderness, they would ask themselves if this was the moment when the stress of their long delay in Chignik finally broke their perception of reality. Though the plane remained on the same course, the water never got any closer, leaving the tantalizing safety of the ocean always just out of reach. The men, as if drawn to a Siren's call, headed directly into thick fog. Martin debated turning around once more in hopes of finding Chignik. He instead pushed on, thinking that the water must surely be near. The fog swirled around them, blotting out the land and sky. Looking for escape, Martin dove to just a few feet above the ground, yet found no relief. No matter which direction he turned, the fog never relented.

He had one option left: climb. If the fog was too thick to see through, perhaps cresting high above it would offer a vantage point, albeit a freezing one, from which they could fix their position. The mountain they saw earlier was now safely behind them, and the maps did not indicate any other peaks in the area. Martin pulled back on the stick. The *Seattle*, weighed down with more than two hundred gallons of gasoline and oil to fight the wind over the long flight to Dutch Harbor, strained to comply. The plane arced higher, taking minutes to rise a distance that normally would have taken seconds. Suddenly, another mountain stood directly ahead. Martin had just seconds before impact to aim for level ground.

The right pontoon struck first. The force of the collision pushed it into the plane's fuselage, shattering its struts. The left pontoon splintered as the top right wing was driven halfway back to the tail. The lower right wing cracked into dozens of pieces, a demolition so thorough that it no longer looked like a wing at all. The wrecked shell of the plane slid for more than a hundred feet up a gentle, gradual slope and finally came to rest on the top ledge of a thousand-foot-high precipice.

There wasn't a sound. Snow covered the nose of the plane, making it appear to be slipping into white quicksand. No trees grew out of the hard ground. Harvey was the first to move. He climbed out of the rear cockpit and checked his body for injuries. He was surprised to find none. Martin recovered from his shock a moment later and pulled himself out of the plane. He, too, scanned his body, finding a few scratches to his face. Miraculously, they were able to walk away from the crash unharmed. Yet their ordeal was just beginning.

They were alone, with no means of communication and only a faint idea of where they had crashed. Both men knew that every choice that awaited them would lead to either their survival and eventual rescue or a painful death in a place so barren that it might be years before someone found their bodies. Martin, though, could not yet fully grasp the potential for tragedy. Overcome by shock, he could not let go of the idea that his world flight was at an end. "In that twisted mass of wreckage lie all my hopes and ambition and the greatest opportunities of any man in recent years forever lost," he wrote. Both of them remained in a daze as they silently packed up the small tin of liquid emergency rations, their pistols, a shotgun, and a fishing pole and began walking south.

Each step took them deeper into the fog. The ground blended into the air, turning everything around them dead white. The men stumbled often and could not tell if they were walking in a straight line. With nothing to orient themselves in the ghostly mist, they felt their sense of balance wane. They stopped frequently to check their course on the compass Martin held. Every stride they took was tentative due to the all-too-real possibility that they could walk straight off a cliff hidden by the fog.

After two hours of frustration, they returned to the plane to seek shelter for the night. The men built a fire out of the smashed wings of the *Seattle* and crawled into its empty baggage compartment to try to sleep. The wreckage was tilted at an angle of forty-five degrees, making it impossible to lie flat, and there was not enough space in the two-and-a-half-foot-wide opening for both men to fit. They took turns in the confined space, each stretching out on top of the other man who was sleeping half exposed in the elements. The bitter-cold wind seeped into their bones.

When they awoke, the fog was still heavy. They sat and waited, keeping the fire burning. By the afternoon, the flames had melted a pit in the frozen ground. The men grabbed a small spade from the plane, cut foot-long bricks of snow and ice, and stacked them into walls. They pulled the remainder of one of the wings of their plane into place as a roof and built berms of snow around the sides to keep out the wind.

With a primitive shelter now protecting them, they smoked their remaining cigarettes and tried to keep warm until the fog relented. There were few ways to orient themselves in the wilderness, giving them the uncomfortable sense that they were floating away. The sky gave no clues. The spring Alaskan sun did not fully set until after ten at night and reappeared six hours later. The fog muted the light, making day and night distinguishable by the tint of the suffocating haze.

On May 2, two days after their crash, they decided to again search for the coast. Learning from their earlier unsuccessful attempt, the men pulled off their heavy, fur-lined flying suits, which were clumsy to walk in, and began their hike clad in woolen pants, flannel shirts, and cotton overalls. One man walked a few paces in front of the other, who would shout if their path appeared to zag off a straight line. They made their way over the mountain and to the top of another ridge where the fog lifted slightly and revealed they were a few paces from tumbling straight down a fifteen-hundred-foot cliff. Spooked by the experience, the men turned back to the creek they had crossed a few minutes earlier and decided to follow it toward the Bering Sea.

Harvey was the first to begin to lose his sight. Snow blindness is a common malady in Alaska in the spring, caused either by damage from the reflection of powerful ultraviolent light off snow or ice, or the freezing of the surface of the cornea. His eyes burned and his attempts to quell the pain by bathing them with clumps of snow fueled further agony. He caught only vignettes of the world around him as what felt like hundreds of grains of sand obscured his vision. A sharp bush he could not see tore a hole in the right leg of his pants, letting the brutally cold air in. He pulled on a pair of tinted goggles and tried to keep up with Martin. They continued along the path of the creek for nearly six hours, Harvey stumbling and tripping most of the way. The sun began to set. The men stopped in a thicket of dead alder bushes and collected the branches for a fire. It was then that they registered the folly of leaving their flying suits behind. While constant motion had kept them warm during the day, they began to freeze in their wet overalls, and the ground was too cold for them to lie down on.

They passed the night without sleeping and in the morning abandoned the idea of following the creek to the Bering coast, which would likely be uninhabited and would offer no driftwood for them to use for fire or shelter. When the sun rose they retraced their steps back to their wrecked airplane and the shelter they had built beneath its wing. Harvey, now fully snow-blind, asked Martin to hand him boric acid from the plane's first aid kit and poured it into his eyes, following the instructions given to them during one of their countless lectures in Virginia.

By the following morning his vision had nearly returned. The fog briefly lifted, allowing the men to survey their surroundings from a nearby peak. They looked to the south and saw a wall of mountains, their tops cloaked by clouds. Nearly hidden among them to the southwest was a lake. Praying that a trapper might keep a cabin along its shores, around eleven a.m., the men began hiking in that direction. Five hours later they estimated that they were still three or four miles away. Again they found an alder thicket and built a fire. For dinner, they shot and ate a ptarmigan, a partridge-like bird native to the Arctic that burrows in the snow. The heat of the cooked meat seemed to warm them from the inside. Martin, particularly, found the bitter, gamy taste of the bird delicious and longed for more. The next morning, they shot another ptarmigan and ate it, then started for the lake with renewed energy.

The men reached it around noon. They scanned along its shoreline with their binoculars but found nothing that suggested the presence of human life. Without noticing it, Martin had begun to lose his sight despite wearing snow goggles, and found that he now stumbled over the terrain. Harvey took the lead, and they followed a stream whose shape appeared similar to one on their maps. Soon, however, the stream bent in the opposite direction they had expected, and they were once again adrift. Martin struggled to match Harvey's pace. By two in the afternoon he was helpless. They stopped in a clearing and Harvey gathered dead-wood and dry grass from a nearby marsh. He built a fire and a bed, and the two men slept for four motionless hours, their first sustained rest since the crash four days earlier. When they awoke, Martin announced that they would each take three teaspoons of their emergency liquid rations rather than the standard two they had been taught to endure in their training. He did not elaborate on his reasons, but the message was clear: They would likely die in this bleak place, and their last moments should be as painless as possible.

Harvey took the lead again and they hiked through a swamp. Martin, whose vision had not fully returned, followed Harvey by the sound of his boots squishing through the damp earth. After what felt like a few hours—neither man had thought to note what time they had set off that morning—they reached a valley where a stream passed through the mountain range. When they tried to reach the water, however, they discovered that the snow blocking their path was fresh enough that it had not yet formed a frozen crust. With each step, they plunged up to their knees, soaking their overalls. Though neither said it aloud, death started to feel welcome.

By three p.m., Martin could no longer go on. Harvey left him with their supplies and hiked ahead to scout out possible routes. He returned before sunset to say that he had seen another body of water—a lake or bay; he could not tell which—about three miles south. The two men were too cold and exhausted to continue that night and camped in an alder thicket. They slept little and were up before dawn.

Shortly after sunrise they reached the water's edge and saw a cabin half a mile away. They hiked along the rocky shore and found that it was empty. They broke down the door and discovered a rifle, a small supply of food, and a tidy stack of wood in the corner that gave the impression that someone had been there the day before. The men, exhausted and half mad with hunger, grabbed flour and baking powder and began cooking pancakes on the small stove. The smell of the melting butter was intoxicating and they barely allowed them time to brown before wolfing them down. They had eaten only parts of two quail-size birds since they'd crashed five days earlier, and their stomachs balked at the reintroduction of food. Each man soon lay moaning on the wooden floor as snow came down heavily outside.

It was still snowing when they woke up the next morning. The wood-stove in the corner was not enough to keep the cabin warm and they sat shivering as large flakes continued to fall without interruption for another day and night. On the morning of May 9, nearly a week and a half after they had crashed, the snow let up enough that they were able to walk outside. Martin took the rifle of their absent host and shot several wild ducks while Harvey hiked along the shoreline searching for clues to their location. He came back with two snowshoe rabbits he'd shot with his pistol but nothing more.

The men again laid out their maps and tried to guess at their position. Nothing around them seemed to match. They decided to search the cabin itself for clues and found a box of condensed milk with a label reading *Port Moller Cannery*. Suddenly, the world outside of the window began to make sense. The body of water was almost assuredly Moller Bay, putting them on the shores of the Bering Sea, less than ninety miles away from where they had taken off from Chignik more than a week earlier. Before them was a desolate sea with hardly any commercial traffic at this time of year and a bay that was largely frozen over and would remain so for at least another month. That they had come across any sign of human life at all was nothing short of miraculous. For the first time, they allowed themselves to believe that they would survive.

After a breakfast of rabbit, pancakes, and gravy, they gathered their belongings and spent a few minutes tidying up the cabin for the owner who had unknowingly saved their lives. They hiked in the direction they believed the cannery was in and hoped there would be at least a skeleton crew of workers present before the summer fishing season. The weather was clear and calm as they walked along the beach. A three-mile-long section of jutting rocks and cliffs briefly forced them inland before they resumed their path on the rocky shore.

As they crossed a sandy beach in the late afternoon, they looked up and spotted a radio tower and smokestack in the distance. They stared at it without moving, silently praying that they would see a puff of smoke to confirm that the building was occupied. Finally one came. Though tired and hurting, the men increased their pace, their feet digging painfully into the sand with each step.

Neither one remembered later who saw the boat first, but there it was, a long rowboat with two men and three woman aboard, all native Alaskans. The men stopped and yelled, waving their arms to grab their attention. They needn't have bothered. On the boat, Jake Oroloff had spotted the men minutes before. The only people in this remote stretch of Alaska were either residents of the native village or seasonal workers in the cannery, and Oroloff knew each one personally. As the boat drew near, Martin and Harvey looked like ghosts of their former selves. The skin on both men's faces had been thrashed from the snow and wind, leaving them blistered and red. Harvey's torn clothing hung loose on his gaunt frame, while Martin hobbled forward with his dirty pilot's hat on his head.

Oroloff brought the men aboard and returned to the cannery. The superintendent rushed down and immediately recognized Martin and Harvey as the lost world fliers. Radio messages soon bounced from ship to ship across the Pacific, announcing the return of two men the world had given up for dead. The naval station at Pearl Harbor, Hawaii, sent the news to Washington, DC, where it arrived just in time for an aide to update President Coolidge before he left the White House to attend Sunday-morning services at the First Congregational Church.

The safe return of Martin and Harvey led the world news the next day, with the *New York Times* devoting five separate stories to their rescue. Boom Trenchard, the head of the Royal Air Force, sent both his personal congratulations and those of the British Empire to the White House. In San Diego, a telegram delivery boy carried a yellow scrap of paper to Mrs. Grace Martin's home, where she remained surrounded by reporters. It read, "Hello, dearest. Safe at Port Moller, 6 pm, today. Crashed against mountain in fog 30th. Neither hurt. Survived next ten days. Good health. Dry your tears. Fred."

"God bless the little messenger boy that delivered that telegram," Grace told the reporters, grasping at once that her husband's survival meant she would no longer have her every moment recorded. "Instinctively I knew he had brought me good news." When pressed for what she would do when she next saw her husband, she smiled and said, "I am going to ask Fred to make the greatest sacrifice he ever made in his life. I want him to promise me that he will never fly again."

Her son, Robert, stood silently crying next to her. When pressed, he admitted that he was not crying tears of joy. He cried because he knew, though no one would admit it, that there was no way his father could continue on the world flight. The X on his map would stay at Chignik forever more, marking the spot where his father went missing and less than a centimeter away from the spot where he was found.

CHAPTER THIRTEEN

"The End of Everything"

IT SEEMED LIKE they had reached the edge of the world.

As the three remaining planes of the American squadron flew toward remote Attu Island, Les Arnold looked down into churning whirlpools created by the merging of the Arctic and Pacific Oceans and thought that nothing that fell into them could survive. In the distance, he could see smoke rising from the peaks of volcanoes, each one looming like a portal to hell. The men pressed on, past all evidence of human existence. After five hours in the air, they landed in the harbor of the most westerly point of North America and the most desolate possession of the United States.

"Attu Island looks like the end of everything," Arnold wrote in his diary.

The barren place felt like their punishment for leaving Martin and Harvey behind. Storms battered Attu from the moment the planes landed, and they were once again stuck. Harding, unable to comprehend a world so at odds with the greenery of his native Tennessee, asked the lone trader on the island when the season would change. "We only have two seasons," the man responded. "This winter and next winter."

Williwaws more powerful than anything they had yet experienced blew hard enough to topple a person over, making it impossible for them to maintain their balance while servicing their planes. The men climbed aboard a US Bureau of Fisheries boat, the *Eider*, and watched from its portholes as the wind flogged their aircraft, expecting every second to see a plane torn from its moorings and smashed into the rocks lining the harbor. If a plane did break down here, so far from home, getting back to the United States would require a weeks-long voyage aboard an ocean steamer through unrelenting storms. Some of the older men who now lived on Attu had come aboard from trading or fishing vessels and never left, preferring the certainty of the island's misery to the grip of the sea. Each moment that the Douglas Cruisers remained intact seemed like a gift, reminding the six American crew members that they had a way to return to the lives they had left behind.

On May 11, nearly two months to the day that they had left Santa Monica and begun their flight, Harding, in the cramped forecastle of the *Eider*, was stirred awake by the sound of crew members of the ship conversing in low tones. Half asleep, he thought they said the words *Martin* and *Harvey* and turned over to fall back into a dream. Then, realizing what he had heard, he leaped out of bed and asked them to repeat what they'd said. The men, half believing it themselves, told him that a radio operator in Port Moller just announced that Martin and Harvey had been found alive.

The impossible had happened. Though they never spoke about it, the American squadron had come to accept that Martin and Harvey were dead. It was the only way to continue. Imagining that they were still out there, somewhere in the cold, brought on a sharp sense of shame that they had deserted two men for the sake of chasing glory. Guilt brought them closer together, creating a sense of brotherhood that did not exist when they left Seattle. "Although Washington ordered us to proceed with the flight, and although we had done everything possible . . . none of us had liked the idea of going on before the search was over," Harding later said.

With Smith in command, the squadron turned to the next leg of their flight with a renewed sense of duty. No matter what happened from here, they would not have to carry the loss of Martin and Harvey. Freed by their conscience, they could once again turn their attention to competing in a race no one thought they could win, inspired by the promise that their flight would show that American pilots and American planes were the best in the world.

It would not be easy. In terms of miles flown, they were now well behind both the French and the British pilots. Ahead of them lay the crossing of the Pacific, a feat that no one had ever attempted. The flight from Attu Island to the most northern island of Japan would entail flying over eight hundred and seventy miles of open ocean without knowing what weather lay ahead—the longest and most isolated stretch of the world flight and the one with the most potential for tragedy. With no radio to communicate between themselves and hardly any shipping traffic over an icy region, a problem as simple as a damaged propeller could have fatal consequences. Martin and Harvey had been shockingly lucky. There was no reason to think that providence would shine on the men on the flight a second time. "It was heartening news to all of us at Attu," Wade wrote of the rescue. "But the flight was hardly started. Who might be next? I shut my mind to the thought, tried to start each new day with yesterday wiped from the slate."

They needed to hurry. Scorecards showing how far each nation's aviators had traveled ran on the front pages of London's newspapers each day. At the same time that the world learned of Martin and Harvey's rescue, d'Oisy, the French pilot, was far in the lead, with 8,380 miles flown, going from Paris to Hanoi in a span of twenty-one days. His blazing pace led to widespread rumors that d'Oisy secretly switched planes at each stop, giving him an unfair advantage that clouded his accomplishment. In response, the French government issued a complete list of all the tools and spare parts carried in his machine when it left Paris, along with a declaration that "the airmen throughout their trip relied solely on these for renewals and repairs."

The French people needed no such reassurance. D'Oisy, in the span of three weeks, had transformed into an international hero and the symbol of a new France. "His extraordinary aerial marathon across Europe and Asia, wherein he vanquished the squadron of four other nations both in point of flying time and distance flown, has put him at the very pinnacle of post-war fame," the *Baltimore Evening Sun* wrote. "Now it is not unlikely there will be a statute erected to him in the French capital." His nickname, Pivolo, and a magpie were used by French artist Cassandre, pseudonym of Adolphe Jean-Marie Mouron, for an influential Art Deco advertisement for an aperitif of the same name. The public hung on d'Oisy's every word and copied his every taste. When his wife mentioned that his favorite work of literature was *Cyrano de Bergerac*, the news ran in twenty-nine Parisian newspapers, and copies of the play were momentarily impossible to find in the nation's capital.

Not since the death of internationally known actress Sarah Bernhardt, whose funeral procession brought tens of thousands of people to the streets of Paris, had one person so consumed the country's thoughts. He seemed to be the manifestation of France's self-image: a place where art was forever intertwined with adventure, its people fearless in both body and spirit. Each detail about his life seemed to make d'Oisy, a short man, grow taller in the eyes of his countrymen. "We had never had a honeymoon and it was going to be this month," his wife told the clutch of reporters who were now a constant presence in her life. "Instead I received a telegraph from Pelletier saying he was going off again somewhere, possibly to Africa, possibly to India. C'est la vie—when you have a very brave husband such as mine."

MacLaren and his British crew, who were at that moment in the northern India city of Allahabad (now known as Prayagraj), were essentially forgotten. Though they were in second place, having trekked 6,350 miles over fifty days, their delays in Greece and India had dulled the shine of their accomplishments. Nor did they feel confident that their position would hold. Close behind them were the Portuguese, who, led by Brito Pais, had reached Pipar, a city in northeastern India, flying 5,700 miles in thirty-six days.

Finally came the Americans, who, having covered 4,210 miles, were more than a thousand miles behind the other nations, despite a head start of seven days. As much as they wished to close that gap, they remained imprisoned by the brutal weather on an island that had only three wooden structures and a permanent human population of just fifty-nine. The men spent their days hunting with the crew of the *Eider* and reading from the well-stocked library of a local fox farmer.

Arnold, the boldest of the group, quickly grew bored and decided to seek out local Aleuts, who continued to puzzle him. Unlike some of the other crew members who had been born or worked in the western United States and felt the influence of indigenous nations, Arnold had spent nearly all his life in the urban area surrounding New York City and had little familiarity with men and women who largely lived off the land. "The natives here are a queer lot," he had written while stuck near Dutch Harbor a week earlier. He perceived their acceptance of food and education supplied by the US government as a form of laziness, yet at the same time he seemed to acknowledge that their way of life had been destroyed by the arrival of men like himself. "The best thing in the world for them would be to have their supply source cut off and make them hunt and fish for their living as their forefathers had to do," he wrote.

While on Attu Island, Arnold spied Aleut women weaving attractive baskets made of grass and wanted one to bring home as a souvenir. He gestured in a way that he hoped conveyed his friendly intentions to a family living near the shore in one of several barraboras, sunken, dome-shaped dwellings dug out of the earth and covered with sod. Each home could fit from six to eight people and relied on the banked walls of dirt to protect against the wind. With an officer from the *Eider* trailing behind him, Arnold was welcomed inside and toured what to him felt more like a storm cellar than a home. On one side were neat stacks of clothes, harpoons, dried fish, and jerked meat; on the other were older Aleut women weaving baskets and making clothing out of caribou hides. Dividing the room was a curtain made of animal skin. Arnold spent a few minutes in the barrabora before racing to the open air of the surface. "Such vile and foul air as we found is indescribable and it was with great difficulty that we could breathe at all," he wrote that night in his diary.

He returned to his bunk without a basket and over the following days his thoughts circled back to the Aleutians. From schoolyard games of cowboys and Indians to history books, he had been taught to see traditional cultures, with their emphasis on communal living and working in harmony with the seasons, as backward at a time when technology was opening up the world to a new future. In person, however, he could not help but recognize Aleutian resilience in the face of the world's most adverse climate and saw the beauty in their works of art. The fleeting interactions he had with the Aleutians did not change his entire worldview, and he continued to see their culture as beneath his own. But the cold days spent at Attu were his first spark of empathy, opening his mind to the possibility that other ways of life had value that could not be measured by success in the air or at war. It was a mental step that his fellow crew members had yet to take. Smith, who preferred the loneliness of his new role as commanding officer to the company of others, busied himself with charts and chores, never giving himself the opportunity to come into close contact with indigenous men and women who did not fit into the social structure of white, Black, or Mexican that he had grown accustomed to in California. The other four American aviators largely kept to the sailors and servicemen they found familiar. Arnold alone appeared to recognize that their trip forced them to see the world's peoples on their own terms, even if it was for a few moments inside their homes. Though Arnold had not yet shed the prejudices of his time and place, the walls built up in his mind by an American culture that prized isolationism and championed racial superiority were slowly beginning to fall.

He had no more time to deepen his understanding of a way of life that remained foreign. Two US Navy destroyers carrying oil, gas, and food for the pilots had been braving severe storms near the Kurile Islands, in the far north of Japan, for more than two weeks and were now running dangerously low on supplies themselves. Any further delay that kept the aviators grounded would run the risk of sailors losing their lives in the battered sea. Each crew member was placed on half rations after local birds they shot proved to be inedible. "The hardships endured by those awaiting the airmen are almost equal to those of the airmen themselves," a London newspaper noted.

Adding to the tension of battling the weather, the US Navy crews had to maintain peace with Japanese naval officers on board who remained skeptical of the Americans' intentions. In order to secure passage through the country and allay Japan's fears that the world flight was a military ruse, Washington agreed to host Japanese observers on American vessels that were in sight of Japanese territory. The men patrolled the boat, ensuring that the Americans lived up to their promise that no photographs would be taken of any part of the Japanese coastline. The lingering sense that foreigners were looking over their shoulders strained both American and Japanese patience, increasing the chance of a confrontation. For the first time, the world flight looked like it would be called off.

Smith knew they would need to leave soon regardless of the weather if they wanted to prevent Washington from grounding them in Attu. Still, the prospect of flying nearly nine hundred miles in a harsh climate with no advance warning of coming storms frightened him. While the men under his command struggled to pass the time, he pored over maps, crafting an alternative plan. In his first real test of leadership, he called the squadron into a small room aboard the *Eider* and closed the door. If they followed the plan dictated by General Patrick in Washington, he told them, they would have no hope of rescue if anything went wrong. Not only that, but there was a real chance that the planes would run out of fuel while battling the wind on a long flight. Yet there was another, safer way: to secretly head to the Komandorskis, a group of Soviet-held islands in the far north of the Pacific and a natural steppingstone on the way to Japan.

Each man knew that landing in Soviet territory could cause a world scandal, given that Washington had yet to recognize the country's Bolshevik government, and might end with the imprisonment of the American pilots, either in the Soviet Union or when they returned to the United States. Before the aviators left their training in Virginia, senior military officials had stressed the need to avoid all contact with the USSR or any of its people. Foul weather did not change that. While in Attu, Smith sent the commander of one of the navy destroyers in northern Japan a request to scout possible landing spots in the Komandorskis in the event of an emergency. "Will not enter Russian waters under any circumstances except to rescue a plane," that officer swiftly responded.

Smith put the choice to his men: they could face the danger inherent in a direct flight to Japan, or risk imprisonment by going along with his proposal. It was a loaded question, and their answer would shape the remainder of their journey. Inherent in such a request was a question eventually asked by all leaders: *Do you trust me?* Smith, at that point, had done little to earn their respect beyond demonstrating his mastery of the air. To go along with him required a leap of faith to believe that he would keep them alive over the flight ahead and also shield them from any potential fallout.

Silence filled the room as the five other men considered their options. Here was perhaps the best pilot they had ever seen, thrust into a role that he had not wanted. If such a person was willing to put his life and career on the line for an idea, then perhaps that was all the convincing they needed. It was ultimately not an impassioned speech or evidence of a foolproof plan that swayed the squadron into placing their confidence in Smith; it was his humility.

Their new route set them on a course to Bering Island, one of the distant members of the Komandorskis. The island, unknown to Europeans until November 1741, got its name when a ship carrying Danish explorer Vitus Bering and a crew of seventy-seven men were shipwrecked there after a storm blew them off course. Barren and uninhabited, the island was overrun with arctic foxes and surrounded by slow, manatee-like creatures described by Bering's German-born naturalist, Georg Wilhelm Steller, and later known as Steller's sea cows. (Steller compared the animal's luxuriant fat to the best Holland butter and observed that they often attempted to come to the aid of harpooned mates, which showed what Steller called an "uncommon love for one another." Overhunting drove the animals to extinction within twenty-seven years of their first sighting, convincing European scientists that species could in fact disappear from the Earth.)

Hungry and suffering from scurvy, the men dug a pit house as a shelter from the snow. For food, they competed with the ever-present foxes. Soon, sailors were sleeping atop the beached carcasses of seals that were too heavy to carry back to their shelter so they would not lose them to scavengers overnight. One by one, crew members perished, forcing those that remained to bury the dead before foxes gnawed off their fingers and noses. Bering died a month after landing on the island. Soon, the only three shipbuilders among the crew died as well. Eventually a Siberian sailor named Sava Starodubtsov, drawing from memory and guesswork, built a new boat from the salvage of the shipwreck. Nine months after reaching Bering Island, he and forty-five other survivors sailed back into the Pacific with barrels of salted sea-cow meat to sustain them and reached the Russian peninsula of Kamchatka three weeks later.

For Smith's idea to work, the aviators had to keep their plan to fly toward Bering Island secret from Washington and the reporters that tracked their every move. For help, they enlisted the captain of the *Eider*, who, as the head of a Bureau of Fisheries vessel, had the freedom to roam the North Pacific without attracting attention. The game plan was simple: The *Eider* would leave a few days ahead of the planes and anchor five miles off the coast of Bering Island so as to evade Soviet patrols. When the aviators reached Bering, they would land in the water on the far side of the vessel and, hidden from view, refill their gas and oil from barrels the *Eider* would toss overboard.

Persistent snow and wind prevented the men from taking off on May 14 as they had hoped. They passed one more day by fishing for cod from the side of a Coast Guard cutter, the *Haida*. That night, each man took a warm bath. "I don't dare mention when we had our last one," Arnold wrote in his diary that night. They were up before dawn and greeted by clear skies. Shortly after eleven, the three planes rose out of the Pacific with Smith in the lead. Below them, heavy swells battered the *Haida*. Every sailor on board hung on to the railings with one hand and waved to the departing planes with the other. Smith was the first to see that the sky in the direction of Japan was black, confirming his fears. He led the men on to the Komandorskis, "deciding to take our chances with the Bolsheviks rather than face the wrath of the storm," he later said. "For three hours we flew out of sight of land, wondering all the time what the Russians would think when they saw three giant planes swoop down out of the sky in this remote region where even ships only come about once a year."

As the men flew, they crossed the International Date Line, the arbitrary boundary at roughly the midpoint of the Pacific that runs along the 180th meridian and by worldwide agreement has separated one day from another since its establishment in 1884. Before then, circumnavigating the planet inevitably led to chaos. The eighteen survivors out of the roughly two hundred seventy men who set out on Magellan's voyage were the first to experience the sensation of losing a day when they circled the globe. When they arrived in the Cape Verde islands near the end of their voyage, they received the surprising news that it was Thursday, not Wednesday as they had thought. "We knew not how we had fallen into error," the ship's scribe later wrote. "Every day I, being always in health, had written down each day without any intermission." Arnold, drawing from his theater past, found the humor in the notion that he was living in two days at once. "Sort of a case of 'As You Like It' . . . that we left Wednesday morning and flew five hours and arrived Thursday afternoon," he wrote in his diary.

They flew over the open sea with only their compasses to guide them. Finally, they spotted Copper Island. Nine miles long and one mile wide, the most eastern member of the Komandorskis would have been easy to miss. "Three hours over the sea and then to absolute strike your mark was a clever piece of navigation and Smith can not be given too much credit," Arnold marveled in his diary that night. When they first met one another in Virginia, Smith's technical brilliance had earned him the admiration of the squadron members; to accomplish remarkable feats while so far from home earned their trust. As the men spent more time in his company, they began to understand that his silence did not mask anger or jealousy. Instead, it was as if Smith parceled out crumbs of his personality, testing to see how they would be received before offering any more. Arnold, who shared his quarters with Smith, noted that with each day, Smith seemed more inclined to laugh at a joke or share a story from his past, as long as the conversation came at his own pace. Though he was the fastest pilot among them, Smith remained the slowest to open up as a person, though he was now beginning to crack.

Seeing Copper Island below them, they knew they were now at the far eastern edge of Asia, making them the first to bridge the Pacific. Two hours later, they reached Bering Island. Soviet radio towers overshadowed the bayside village of Nikolski, reminding them that whatever happened here could immediately be broadcast all over the world. The *Eider*, as planned, was five miles offshore. Smith circled the boat but could not land because the sea was too rough. The captain of the *Eider*, realizing the problem, steamed two miles closer to land and dropped buoys on the side of the ship facing away from the shore. The three planes landed at roughly two thirty in the afternoon and taxied through the choppy, icy water toward the oil and gas barrels that were their lifelines.

As he neared the buoys, Smith saw a Soviet vessel steaming out from shore toward them. Five bearded men—including two in military uniform carrying rifles—were aboard. This was exactly what he feared. Smith signaled to his men to remain in their cockpits in case they had to take off immediately. Three small boats launched from the *Eider*, entered the water, and stationed themselves next to the planes. The men spoke in hushed tones as their aircraft rose and fell with each passing wave and waited for the Soviets to close the gap.

When they were within shouting distance, the Soviets yelled something to the Americans, who could not understand them. Their guns, however, were not pointed at either the airplanes or the *Eider*'s crew, which Smith took as a signal that they were friendly. He slowly climbed down from his cockpit into the *Eider*'s lifeboat and motioned for the Soviets to follow him back to the larger ship. They complied and were soon standing on the *Eider*'s deck, unsure of what would happen next.

From the hull came an American sailor from Chicago whose family was from Lithuania and who could speak piecemeal Russian. With him as their translator, the Soviets firmly but politely refused to let the Americans land on the island until they had secured permission from Moscow. Smith assured them that they had no ill intentions and told him the pilots were simply "birds of passage winging our way around the world." Before returning to the island and its radio equipment, the Soviets ordered the Americans to remain aboard the *Eider*. The men, who feared falling into foreign custody, were happy to agree.

As soon as the Soviets pushed off, Smith and the other men raced to service their planes and refuel, knowing they might need to take off again quickly. The captain of the *Eider* radioed the *Haida* in Attu informing it of the American aviators' contact with Soviet servicemen. Within minutes, the *Haida* was steaming toward Bering Island in case it was needed. A few hours later, a Soviet boat again arrived, this time with a man carrying a large container of vodka. He handed it to the Americans. Smith thanked him heartily for the gift, but as soon as the man was gone, he forbade any member of the crew to drink it. The crews worked on their planes deep into the evening. At ten, when it was still light enough to be able to read in the cockpit, they boarded the *Eider* and slept in small bunks. When they awoke at four thirty a.m., it was again broad daylight.

They readied their aircraft and broke the silence of the morning with the hum of engines as the planes taxied into position. As they prepared to take off, the Soviet party again arrived. With regret, they informed the Americans that Moscow denied authorization and they must leave immediately. Smith thanked them for their courtesy and signaled to Nelson and Wade that it was time to go. The three planes lifted into the air a few moments later. "I suppose the Russians are still stroking their beards and wondering what it was all about," Smith later wrote. In what would be one of the many trials of his leadership, Smith had remained as cool and confident as he had when he walked through the gates of Langley in Virginia. Here, in the cold waters near Siberia, the men in his squadron began to believe that there was more to him than they had expected.

The planes headed southwest, passing the jagged white mountains of Kamchatka. Snow squalls and fog forced them to fly low over the ocean, skimming the waves above an offshore trench that is among the deepest fissures in the world. If they crashed in the isolated waters, their planes would sink more than five and a half miles, a distance greater than the height of Mount Everest. The snow turned to heavy rain as the men flew on, leaving them drenched and shivering in their cockpits. Icicles soon formed on their bodies and they would occasionally swat them away, causing a tinkling of breaking ice they could faintly hear despite the roar of their engines.

Finally, five hours after setting off from Bering Island, they spotted an American destroyer and two Japanese battleships waiting for them in Kashiwabara Bay. Sailors waved at them through the drenching rain as each ship blared its sirens. A thirty-one-year-old Associated Press reporter named Linton Wells aboard the American vessel convinced its radio operator to send an urgent message to his office in San Francisco announcing to the world that the American fliers had landed in Japan at 11:35 a.m.

As Smith and the other men boarded the American destroyer, messages of congratulations came in from across the globe. Among the first was from Secretary of War Weeks: "Yours is the honor of being the first to cross the Pacific by air . . . the Army has every faith in your ability to add the circumnavigation of the globe to its achievements." Wells's Associated Press story ran on the front page of dozens of papers, announcing that "the three United States army world flyers reached this ice-fringed bay bordering the Arctic this morning" as they "blazed a trail through skies never before invaded by an airplane."

Reaching Asia safely gave the American men hope that they would finally escape the confines of ice and snow. But they knew they were merely replacing one danger with another. Until now, the greatest threat had been the harsh physical world. In Japan, their exposure to the cold would retreat, and in its place would come the potential for war.

CHAPTER FOURTEEN

The Seeds of War

A s the black limousine carrying Albert Johnson slowed to a stop in front of the White House, he had never been so close to fulfilling a dream. Slender, with a mop of wavy gray hair parted in the middle that gave him an unfashionably boyish appearance at the age of fifty-five, Johnson carried himself with the certainty of a man who believed his time had come. He had accumulated power in doses, inching higher over the last twelve years from his position representing a congressional district stretched across a lightly populated area of western Washington to the chair of the House Immigration Committee. All of this came despite his having neither the money nor the charisma that normally opened doors, convincing him that it was his intellect and ideas alone that catapulted him into importance. Under his watch, the committee had transformed into one of the most influential on Capitol Hill. Now, as he stepped out of the car and looked over the South Lawn, he could not help but think he was edging closer to the day when he would have a similar view from behind the desk in the Oval Office.

For now, at least, he was in a position to dictate the nation's future to the president. He had introduced a bill, the Johnson-Reed Act, a few weeks earlier that reflected his worldview that the United States must cleanse itself of undesirable immigrants—a group that he defined as those without Northern European heritage. The bill limited the number of visas issued to newcomers from each nation to 2 percent of their numbers represented on the 1890 census, a move intended to stem the tide of Italians, Jews, and Greeks arriving on steamships into New York Harbor. Its most explosive aspect, however, was a provision that prevented anyone who was ineligible for citizenship from stepping foot in America—effectively banning any person from Japan from the country.

Exclusion of the Japanese had been the fuel for Johnson's transformation from a newspaper reporter to a politician more than a decade before. The son of a farmer, Johnson and his family had moved to Hiawatha, Kansas, in 1869, when he was an infant, and he grew up in an atmosphere where the Civil War seemed to live on. As a prank, Johnson once hung the Confederate battle flag from the family barn, dooming his father's candidacy for the office of district judge on the Republican ticket. His first job was the editor of a self-published newspaper, and his career eventually took him to the *St. Louis Globe-Democrat* and the *Washington Post*. He was lured west to the state of Washington by the owner of the *Tacoma News*, who offered him a job in 1898 with the promise that "you will find that the city of Tacoma is the city of destiny with opportunities and possibilities beyond that of any place in all the Universe. You can return to Washington as a Congressman or Senator if you wish."

As editor, Johnson remade the paper into a conservative Republican broadsheet, warning the city of twenty-eight thousand people of the menaces of Bolshevism, labor unions, and environmental regulations. In Tacoma, he noticed Japanese laborers building the railroads of the Pacific Northwest. "I began to call attention to the situation in every way I could," he later said. He grew paranoid that the young Japanese men and women he employed in his house as domestic servants were spying on him. After one young man who had worked for Johnson fell sick and died while on the ocean voyage back to Japan, Johnson learned that he had been the son of a wealthy banker and did not appear to need to work. Johnson told anyone who would listen that the man had been a secret agent covertly sending information about Johnson's family to Tokyo because of his opposition to Asian immigration.

He ran for Congress in 1912 on a platform that shutting the nation off to Asian newcomers was the only way to maintain its character. "The average American is suffering from an overdose of the unassimilated foreigner," he wrote. "It will mean lower standards of living. . . . A check on immigration must be provided now." When he narrowly won his first election, he brought his cause to Washington. "The day the United States found it necessary to conserve its resources was the very day to have put up the bars against an ever-increasing immigration," he argued in an early speech. By 1918, he was the chair of the House Immigration Committee, and in 1921 he shepherded a measure through Congress that was designed to increase the percentage of immigrants from northwestern Europe. But he felt like the law didn't go far enough. On March 17, 1924, he introduced a bill that, forty-two years after the Chinese Exclusion Act, barred Japanese immigrants from the country for the first time. "Our new immigration legislation is America's second Declaration of Independence," Johnson said.

The act was seen as a grave insult in Japan, which considered itself an equal to the United States. Twenty years earlier, Japan had defeated Russia in an eighteen-month-long war fought on land and at sea, marking the first time in modern history that an Asian country triumphed in battle against a European opponent. The victory elevated the country to a place among the world powers and led to a grudging respect in Washington and European parliaments. Japan, which was not as industrialized as its world rivals, remained sensitive to any suggestion that it was second class. "The action of the American Congress in passing the exclusion legislation amounts to a challenge to Japan," a prominent Japanese newspaper warned. "The nation must prepare for whatever condition may come, even war." In America, editorials warned that the immigration bill could upset a fragile peace. "The seeds of conflict have been sown. Seeds grow," wrote Charles P. Steward, a columnist whose work was published across the country.

Johnson's approach was widely seen as a blunt instrument at a time when tact was necessary. The chairman of United States Steel Corporation told reporters, "I don't think we ought to slap them in the face. . . . It is all right to limit the number of immigrants from Japan, but the way to do it is to enter into an agreement with the Japanese." Politicians who had in the past argued for racial restrictions to citizenship drew a line at the Japanese exclusion. Senator James Reed, a Democrat from Missouri who was not the namesake of the Johnson-Reed Act, said on the floor of the Senate in 1916, "I would not say that all people who are not of the white race are bad people, but I say that no man not of the white race ought to be permitted to settle permanently in the United States of America." But when he read the text of what Johnson proposed in 1924, he told reporters that he intended to vote against the measure because he did not believe it wise "to go to the extreme in restrictions."

The opposition included President Calvin Coolidge, who said that the bill "is unnecessary and deplorable at this time . . . if the exclusion provision stood alone I should disapprove it without hesitation." But Coolidge, who had been in office less than a year after the sudden death of President Warren G. Harding, had little power to act. Taking advantage of anti-Asian sentiment in California and other western states, Johnson assembled a veto-proof majority for the bill. The only question was when it would go into effect.

As Johnson strode toward the White House, Coolidge was waiting inside in hopes that he could convince him to postpone the bill to soften the blow to Japan. Johnson was in no mood for compromise. That day, a handful of newspaper editorial boards across the country urged the Republican convention to nominate Johnson for vice president or even president if Coolidge pulled out of the race. "The Washington congressman has always been a hard and consistent worker, this being demonstrated by his arduous and splendid fight for a proper immigration policy for this nation," the *Tacoma Daily Ledger* wrote. America, it seemed, was destined to follow Johnson's lead, closing itself off from anything that happened beyond its shores.

Half a world away, the six American aviators tried to sleep in their bunks on a destroyer anchored in the northern Pacific as it was tossed by the wind. When they awoke, they understood how far they had traveled from home. "The presence of the Japanese destroyers with their snappy-looking little sailors contributed chiefly, I think, to the illusion of a new world," Wade said. "And when we looked at the unpronounceable names on our maps, that helped too."

Until now, the men had largely been able to shield themselves from close contact with other cultures. Arnold was the only one who attempted to see Aleutian life on its own terms, and that ended with him running out of someone's home. In Japan, for the first time, they were confronted with a powerful, militarized country with a language and rituals utterly different than anything they had experienced in America or during the war in Europe. Even Nelson, who had twice sailed around the world, had spent much of his time roaming the seaside bars of port cities, where the chief distinction between places was the type of alcohol they served.

It was as if a curtain had been drawn back, revealing a world of color instead of black and white. The men entered into it with trepidation, unmoored by the sense that they had nothing familiar to latch on to. Smith alone seemed unfazed. His focus remained on the fact that they were thirty-one days behind schedule, and he pushed the flight to carry on as quickly as possible. Within a day of crossing from Attu, the squadron was airborne again, flying seven hours south through weather that Wade called the coldest they had yet experienced. The men stamped their feet in the cockpits to confirm that they could still feel them. When they looked down, they saw people waving to them from boats and seaside villages. "It was nice for a change to . . . see people after the desolate stretches we have travelled," Arnold wrote in his diary.

It was unclear until the moment the Americans took off from Santa Monica whether Japan would agree to let them or any other nation's pilots enter the country. The growing number of European expatriates and the rising influence of Western culture in Japan were seen as threats by its military leaders. The government relented but remained wary of the foreign airmen and destroyers parked off its shores at a time when Japan's air capability was limited to the handful of European-made aircraft in its possession. "If the British and Americans seek only to demonstrate the feasibility of traveling the world by air, Japan can be content with her role of onlooker; but if their flights are preparation for expansion of their military aviation defense, Japan must adopt plans to meet the situation," argued the *Asahi Shimbun*, one of the oldest and most respected newspapers in the country.

American reporters saw the country's small air force as a sign that it was not yet in the realm of world powers, looking past the insignificant number of aircraft in the possession of the US military. The world flight, by its nature a clash of cultures, was reshaped by some commentators as a clear example of racial hierarchy. "Intelligent Japanese are aware of their country's backwardness in aviation," a wire story ran in the *Arizona Republic* and dozens of other papers nationwide. "Therefore their admiration for the exploits of the Anglo-Saxons, although genuine, is accompanied by regret that they cannot enter the competition for the globe-girdling honors."

Once the American aviators arrived, they became a spectacle. Foreign men, foreign planes, foreign vessels—it was all too much in a country that remained reluctant to welcome outsiders after more than two hundred years of near-total isolation under the Tokugawa shogunate. As the squadron landed in a lake just off Hitokappu Bay (now known as Kasatka Bay), several hundred schoolchildren who had walked the nine miles from a local town in their uniforms waited on the shore to get a glimpse of them. When the men walked past after docking their planes, some of the children reached out to try to touch their flight suits. They had never seen anything like them before.

Fog the following day grounded the Americans. They walked down the main street of a local town, happy to once again see trees and horses after their experience in the Arctic. An elderly Japanese man smiled, bowed to them, and indicated that they should follow him. The man led them to his house. There, the Americans for the first time felt the shame of outsiders who did not know how to follow local customs. "Thus far the only thing regarding our world flight that Gen. Patrick . . . had overlooked was to give us a course in Japanese etiquette," Wade later wrote. "Worst of all, however, was our embarrassment in not being able to make our feet inconspicuous by sitting on them after the fashion of our honorable host."

The men fumbled when taking off their shoes and felt out of place in the ornate home and surrounding garden. Their elderly host served them tea and attempted to carry on a conversation with them in gestures, given that the Americans' only Japanese word was *arigatou*, meaning "thank you." Harding was the first to realize that the men were being rude by not loudly slurping their tea. He attempted to follow the example of their host and inadvertently sprayed the drink over himself and Wade sitting next to him.

That evening, the American aviators were invited aboard a Japanese destroyer. They watched sumo wrestling bouts, amazed that the men were competing shirtless while they sat in their heavy flying suits to guard against the chill. "The men were wonderful physical specimens and I have a new respect for their strength and prowess," Arnold wrote that night. They ate cakes and drank wine with their hosts and later that evening invited them aboard a nearby American destroyer to watch a silent movie.

When the fog cleared, they flew 485 miles south to the fishing village of Minato, which put them on the main Japanese island of Honshu for the first time. Smith had asked that the fliers receive no formal greeting or ceremony upon arrival so that they could make up some of the time they had lost in Alaska. The Japanese navy had told him that they would comply, yet as he circled the landing site, Smith looked down onto a crowd of hundreds of people waving American flags. Giant fireworks exploded in the air as soon as he touched down onto the water while small boats carrying fuel and oil launched from a nearby wharf to meet them.

As he serviced the plane alongside Arnold, Smith debated whether the squadron should leave as planned, offending the crowd, or go ashore and put another hole in their schedule. The weight of social obligations was one he felt unprepared to carry. As a pilot, he was the finest of the group; as its public face, he was hopelessly out of his element. Each question removed from the world of aviation and navigation felt like it was coming in another language, and deciphering them took time he would rather have spent flying or preparing to fly.

Until now, his social ineptitude had not mattered. But in Japan, a country that placed a premium on social grace, he felt the glare of attention and longed to shrink into the shadows. He found himself leaning on Arnold, a man who loved the spotlight, for guidance. The two conferred and agreed that they would ask the US Navy officer who had supplied their oil and gas to send their regrets to the crowd. The squadron, with Smith in the lead, took off from large swells shortly after one p.m. and flew south toward Tokyo, where more attention awaited them. Four hours later, they reached Lake Kasumigaura, about fifty miles north of the capital. Some twenty thousand Japanese had gathered on its shores, many of whom had never seen an airplane before.

For the six Americans, the crowd—the largest they had seen since Seattle—made them at last realize the significance of what they were doing. They were not just a handful of military pilots anymore, anonymously traveling through the world. They were now global celebrities, their every move recorded by an international press. What they ate, how they dressed, where they had grown up, how they had acted as children—it was all out there for public consumption, turning them into characters in an ongoing story. "There were photographers to the front of us, photographers to the left of us, photographers to the right of us, on platforms, on poles, and even on the roofs," Arnold later said. "There were newspaper correspondents from all parts of the world—French scribes with beards, Englishmen with monocles, and Americans with straw hats and horn-rimmed glasses."

The reception by cheering crowds despite the chill of the American immigration bill made the aviators appear to be the ambassadors of a new era, one in which aircraft had the power to connect distant branches of humanity and leave politics behind. "Why does the entire reading public grab its daily paper to get the latest information about the around-the-world flyers? Not because everybody is engrossed in aeronautics.

Most of us are not. . . . It is human skill, daring, and endurance pitted against the powers of nature," noted an editorial in the *Long Beach Telegram* celebrating the arrival of the American aviators outside of Tokyo. "People on opposite sides of the globe are made akin. . . . Any national antipathy aroused by the exclusion issue was lost in a profound emotion. There were no American and no Japanese, but just human beings stirred by the immemorial drama of man defeating nature."

The aviators, who had flown ten hours that day, retired to accommodations that Arnold noted were as luxurious as anything in New York City. The next evening, senior officials in the Japanese navy took the men to an upscale restaurant, where they were attended by geishas in bright silk dresses. Smith alone proved adept at using chopsticks, while Arnold marveled that sake was heated instead of put on ice like white wine. "Japan surely is a topsy-turvy land," he later wrote. "Or is [it] that we ourselves are queer?"

The flight schedule mandated an eight-day stay at Lake Kasumigaura so that the aircraft engines and pontoons could be overhauled. The six aviators were given two days to visit Tokyo. The city was still recovering from a devastating earthquake eight months earlier that had killed more than a hundred thousand people and erased entire blocks. Fragile, temporary structures dotted the streets and corners. Black soot blistered the sides of buildings that had survived the blaze, and great cracks ran along their foundations. Among the few edifices standing unhurt was the Imperial Hotel, built in 1919, designed by American architect Frank Lloyd Wright. It was in an H formation with interlocking timber beams that would sway rather than collapse during an earthquake. (Wright's son John assisted on the project but had a falling-out with his father over his salary; when he returned to America, he patented the interlocking design and released a miniature version in a new toy he called Lincoln Logs.) Despite the damage around him, Smith was struck by the resilience of the men and women he met, seeing a reflection of himself in their willingness to endure. "There is a wonderful spirit of optimism in the air," he later said. "Their dream is that the most beautiful city in the world may arise out of the ashes of old Tokyo."

Crowds milled in front of the hotel where the Americans were staying and followed them everywhere they went. To get through, the men "adopted football tactics, forming a V and forcing their way through the . . . photographers, reporters and spectators," one journalist noted.

The crush of their newfound celebrity felt overwhelming, especially after nearly a month of fighting the weather through areas nearly devoid of humans. "The fliers apparently are overcome by the attentions," the *Chicago Tribune* wrote. "They faced the storms and dangers of the frozen north, but they shied before the Tokyo crowds and stood absolutely silent before the American ambassador."

Smith, particularly, tried to hide from the spotlight, downplaying their accomplishment as little more than "routine flying" in one interview in which he again said he wished that Martin had not crashed and was still in command. "I do not catch the idea of all these extravagant comparisons," he told one reporter. "We do not consider ourselves Magellans of the air. As I remember it, Magellan met his death just after crossing the Pacific. Certainly we do not hope for that comparison."

The little things suddenly took on new importance. When Arnold and Wade walked into one upscale department store, the owner raced up to them, bowed, and begged their forgiveness for not putting up special decorations. In a meeting with the minister of war, each man received a silver sake bowl engraved with an image of the Douglas World Cruiser, and they all struggled to remember the proper etiquette to convey thanks for a gift. The president of the University of Tokyo hosted the men for a formal dinner, in which he told them, "The honor and pride [of their flight] are to be shared by all mankind, because they are a manifest expression of moral and intellectual powers in the human race." In one restaurant, Arnold was momentarily confused when he saw a person's hand apparently floating in a shadow on the wall behind him. The next second he saw the blinding flash of a camera and gathered it was a photographer hiding in the corner.

Thousands of miles from home, the American aviators felt a new duty to connect with a people they had never considered equal to themselves. "With the realization of the significance of the flight, our sense of responsibility increased," Wade later said. "It was no longer just a personal adventure. . . . We started watching ourselves and our actions on the ground. Diplomatic correctness became as important as our aerial skills." Used to looking out for each other while in the air, the overwhelmed Americans banded together under the glare of attention.

Amid the optimism, it was easy for them to overlook the things they didn't want to see. The possibility of war buzzed faintly in the background, not loud enough to gather notice yet present all the same. As the Americans worked on their planes, Japanese military men took dozens

THE SEEDS OF WAR

of pictures of each part of the engines and frames, as if creating blue-prints to follow. The Americans were not permitted to take photographs of anything they saw, whether on land or in the air. In each place they visited, from the smallest village to the sprawling city of Tokyo, children marched in military formation, often chanting battle songs known as *gunka*. Back at home, US newscasters told their audiences that the scenes of friendship were for show and that they should prepare for war. "The real reason for the world flight is to discover a short route to Asia in case of any trouble there," a host on WJZ in New York City said.

To the six American pilots, however, an armed conflict with Japan felt unthinkable after a few days in the country. This was a place where, when Nelson accidentally walked into a rice paddy up to his waist when returning home from a nightclub in the darkness, he was immediately helped by strangers, and where Arnold laughed loudly with Japanese officials and his translators about the hardship of the aviators having to drink beer and sake because the US military suspected that the water in Tokyo was not clean. It felt like a storybook, and they did not want it to end.

On the other side of the world, on May 26, President Coolidge signed the Johnson-Reed Act, splintering the relationship between the United States and Japan. A few newspapers ran gleeful articles celebrating what they saw as a coming era of national racial purity, with headlines such as "Click! Gates Are Locked Against Orientals with Signing of Alien Bill" in the *Cincinnati Enquirer*. But for the men on the world flight, the bill felt like it belonged to a distant past, unrelated to the new future they were building with each mile in the air.

"As we flew on and on toward China, my engine was running so smoothly that the ship seemed to be flying herself," Nelson wrote during his final days in Japan. "I dropped into a reverie, and seemed to see dozens of giant planes passing me in the sky with passengers making weekend trips between Shanghai and San Francisco, just as they do now between Paris and London. It seemed to me that the airplane was designated to be the agency that would bring the races of the world into such intimate contact with each other that they would no more feel inclined to wage wars than the people of Oregon feel like fighting the inhabitants of Florida. If our flight helps in any way to hasten this era, we shall be repaid a million times over for our efforts."

CHAPTER FIFTEEN

"A Tonic"

T HE RAIN WOULD not stop. It came down in sheets, swelling the streams and harbor until there was no distinction between land and water. Even when it was not raining, the sky remained heavy with mist, as if the storm were intent on preventing the sun from coming out and undoing its hard work. Within a few days, it would be the official start of monsoon season, a three-month deluge during which a total of more than nine feet of water often poured from the sky. Compared to that, this unrelenting rain felt like a dress rehearsal, a time for the clouds to work out the last kinks and ready the earth for the misery that was to come.

Archibald Stuart-MacLaren sat in the cockpit of his plane, soaked to the bone. Every part of him ached. Over the last month, he had spent more days on the ground than in the air. In Parlu, India, the intense heat had melted the glue holding his plane together, leaving him stranded for more than two weeks. He finally repaired the fabric and a busted crankcase and flew to Calcutta, where he found himself stuck again due to an engine that would not comply. He waited days for a replacement, knowing full well that he was trying his government's patience with his lack of progress. When the new parts finally arrived, he flew to water-logged Akyab, in the British colony of Burma (now Sittwe, in the country of Myanmar). He was thirty-three days behind schedule, flying into weather that he had hoped to be well past at this point. Each raindrop that splattered on his head felt like another reminder of his failures. Now, under an unrelenting sky, he gave the order to Plenderleith, his pilot, to start the engine and attempt takeoff.

The heavy plane strained through the harbor as if tethered by an invisible chain. Finally it became airborne and turned in the direction of Hanoi. Then, without so much as a gentlemanly warning, the plane simply stopped working. Engine, propeller, flight stick—they all jammed at the same moment, united in protest against the miserable conditions. The plane, now more rock than aircraft, plummeted from the sky and crashed hard into the harbor. MacLaren and his crew bailed out of the sinking plane and attempted to swim to shore. A passing fishing boat picked them up. They all turned back to see their plane bobbing on the water, as if unsure whether it felt like going through with its plan of self-sabotage. Its back and wings appeared broken, like a bird that had crashed into a tree and was stuck somewhere between dead and alive. Finally, after a few more moments of indecision, the aircraft began its slow dive. Once it settled, only the back tip of its fuselage remained visible above the water, marking its spot like a gravestone.

MacLaren, fearing that he was now the second British aviator to see his hopes of a world flight die in Southeast Asia, soon found a dredging boat and convinced its crew to pull his aircraft out of the harbor. He inspected it as it lay dripping on the dock, hoping for some miracle that would cause it to become reanimated. He found none. The plane, his dreams, the mission—all appeared lost.

"The deepest sympathy is felt by everyone for Squadron Leader MacLaren's latest misfortune in his world flight," the *Grimsby Evening Telegram* reported as soon as word of his accident was cabled back to England. "Nothing but bad luck appears to have been his lot since he started on his great adventure, and the crash at Akyab is the hardest stroke of all, for it has rendered his machine of no further use."

MacLaren's only lifeline was a spare airplane that the Royal Air Force had parked five hundred miles north of Tokyo in case he needed to strip it for parts once he successfully reached Japan. But there appeared to be no way of reaching it. Finally out of options, MacLaren and his two-person crew turned to the pressing task of finding shelter, unsure of how long they would be marooned in Akyab with nothing but the rain to distract them from their fate.

IN JAPAN, LIEUTENANT Colonel L. E. Broome of the Royal Air Force—the man who, two months earlier, had asked General Patrick if it was possible for the Americans to start on their flight at once so that they could have a proper race with MacLaren—knocked on the door of Smith's room at the Imperial Hotel. He was there as an advance scout for the British flight and looked forward to meeting his rivals in person.

Smith opened the door and let him in. The other five American aviators were in various states of readiness, jostling for position in the bathroom as they combed their hair and put on their uniforms for the day's events. Broome found it hard to reconcile the cheery, laughing men he encountered with the tales of the suffering they had endured. It was as if he had been given access backstage and allowed to watch the men before they transformed into the roles they needed to play while in public. He traded stories with them for over an hour, comparing their experiences with his own traveling the world leaving supplies of gas and food for MacLaren.

A knock came at the door. A Japanese man walked in carrying a message for Broome. He opened it and read: "MacLaren crashed at Akyab. Plane completely wrecked. Continuance of flight doubtful."

Broome said nothing to the other aviators and stared ahead. The Americans, suddenly aware of his silence, shared glances. After a moment, without a word, Broome handed the piece of paper to Smith, who read it and then passed it down the line. "Two years' work gone west," Broome muttered. The room remained quiet, each man imagining MacLaren and his wrecked machine. Since their start in Santa Monica, they had experienced enough close calls that it was easy to put themselves in his position, and they could not bring themselves to feel joy at the failure of a rival. They wanted to win, but not this way. In his mind, Broome began composing a request to the British navy to bring MacLaren's spare plane to him in Burma, despite knowing full well that it would be declined due to the cost and complications.

Suddenly, Smith spoke, his voice not much louder than a whisper. "We'll get the machine to MacLaren somehow," he said. "Let's come upstairs to Commander Abbott's bedroom and have a talk with him."

More than any other man there, Smith knew the firsthand pain of being let down by something out of his control in a moment of need. He had once lost his aircraft to a mechanic's error during a race across the United States. At that time, he had talked another competitor into giving up his own plane. Now, he felt, it was time to repay the favor. Throughout his life, Smith had been driven by an innate sense of fairness, the byproduct of the hours listening to his father preaching. Take your time and do the right thing, and you will be rewarded, he had been told; skip a step or look past another person in need of help, and your soul will suffer.

Broome, still in shock, followed Smith to the room of Captain John S. Abbott, the commander of the US Asiatic Fleet. Within five minutes, they had a plan to load the spare British plane onto an American destroyer and bring it to Hong Kong, where it could be transferred overland to MacLaren in Burma. They cabled Washington for approval and received a prompt go-ahead. By the end of the day, American sailors were cutting pipes and dismantling the radio tower on the USS *John Paul Jones* in order to squeeze the cases containing the parts of the British plane between its engine room and main mast. Broome sent a cable to MacLaren, who responded with just two words: "Well done."

The world press was shocked by the American effort to help MacLaren, especially as it seemed highly unlikely that the men under Smith's command would circle the globe first. It was tantamount to a gladiator offering his foe a sword to slay him with. "This sporting offer to assist a friendly rival is most deeply appreciated by the organizers of the British flight," London's *Guardian* newspaper marveled.

For that moment, at least, the airplane seemed to be fulfilling the best version of itself: a machine that, instead of unleashing violence, brought cultures together in a shared human pursuit. Whether the spell would last was, of course, uncertain. But it was a sentiment felt as far away as Shanghai, where d'Oisy, the French pilot, was stuck after crashing on a golf course and wrecking his plane in a sand bunker. "Since the airplane is demolished beyond repair I have decided to terminate the undertaking," he announced at a reception in his honor at the French consulate. He wept openly alongside French officials, who presented him with a massive white jade vase to celebrate his achievement.

The following day, a Chinese general named He Fenglin offered d'Oisy his pick of several planes in his fleet. He selected a French-made Breguet, overjoyed that his flight was reborn. All the world celebrated that the Frenchman it had grown so fond of would not be exiting the stage as it had feared. All the world, that is, except d'Oisy's wife. After weeks of suspicion that French officials were keeping secrets about her husband's flight from her, she had told reporters that she looked forward to his return. "I'm glad it's finished," she said. "I've had enough of glory." The airplane d'Oisy selected proved not to be airworthy and it took several days to find a replacement. He resumed his path toward Hong Kong, taking care to avoid Nanking after a rival Chinese warlord, Chih Hsich-Yuan, threatened to seize the plane if he landed there, which served as d'Oisy's dangerous introduction to the reality that the country was splintered under dueling military fiefdoms.

The world race, which had seemed to come to an abrupt end when the pilots of two nations crashed their airplanes, was back on. For the first time since their takeoff from Santa Monica, the Americans felt like they had the upper hand. They were the only fliers so far who had crossed an ocean, a mental and physical hurdle that more than made up for their lack of total mileage. Their reception in Japan made them feel as if their journey, though not yet completed, had already changed the world for the better. As they prepared their planes for the flight toward southern Japan and Asia, a number of high-ranking Japanese officials surprised them with a request to see them off personally. "They looked upon the circumnavigation of the world by air as an event sure to usher in a new age, and an age in which they intended Japan to play a leading part," Arnold wrote.

Their slow pace through Alaska, however, now put the Americans squarely on pace to reach southeastern Asia just as the monsoon season began in earnest, bringing with it the likelihood that their planes would become incapacitated by the rain. Perhaps because of the dangers they faced, Smith found himself growing into his role as a leader. He spoke to Abbott shortly before the men left Tokyo and received his assurance that the aviators would have navy ships close by until they reached Calcutta, which would prevent the men from ending up stuck like MacLaren. With that, Smith led the squadron of three planes through a typhoon to Kushimoto, one of their final stops in Japan. The planes landed, and the men boarded a US Navy ship to sleep in its cabins. Late that night, a sailor on lookout duty told Smith that one of the planes was drifting. Rather than wake up the other men in his squadron, Smith gathered a crew of sailors and led them out into the driving rain to attach another anchor to the errant plane.

The following day, another contingent of Japanese officials presented the Americans with gifts. Smith noticed, however, that there were only three presents, apparently signaling that they were intended for the pilots but not the mechanics. He pulled the officials aside and asked them to find three more so that each man could have one. Until six were available, he said, he would refuse any gifts presented to them, ensuring that no man felt like he was second class. "He explained that we were simply six American airmen flying around the world together, and that we were all on equal footing," Arnold wrote. "This was mighty decent of Lowell and we all appreciated it." No one felt the kindness of the gesture as much as Ogden, who was sensitive about his lower rank. That evening, Smith sent a cable to Washington requesting that Ogden receive a promotion so that he, too, was a lieutenant. Soon, the men were equal in the eyes of the military as well.

The public responsibilities of commanding the mission remained a source of discomfort for Smith and he tried to hurry the pace toward mainland Asia, where there would be fewer ceremonies and public attention. No matter how far they flew in Japan, there were always people waiting for them. On June 2, the men reached Kagoshima, the southernmost city of Japan proper. Towering above the bay stood Sakurajima, one of the most active volcanoes in the world, which belched smoke and ash every few hours. In the shadow of its peak, the "shore was black with people," Arnold wrote. More than twenty thousand schoolchildren waited in neat lines waving American and Japanese flags, and they burst into "My Country, 'Tis of Thee" when the aviators reached the dock. The men, overwhelmed by the reception, handed out souvenirs and trinkets to the throngs of children. In America, the exclusion bill was now law; in Japan, there seemed to be open arms for the US aviators. "We saw not the slightest evidence" of anti-American sentiment, Arnold wrote. "They seemed to feel that ours was the type of undertaking that might inspire the younger generation." ᴙꜰ Lᴏᴀᴛs

Smith felt restless as the men waited in Kagoshima for two nights as naval ships got in position to offer assistance if necessary for their flight to Shanghai. Finally, on June 4, the men were greeted with clear skies. The lake surface was too glassy for the planes to easily take off, forcing the men to taxi in circles through the bay to build up waves in order to break the pontoons free from the suction of the water. Frustrated, they began throwing unnecessary items overboard, including their change of clothes. The *Boston* and the *New Orleans* were soon airborne, but the *Chicago* could not escape the surface tension no matter how hard Smith pushed the engine. He signaled to the two airborne planes to keep going, and he and Arnold returned to their mooring. There, they changed into bathing suits they had been given by the city of Portland, Oregon, and spent hours diving beneath the plane to find what was wrong with the pontoons. They discovered that a small metal strip had been torn away, which prevented them from generating enough resistance to achieve lift.

For the first time, Smith was separated from the rest of the squadron. Wade and Nelson flew ahead toward Shanghai, replaying in their minds the last two weeks in Japan. "It was so wonderful that we were still in a bit of a daze," Nelson later wrote. They soared for six hours over open water, watching the steamships and junks—a type of Chinese sailing ship—below. As the planes neared the Yellow Sea, Nelson noticed a burning smell. He told Harding to take control while he inspected the engine. Despite the chill of their high altitude, the metal seared his skin. His eyes darted back and forth across the machine, looking for the source of the smell before it grew into a fire that would bring them down far from land. He found an exhaust pipe that had become overheated and cracked, burning the rubber off the engine's ignition wires. Had it happened an hour or two earlier in their flight, they would likely have had to abandon the aircraft out of fear that the engine would combust. Instead, Nelson felt that the engine would last long enough for them to reach China. The men flew on for forty-five minutes, the line between life and death growing smaller by the second as the rubber continued to burn.

When their plane reached Shanghai, they almost did not have space to land in the bustling harbor. Junks, sampans, steamboats—seemingly anything that could float was crushed together, all filled with people straining to see the Americans. Shanghai was among the most cosmopolitan cities in the world, home to large contingents of Japanese, Indians, Parsees, Koreans, Turks, Punjabi, Javanese, Russians, Malays, and Europeans. "They all appeared to be on the river in boats waiting to see us," Nelson later said.

He and Harding touched down into the water and dodged small boats as they taxied to their mooring. As soon as the plane was motionless, they asked to be taken to a machine shop. There, in a Chinese shipyard, Nelson worked late into the night building several new exhaust stacks, making replacements for not only the one that had nearly brought his plane down but for those on the other planes as well. Though he was now thousands of miles away from Santa Monica, he acted like he was still back in Douglas's factory, continually tweaking the plane until it had no more weaknesses. He worked through the reception for the crew held by representatives of the powerful Standard Oil company, which was promoting the American fliers in advertisements that ran in newspapers across the United States. It did not feel like a loss. For the men, the novelty of celebrations had worn off after their experience in Japan and the group tried to avoid them. "We were sorry to miss meeting these folk, but I am afraid we were the cause of similar disappointments all along the line," Nelson later said. "Our work was first, for we were not on a joy ride."

They could not avoid every obligation. While waiting in their hotel for Smith to land, the men were ushered into a limousine and taken to the home of a prominent merchant. The doors of the home swung open to reveal men in tuxedos and women in evening gowns, tiaras, and ostrich-feather fans. An orchestra began playing American music as the dazed aviators walked in. Young girls in dresses appeared a few paces before them, dropping rose petals along their path. "The movie stars of Los Angles could do no better than this," Nelson wrote.

Smith landed the following day, and another ball was hastily planned. He declined the invitation and instead installed the new exhaust pipes that Nelson built, working on his plane in the harbor by lantern light. When he and Arnold returned to the hotel in their greasy coveralls, the doorman ordered them to enter by the servants' entrance, leaving Arnold laughing about his quick change in status from the night before. But Smith was past social niceties, consumed by the newest problem he had to solve: With the harbor so clogged, the planes, loaded with enough gas to reach their next destination, would not have room to take off. Smith changed the route, adding a new fueling stop along the way, and hoped the planes, now lighter, could maneuver more easily through the river traffic. Even then, the *New Orleans* barely missed scraping the mast of a junk as it climbed from the water.

The weight of celebrity followed the men everywhere they went. Taking to the air became their escape. They flew low over the Chinese coast, close enough to peer into the windows of houses and smell the aromas coming from villages and rice fields. To amuse themselves, they picked out small ships on the coast, dived toward them at full speed, and pulled up at the last second. Such pranks allowed them, for at least a few moments, to once again feel like young men on an adventure, unburdened by the need to represent their country to the world. "It was fun for us, and I dare say it helped to break the monotony of life on board the junks," Ogden wrote. The man who enjoyed it the most appeared to be Smith. Here, far away from cameras and the pressures of the race, he granted himself the freedom to open up to his squadron, showing that there was more to him than timetables and silence.

Each landing meant more ceremonies, more balls, more obligations. With MacLaren waiting on his new plane and with d'Oisy flying a replacement, the race seemed to be theirs to lose. Becoming the only nation to successfully circle the globe would go a long way to restore the reputation of American aviation and perhaps lead the country to embrace the possibilities offered by air travel. Even now, they were changing minds back home. "The round-the-world flight of the army airmen is well under way, and has already afforded a convincing demonstration of American pluck and ability," noted an editorial in the *Virginian-Pilot*.

Cities started to become a blur. The island city of Amoy (now known as Xiamen) in China; the busy seaport of Hong Kong; the Pearl River Delta colony of Macao, at the time a possession of Portugal (and now a bustling gambling hub under Chinese control known as the Las Vegas of the East)—at each one, the Americans followed the same routine of refueling and servicing their planes and then attending formal ceremonies and lavish parties held in their honor. Flying by day and glad-handing by night took a toll even on Arnold, a man who had never turned down an opportunity for fun in his life. His diary entries shrank to a few fragments jotted down with less thought than a grocery list.

Smith, as the squadron commander, found it the most difficult to avoid the attention. He did not want to be on a stage under the best conditions, and he especially did not want to be in front of other people while wearing an increasingly dirty and foul-smelling flight suit, the result of throwing most of his clothing overboard to minimize weight. Now anticipating that they would be photographed and put on display wherever they went, the men started sizing up the naval officers aboard the ship waiting for them at each stop, searching for men who were of similar height and build as themselves. They then asked to borrow the unsuspecting officers' formal uniforms for that evening. The ploy allowed them to pass as the debonair world adventurers that their admirers hoped to see, not the tired and overwhelmed men they actually were.

In Haiphong, then a part of French Indochina and now an industrial center of modern Vietnam, the Americans were invited to a ball in their honor hosted by the French governor-general. Again, before the event, they found naval officers who were roughly their size and again borrowed their clothes. The six men dutifully appeared at the ball, none of them understanding any French, and drank in the soft luxury of the moonlit evening. As the music played, a French interpreter told them that Brito Pais, the Portuguese aviator, had just arrived in Rangoon,

Burma. The race, which had faded into the background, suddenly took on a new urgency. "This news of the progress of the Portuguese was like a tonic to us," Smith said.

The men excused themselves from the reception and hurried back to the waiting American destroyer. They were up at dawn the next morning and prepared to fly to Saigon. For Smith, the renewed focus on flying—and flying alone—revived him, and he imagined his machine shared his passion as he readied it to soar into the hazy sky. "Our Libertys seemed to be humming a song of joy and contentment as we warmed them up to the accompaniment of the temple bells of Haiphong," Smith later wrote.

He had no way of knowing how fleeting his joy would be.

CHAPTER SIXTEEN

Tiger Country

No MATTER WHERE in the world the pilots landed, the sight of the American airplanes caused a sensation. In large cities, thousands of people crammed onto the shore to watch the squadron take off or land; in smaller places, like here in Haiphong, the presence of the world fliers clogged the river with boats of all kinds and sizes, each person aboard wanting to get a peek at what the future would bring.

Smith was by now used to the attention, though he never warmed to it. He started his engine and signaled for the men behind him to follow. In a few minutes, he hoped he would be in the sky, where he felt most at home. Until then, he tried to keep a lane in the river clear of obstacles, allowing the planes in the squadron to gather enough speed to take off.

The calm water did them no favors. There were not even ripples on the current that could help the pontoons break free. An hour passed without a successful takeoff, then two, then three. Losing his patience, Smith led the men ten miles down to the mouth of the Gulf of Tonkin, where there appeared to be enough wrinkles on the water to enable the planes to lift. After a few more attempts, he took to the air first, followed by Nelson. Wade, however, could not get free, no matter how hard he pushed his engine. He went back up the river, giving himself ample space for what he planned. Once he was ready, he zoomed along the water at a speed of fifty-five miles per hour, dodging and swerving between sampans with just feet to spare. After twelve miles of this, he succeeded in breaking the vacuum under his pontoon and felt himself lifting into the air. He climbed until he was even with Smith and Nelson, who had been circling above, and the squadron turned in the direction of Saigon.

The planes flew over the dark green earth, its contours swallowed by the jungle. Occasionally, the wilderness would recede and reveal flooded rice fields, tended to by farmers trailing water buffalo bound by wooden

After the end of World War I, General William "Billy" Mitchell was one of the few voices arguing that aircraft would change the world. Though he was often ignored during his lifetime, he is now widely seen as the father of the modern US Air Force. *US Army*

As a young designer in Los Angeles, Donald Douglas worked out of a rented room in the back of a barbershop while trying to get his own company off the ground. The success of the Douglas World Cruisers made him a household name.

Santa Monica Public Library

The Douglas World Cruisers were made from wood and canvas and held together with glue. Here, Douglas employees sew the heavy canvas to a rear section of the prototype plane.

Santa Monica Public Library

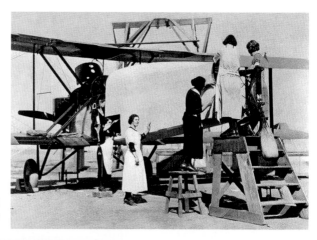

At the time he signed the contract to build the World Cruisers, Donald Douglas employed fewer than one hundred workers. Here, on the Douglas factory floor circa 1924, employees design and build components in what was once a movie studio in Santa Monica. *Santa Monica Public Library*

More than twenty thousand people gathered at Clover Field in Santa Monica, California, in March 1924, to watch the four Douglas World Cruisers begin their flight around the world. The site is now the home to the Santa Monica Airport. *Santa Monica Public Library*

Major Frederick Martin with his wife, Grace, and his son, Robert, before the world flight officially began in Seattle. When Major Martin later crashed in Alaska, reporters hounded Grace for any reaction to her husband's disappearance.

University of Washington Museum of History and Industry

British aviator Archibald Stuart-MacLaren (*in rear*) along with his two crew members. *Courtesy of Vanessa Ascough*

The Vickers Viking used in the British attempt to fly around the world. A type of aircraft known as a flying boat, the plane would land with its hull directly on the water without the use of pontoons. *Courtesy of Vanessa Ascough*

Major Martin and his mechanic, Alva Harvey, after they had been lost in the Alaskan wilderness for ten days.

One of the American planes landing at Lake Kasumigaura outside of Tokyo.

Hundreds of Japanese schoolchildren waving American flags greeted the three American planes despite increasing national tensions due to the 1924 Johnson-Reed Act, which prohibited Japanese from entering the United States.

Japanese military officials allowed the American squadron to enter Japan on the condition that they be allowed to inspect and photograph their aircraft. Here, Lieutenants Lowell Smith and Leslie Arnold stand near the *Chicago* while it is parked in a hangar outside of Tokyo.

Smithsonian National Air and Space Museum

An American plane soaring over junks as the squadron arrives in China.

Lieutenant Erik H. Nelson (*left*) and Lieutenant Jack Harding make repairs to the engine of the *New Orleans*.

Lieutenant Smith (*center*) shakes the hand of Mrs. MacLaren after the American aviators land outside of London. While in Japan, Smith pushed the American military to bring one of MacLaren's spare planes to him so that he could continue on his attempt to fly around the world.

One of the American planes landing near an iceberg in Greenland.

The last moments of the *Boston* before it sank in the North Atlantic, as seen from the USS *Richmond*. Among the journalists on board to document its loss was Damon Runyon, whose short stories were the inspiration for the musical *Guys and Dolls*.

Italian aviator and political figure Antonio Locatelli (*center*) hoped to beat the American squadron around the world by flying a faster monoplane. When his aircraft went down off the coast of Greenland, American sailors saved him and his crew and brought them to New York City.

Lieutenant Nelson, in the *New Orleans*, as the squadron flies from Boston to New York City.

The six American aviators who completed the world flight, alongside General Mason M. Patrick (*second from left*). From left, the aviators are Lieutenant Harding, Lieutenant Smith, Lieutenant Wade, Lieutenant Ogden, Lieutenant Arnold, and Lieutenant Nelson.

President Calvin Coolidge (*left*) stood in the rain for several hours to be on hand for the arrival of the American squadron in the nation's capital. Smith (*center*) greeted him and demonstrated the features of the Douglas World Cruiser.

Lieutenant Nelson (*center, hatless*), with a policeman nearby as guard, striding along the shores of Seattle after the squadron had landed, completing the first flight around the world. *University of Washington Museum of History and Industry*

Lieutenant Smith (*left*) and his mechanic, Lieutenant Arnold. A study in contrasts, the soft-spoken and press-shy Smith often leaned on the gregarious Arnold, a former actor, to take his place in the spotlight at balls and receptions across the globe.

yokes. Soon, even those gaps in the dense landscape became rare, part of what appeared to be a never-ending canopy hiding the ground below.

After Smith had flown for more than one hundred and fifty miles, the plane's engine began to overheat. He landed the *Chicago* in a small lagoon called Kuavictorpalms. Arnold filled the radiator with salt water, and they were soon airborne again. The problem, however, was not solved. Within minutes, a stream of warm water spurted into both men's faces from somewhere in the machine. The jungle below was too dense for them to land and the sea was too heavy. They flew on for another twenty minutes, looking for a place to set down. The motor began knocking, and the thin layer of cotton covering the fuselage turned burning hot to the touch. Smith, in the cockpit, feared that the plane would catch fire at any moment.

He spotted a lagoon three miles inland and dove for it. It was surrounded by jungle and devoid of any railways or roads that could lead them toward help. At that moment, those concerns didn't matter. The *Chicago* glided into the lagoon, its placid blue water surrounded by palms and the broad green leaves of banana trees. Arnold jumped out of the rear seat with a fire extinguisher but did not have to use it. The men examined the engine to find a shattered connecting rod had poked a hole in the crankcase. Further inspection revealed that a cylinder had cracked as well. The engine was useless.

The two other planes soon landed. Together, Smith, Nelson, and Wade tried to find the lagoon their squadron was in on the map but could not. With the heat rising, the crews of the *New Orleans* and the *Boston* gave Smith and Arnold all of their remaining drinking water and promised to return as quickly as possible on foot with a new engine. The two planes took off, leaving Smith and Arnold alone in a lagoon that was not on any maps; in a country they were reasonably sure was French Indochina; on a continent that was very far from home.

For the second time, the acting commander of the American world flight squadron had been forced down and left behind. Smith, with Arnold at his side, took stock of their surroundings. Seen under any other circumstances, the landscape would have seemed close to paradise. The sun glistened on the water as a breeze blew in, as if inviting them to linger. Yet after a moment they realized that they were likely not alone. The lagoon was full of what appeared to be fishing traps made of bamboo poles that had been driven into the mud, opening up the question of when the owner of them would return. Arnold tied the tail of the plane to one of the traps. Insects buzzed around them. The muffled calls of unseen birds echoed through the clearing. Occasionally, they heard the plunk of a crocodile slithering into the water below them, giving Arnold goose bumps despite the unwavering heat.

After roughly half an hour a man in a dugout canoe approached them cautiously. His hair was black and he spat crimson juice out of his mouth as he chewed what appeared to be a betel nut, a mild stimulant. Though he spoke no English, when he yelled at the men and poked a paddle at the *Chicago*, his message was clear: He was the owner of the traps, and he did not appreciate finding a plane tied to them, no matter whose it was. Smith and Arnold untied the rope from the bamboo stakes, pushed farther out into the lagoon, and dropped their anchor there.

Soon more men appeared in canoes, although where they came from was a mystery to Arnold, who saw no nearby dwellings. They were naked except for breechcloths and spoke rapidly among themselves in a language neither American could understand. Then they approached, tentatively at first, and soon seemed to accept that neither Smith nor Arnold posed any danger. "The natives became friendly when they found no harm was likely to befall them; in fact they were just a bit too chummy," Arnold later wrote.

The indigenous men climbed aboard the plane, their weight submerging one of the pontoons. Smith and Arnold tried to limit the numbers to keep the plane from sinking. The effort to maintain order in the thick tropical heat exhausted them, and they drank their entire supply of fresh water. Smith seemed to wither as the heat intensified. As they sat there debating whether to go inland to look for a brook or stream, a man in a white robe paddled by. He asked the aviators, in French and with accompanying gestures, for cigarettes. When they responded they had none, the man rowed on, ignoring Smith's and Arnold's request to point them in the direction of fresh water.

Not long after, the fisherman who had been the first to approach the plane returned and offered several bananas and coconuts to the men who dropped out of the sky. He cut open each coconut and instructed the Americans on how to drink its milk. He then offered them water from the bottom of his canoe. Smith appeared ready to take it, but for once Arnold stepped in to maintain safety, not allowing himself to go along with whatever life threw at him. Remembering their training in

Virginia, he declined for both of them, fearful of contracting dysentery from foul water. In the air, Smith was flawless; on the ground, his body was more vulnerable to the elements than other members of the squadron, and Arnold saw that he needed to protect him.

The infusion of food and liquid revived the Americans, who had felt themselves slipping away in the relentless heat. Smith's renewed strength proved temporary. Sweat poured down his face and arms and left his normally pale face crimson. Though he was comfortable in the deserts of California and Mexico, he had never experienced the sweltering, heavy temperatures of the tropics, and he longed to climb to higher altitudes where he felt safe. He sat next to Arnold and watched the sun slowly dip out of the sky, all the while imagining how glorious a drink of water would be.

As the two men attempted to gather material to use for bedding, a sampan carrying three French missionaries arrived from what they said was a village three and a half miles away. Arnold, with perhaps a dozen French words at his disposal, tried to communicate that they were desperately in need of more water. "Smith, whose outward display of mirth rarely goes beyond a whimsical smile, roared with laughter at my pidgin French and pantomime," he later said. The missionaries offered to take Arnold back to their camp. He agreed, and warned Smith again not to drink any water until he returned.

Arnold paddled off, trusting the men to lead him into the dark.

NELSON HAD TAKEN command in Smith's absence. He navigated the path to the city of Tourane, about an hour away from the unnamed lagoon. As soon as they landed, he hunted down a local Standard Oil agent who knew the area well. Together, they drove to the man's palatial home and scoured a detailed map of French Indochina for a place that matched what Nelson had seen earlier that day. At the time, the colony was larger than France itself, stretching through parts of present-day Vietnam, Cambodia, Laos, and China, and details of the interior were little more than guesswork on most colonial maps. After finding what looked like the place Smith and Arnold went down, Nelson ordered Wade, Ogden, and Harding to guard their planes and drove with the Standard Oil agent to Hue.

They traveled along a gravel highway cut through the jungle. The road was new, and at times it ended at small docks, where barges were necessary to take them across rivers. After three hours, they reached Hue, and Nelson was told that not only were they most likely in the wrong place but no airplanes had ever been seen in that part of Asia. Unwilling to give up, he insisted that the men take him to the lagoon on his map. It was impossible to reach by car, he was told, so they would need to go most of the way by canoe.

He bought sandwiches and water at a local hotel and packed them away to give to Smith and Arnold. With indigenous Vietnamese as his guides, he boarded a canoe and pushed off into the night. As they felt the current picking them up, his guides threw cooked rice into the river and evidently said a prayer. The men gestured to him to keep his voice down to avoid attracting tigers or crocodiles, both of which he later learned were in ample supply. Not that he would have been able to see them before it was too late. "It was pitch dark, not even a star," Nelson later wrote.

They reached a plantation after thirty minutes on the river. The owner, awakened by the sound of his dogs barking at the passing canoe, came out and invited Nelson inside. There, Nelson and the man studied the available maps of the region, but this time they could find no lagoons that matched Nelson's description. Not willing to let Nelson down, the plantation owner told him of a local Vietnamese priest who lived a few miles inland. If anyone could find the lagoon, the man said, it would be him.

Nelson found himself in a party of five men walking single file through the jungle in the dead of night, all hoping that they were not attracting the attention of curious tigers. The man in the front of the line cut their path with an ax. Every few minutes they passed what appeared to be shrines with food and other items left as offerings. The darkness of the night, the denseness of the jungle, the whispered conversations in a language he did understand—together, they left Nelson feeling lost, unsure of where he was and how he would ever return. "Just how far we hiked I do not know," he later wrote.

Eventually, they arrived at the thatched house of the priest. In a brief conversation with the help of interpreters, the man said that he had neither seen nor heard of any airplanes. Nelson felt his stomach drop. After all he had done, he feared that it now amounted to nothing more than a pointless mission, while Smith and Arnold remained in the wilderness with neither food nor any means of contacting help. The sense of futility he had felt while searching for Martin in the wastelands of Alaska flooded back, and Nelson tried to drown it with action. He asked the priest if he could inquire whether others in the surrounding villages had heard anything of an airplane. As men carried his message onward, Nelson waited in the dark clearing, too tired to sleep, too scared to give up his last hope.

Minutes or hours later—Nelson was never sure how quickly time passed in the jungle that night—two fishermen appeared and said that they had seen monsters flying through the air. With the help of an interpreter, they pointed Nelson in the direction the beasts had traveled. Again the search party boarded the boats and floated down the river. Every few moments they called out Smith's and Arnold's names. Nelson, unable to stay awake any longer, lay down in the bottom of the boat. He closed his eyes and drifted into a dreamless sleep, unbroken by the sound of the names of his lost crew members echoing through the dense wilderness.

HE COULD NOT take it anymore. As Smith waited for Arnold to return, he felt the heat draining his resolve. He sat on the top wing of the plane with a flare gun in his hand, mosquitoes swarming on his arms. After Arnold left, the native men surrounding the lagoon became bolder in their curiosity and attempted to climb from the pontoons up into the cockpit. In desperation, Smith grabbed the flare gun and fired a round above their heads. The men scattered but remained a few yards away as if testing him. Tired and desperately thirsty, he watched them drink water from their canoes. He longed for any measure of relief from the sultry air. A man offered him a cup. Unable to stop himself, he guzzled several deep swallows of the water, forgetting all his training. He then returned to the top of the wing and resumed his losing effort to keep the mosquitoes at bay.

Occasionally, he heard a buzzing sound and looked to the hazy sky, hoping to see an American plane but dreading that he would see MacLaren. The British pilot had by now received his spare aircraft and resumed the race. His path would likely take him directly over this part of French Indochina. With the sky blocked by clouds, Smith filled it in with his fears. The world, he knew, was going on without him, and nothing gnawed at him more than the feeling of inaction. Gazing up at another plane moving above him while he was stuck here would be agony, yet he could not keep his eyes from scanning the skies.

Arnold returned an hour later carrying wine and boiled rice that he had obtained from the local missionaries. The two men ate, washing down the food with slugs from the bottle. Unsure of the time, Arnold made a bed for himself on the bottom wing of the plane while Smith curled up in the baggage compartment. Within minutes they were asleep.

When they woke up, they had no idea how much time had passed. The sounds they heard seemed to be coming from their dreams, leaving them momentarily lost in the confusion between consciousness and sleep. Smith was unsure if he was truly hearing something or having a nightmare of MacLaren flying directly above. Distant at first, the sounds became louder and clearer, revealing themselves to be human voices. As he shook himself awake, Smith realized that he was listening to his own name being called by unknown men in an accent he did not recognize. He banged his arms against the side of the plane to alert Arnold, and together they called out in the darkness.

Moments later Nelson walked into the clearing. Seven days earlier, the three American men had been part of a parade that brought the city of Tokyo to a halt; now, in an unmarked lagoon, they embraced under a dark sky with only crocodiles and swarming bats as their audience. Nelson offered the sandwiches and water he had purchased at the hotel, a time that in the refracted world of the jungle felt like days earlier but had in fact been that same night. Smith, reawakened by the water to his responsibility of keeping accurate records of the flight, asked Nelson what time it was. He looked at his watch and saw it was three a.m., making it June 12. It was then that Nelson remembered that it was his thirty-fifth birthday. The men celebrated by downing the remainder of the wine and toasting to the success of their mission.

By morning they had gathered a team of native Vietnamese to tow the *Chicago* along the river to Hue. At dawn, the sampans—each filled with ten men, all naked to the waist—pushed off from the shore. Smaller boats flitted next to them in the water, filled with women from local villages and supplies of water and cigarettes. At the front of the procession, a man in a small boat beat a drum, providing the rhythm for the oars. For the next ten hours the men rowed without stopping, bringing the plane twenty-five miles downriver.

Smith and Arnold pulled the cushions out of their cockpits and sat in the shade on the lower wing. Occasionally, the boats passed elephants throwing water over each other from their trunks. Coconut trees, swollen with fruit, hung over the water. "Our greatest regret was that we hadn't a camera. Every bend in the river revealed a view that would have been worth photographing," Smith later wrote.

Eventually, the boats reached the spot where Nelson had left his car the previous night. He hopped off a boat, drove ahead, and rounded up local men to guard the plane once it reached Hue. He then returned to Tourane, where Wade had secured a new engine for the *Chicago* from an American destroyer. Nelson and Harding then drove back to Hue to help rebuild the damaged aircraft, and Ogden—the youngest of the men—accompanied the engine in a truck driven by a local man. Wade stayed back with the two remaining planes.

The success of the American world flight rested on the truck carrying the new engine, Ogden, and a hellbent driver who set out into the sunset. It was soon so dark that Ogden couldn't tell how fast they were going or what lay outside his window, only that both were too extreme for his liking. "The driver of that lorry cared little for his own life and less for mine," Ogden said later. The truck climbed up a steep and bumpy road, the first clue they were cresting a mountain. Occasionally Ogden could see the eyes of an animal in the jungle gleaming back at him in the night. The bumping momentarily ceased when the truck lost its grip on the road and drove into the brush, making Ogden briefly feel like he was once again flying. After thirty minutes of pulling and pushing, the truck was once more back on the road and being driven with the same reckless abandon. Over the next several hours, the truck careened into a pile of rocks, veered off the road into a tree, and nearly slid off the lip of a valley. "My heart stopped beating at least ten separate times that night," Ogden later wrote.

The sun was rising over the coconut trees when Ogden finally reached Hue, where Smith and Arnold had beached the *Chicago* under a bridge. He jumped out of the truck, and together the men hoisted the malfunctioning engine from the plane and dropped it on the beach. They then lifted its replacement into place. Over the next four hours, Ogden installed the motor and got the machine working again, a job that he later said he had never done as quickly. When he was finished, Nelson, Harding, and Ogden returned to Tourane in the car that Nelson had borrowed from the Standard Oil agent. Smith and Arnold took off from the river in Hue and flew to join them, closing in forty minutes the distance that automobiles had taken all night to cover.

The next morning they were all together again. In the span of seventy-two hours, they had become lost in an unmarked jungle, driven through the dead of night, convinced native Vietnamese to tow a broken-down plane over twenty-five miles of a river by the strength of oars alone, and secured and reinstalled a new engine. Each man had faced adversity and contributed equally, strengthening the bonds between them in a way that parades and formal dinners could not. In Alaska, their decisions under pressure had largely been dictated to them by Washington. Here, they had depended on their own judgment and come out the better for it. An immigrant auto mechanic had come to the aid of a failed Broadway actor and the son of a preacher, and a descendant of the *Mayflower* and a man who had never been outside of the South until his adulthood revived the planes in order to keep their quest alive. They were a living example of the American melting pot, demonstrating through their teamwork that the nation's strength lay in variety rather than exclusion.

The reunited squadron flew on to Saigon, then known as the Paris of the Orient, where they spent a day refueling and servicing their planes. That evening, the men borrowed clothes from sailors on a nearby American ship and walked through the city streets. They found a sidewalk café and sat down at a table. A waiter approached and told them that they could not be served because they were not wearing jackets. The men tried to explain that they were pilots on a world flight and did not have formal wear with them.

"All he said to this was that he knew who we were, but that it made no difference, and we would have to go away at once," Wade later said.

In Japan, they had been hailed as the symbols of a new technological age; in Saigon, they were refused service for not adhering to a colonial social code. As the men walked down the street to find a new restaurant, they felt stuck between two worlds, unable to reconcile the era they were creating by their flight with the one they were leaving behind.

CHAPTER SEVENTEEN

"The Outlying Borders of the World"

THEY AWOKE BEFORE dawn. As the Americans climbed into their cockpits shortly after four in the morning, the first hint of light broke above them. The sun climbed slowly, unfurling streaks of soft pink and purple across the sky. In another time and another place, the colors etching the clouds above the thatched homes and bright pagodas of the city would have made them stop and admire the view. But here, in the humid morning air of Saigon, the golden light brimming over the palm trees was a sign to get moving before the full fury of the day's heat descended.

Smith, in the lead, glided through the river, his plane shimmering in the reflection of the sunrise on the water. The three planes climbed into the sky and flew east toward Siam (present-day Thailand), following a muddy river that reminded them of the lower Mississippi. Smith insisted that they remain close to the shore rather than taking a more direct route over the lightly populated mangrove swamps of what is now Cambodia. Here, in what the American press was calling the "back stretch" of the flight's path, the prospects of rescue, should it be needed, were slim. Though not superstitious, Smith recognized that good fortune had smiled upon Martin in Alaska and saved them from the lagoon, and there was no reason to expect a third miracle.

Soon they were over the sapphire waters of the Gulf of Siam (now the Gulf of Thailand). As the men flew, Smith looked down at the dozens of small islands they passed, each fringed with perfect beaches and coconut trees. A few days earlier, he had been stuck in a lagoon that looked similar and forced to imagine what would become of him if he were not rescued. For the first time since he left Santa Monica, he thought of his own future, one that was not dependent on a race for meaning. "So enticing were they that we flew lower, to explore them with a view to coming here on our honeymoons—that is, if any of us really do get married," Smith later wrote.

The daydream quickly passed. The men landed in the Menam River (now known as the Chao Phraya River) and secured their planes in the busy Bangkok waterway. Two planes needed minor repairs, forcing the men to spend a second night in the city. Smith, as usual, kept to himself, filling his time checking and rechecking their equipment and asking for the latest weather reports for the route ahead.

The other men spent time fixing the engines or sleeping aboard an American destroyer anchored in the bay. Their day-to-day lives were so intertwined that when given the opportunity, the aviators often scattered, each man needing time to himself. Arnold, his responsibilities complete, took a tour of the cosmopolitan city. At the onset of the race, he had been a libertine, powered by a thirst for experience that had made his home-town in Connecticut feel like a jail cell. Several hours free in Bangkok for such a man seemed likely to result in an epic hangover, a night in prison, or both. Yet as he strolled through the city streets, he felt a for-eign sensation—peace. He had wanted the world, and now, with Smith as his pilot, he had found it. Flying thousands of miles and visiting doz-ens of cities soothed the restlessness that he had felt since he was a child, haunted by the suspicion that there was always something better around every novel corner. It was as if an itch had finally been scratched, and he was now free to devote his attention elsewhere.

More than any other man on the flight, he looked forward to the downtime. He knew that he had originally been an alternate, someone's second-best choice, and he was lucky to be on the mission at all. For most pilots, that would have been a blow to the ego that they would spend the rest of their life trying to heal, every moment another chance to prove everyone wrong. Arnold took it as a gift—in a squadron full of the best aviators America had to offer, he alone did not need to win a race or re-build an engine to ensure his place in the world.

Naturally curious, he immersed himself in the city, unbound by routine and determined to turn it into more than a refueling stop. He visited several pagodas and temples, observed the patterns of daily life, and pictured what his life would be like if he lived there. In the early afternoon, he found himself standing before a giant gilded statue of the Buddha reclining, and for the first time he felt small in the presence of a tradition that was not his own. "The Siamese are a very keen race—

smart, courteous, kind, and very likable," he wrote in his diary that night. "It would be most interesting to stay here long enough to see more of the country, to learn and observe some of its customs, and to see some more of its worthwhile sights."

Though they shared one plane, Smith and Arnold met each day with nearly opposite approaches. Smith, carrying the responsibility of leadership that he had never asked for, directed his efforts toward completing the race as quickly and safely as possible. Arnold, sitting in the cockpit behind him, wanted nothing more than to marinate in places that were so different from what he had known. For Arnold, the fact that a race was on seemed trivial compared with the opportunity to inhale all that the Earth had to offer; for Smith, there was no greater experience than winning.

Once the planes were fixed and secure, an official brought the full squadron to the home of a minor Siamese prince who wished to meet them. They walked through rooms decorated with huge carved elephant tusks, their walls glimmering with gold leaf. When they were ushered in to meet the prince, they saw a photograph of General Billy Mitchell, the man who had come up with the idea of a round-the-world flight, on a nearby table. Mitchell had visited the country a few weeks earlier on a hunting trip. From the way the prince spoke about him, it was clear that Mitchell's exile from Washington had not dimmed his enthusiasm for the flight in the least. He was no longer in America, but he was still fighting for the world to recognize American aviation. "Everyone in Siam was loud in praise of the man who has fought so hard to make the people of America appreciate the fact that the world has at last reached the era of travel by air," Wade later wrote.

The unexpected reminder of Mitchell intensified Smith's focus. That night, he made an announcement, without first asking for the input of the crew: Rather than continuing on the planned route that hugged the shore of the Malay Peninsula for nearly a thousand miles, they would fly the 430 miles across it, most of which was made up of dense jungles and mountains. The shortcut would save a day or more. If all went well, they would reach Rangoon by nightfall. Given the terrain, there would be no body of water on which to land the planes over the course of the shortened route, and no way for the aviators to be rescued even if they somehow survived a crash.

There was no need to take such a risk. The squadron had flown roughly 10,795 miles from Santa Monica and had another 14,530 miles to go to complete the circle of the Earth. D'Oisy, the charming French pilot who had held the lead in the world race, was no longer a threat. His plan to fly without scheduled stops or reinforcements had worked better than anyone thought possible, and he had landed in Tokyo as a global celebrity and a symbol of the freedom of movement made possible by the airplane. Even he, though, could not find a way around the impossible. There was simply no way to cross the Pacific without a chain of ships and men waiting with oil, fuel, and other supplies. After flying across Europe and Asia faster than anyone in history, his race was over.

The fact that he had quit before he killed himself in a reckless attempt to keep going made the world love him even more. Tokyo held a parade in his honor. Invitations to balls and festivities celebrating his achievement came in from across Europe, South America, and the United States. From India, British aristocrats sent word that he was welcome on an upcoming tiger hunt; in California, a public relations man inquired whether he needed his services to plan a tour across the country. France announced that he was immediately promoted to captain. D'Oisy, however, preferred to retreat into the shadows, content that the spotlight would now shine on someone else. "I am very happy that it is all behind," he told reporters, and turned his attention to working out the problem of how exactly he would get back to Paris because he was no longer in possession of a plane that he could fly there.

The Portuguese, led by Brito Pais, were also out of the running. Unable to find Macao through the cloud cover, the men searched for a landing spot until they unexpectedly saw the city of Hong Kong below. The plane circled the city until it was nearly out of gas, finally coming down in a hillside cemetery. The hard landing damaged its wings and engine, putting it in no shape to go on.

The world race appeared to be down to the Americans and the British, though Pedro Zanni, the Argentinean ace, announced that he would launch his own flight in the coming days. Zanni had secured a Fokker aircraft, built by the revered German manufacturer, in Amsterdam, and told reporters that he would follow the same route as MacLaren. "Major Zanni believes that the speed of his plane will enable him not only to evade the monsoon in India, but also to beat the American world fliers," a British paper noted. MacLaren, at that point, was nearing Hong Kong, having narrowly escaped Rangoon and its unceasing storms. "Rainfall here stupendous; have never seen like before," he wrote in a telegram to London.

The American press grew desperate for any news, something to satisfy the readers who were demanding to know what was happening with the fliers even if they could not locate the squadron's whereabouts on a map. "When they were struggling with Alaskan unpleasantness or skirting the Japanese and Chinese coasts, the public had a fair idea of where they were and what they were seeing. But now . . . one feels rather at a loss," a columnist for the *Baltimore Evening Sun* wrote. "It is possible that the small boy with a scientifically arranged stamp collection may be coming into his own as a guide for adult relatives through the outlying borders of the world. But if he . . . is not able to help, the average reader may be lost beyond finding in the strange lands east of Suez."

The far parts of the globe became newly relevant because the public knew that six Americans they had grown fond of were out there. "If these round the world flight attempts serve no larger purpose, they will serve at least to teach millions of landlubbers a lot more geography than they have known before," the *Dallas Journal* wrote. "It isn't that we are ignoramuses. It is merely that we have not made a meticulous study of the map of the world. These round the world flights are going to instruct us mightily."

No matter that geography was not America's strong suit. The nation was in the lead in the greatest race the world had ever seen, and it could not contain its pride. "The name of America and Americans is on more lips, on account of this feat, than perhaps ever before," the *Long Beach Press-Telegram* wrote, its enthusiasm drifting into hyperbole. "This is going to help bind nations more closely together in bonds of common understanding and common sympathies." With news slow, the *San Francisco Examiner* resorted to running a long story about a young woman who saw the American squadron flying overhead while on a steamship home from Japan. The only grumbling that could be found over the race came from Australia, where a prominent columnist complained that "the English papers serve no useful purpose in enlarging their description of the aerial flight. It is not a 'round the world' one, no flight will ever be till it does the girth. It is a round-the-top-of-the-world flight, the coast of the three continents that lend themselves to it being followed practically all the way."

Smith knew that his squadron had a slight advantage over MacLaren in terms of total miles flown but felt that it was precarious. MacLaren's machine was new, and he had the benefit of flying away from the fierce storms that Smith knew lay in their path. The Americans had proven that the Douglas plane could withstand the brutal temperatures of Alaska and the Aleutian Islands. No one had yet demonstrated that an aircraft, much less three of them, could handle the unceasing monsoons. "It is the tradition in the British Air Ministry that no airplane has ever crossed India in the rainy season. Our pilots must attempt it," the *Tulsa World* warned its readers.

On the morning of June 20, the three American planes taxied up and down the glassy river in Bangkok, churning up enough wake to allow them to take off. After a few hours of frustration, they were airborne, flying toward a great expanse of green while the pagodas of Bangkok inched away from view. As the men flew deeper over the forest, they began to pass through clouds of steam rising from the damp ground below. Strange and unexpected air currents gripped them, making them momentarily lose control. Thrusts of air tossed their planes up and down, leaving them feeling like they were riding unbroken horses hundreds of feet above the ground.

There seemed to be no way to spot the fissures or any way to escape. Nelson and Harding, sitting in the *New Orleans*, felt the current drag down their plane while the *Chicago* and *Boston*, flying just to the right of them, were unaffected. Unable to fight against its power, Nelson banked sharply to the left and for a few long moments flew back the way they had come until they cleared the air mass and found themselves riding a rising current. One particularly bumpy air pocket snapped two wires from the *Boston*. Wade decided to fly on with wires dangling from his wing, rather than turning back to Bangkok or trying to descend.

The squadron reached Rangoon just as rays of the setting sun glowed from the spire of the golden Shwedagon Pagoda that rose over the city. In *Letters of Travel*, Rudyard Kipling, in his first visit to Burma, called the nearly four-hundred-foot-high structure one of the most sacred sites in Buddhism, a "golden mystery . . . a beautiful winking wonder." Smith used its reflection as a beacon to find his way to the mooring buoys set up for them in the densely packed Irrawaddy River and maneuvered between boats to prevent any from clipping his wings.

The shortcut had worked. Though he told no one, Smith had felt ill for most of the flight and struggled to remain awake now that he was no longer in the sky. With his fever rising, he did not notice Arnold fall off the side of the plane while attempting to secure its wings. As Arnold treaded water, he watched as the *Chicago* sped up the river in order to avoid a collision and fought against the swift current that the men had been warned typically drowned at least one person a day. Smith turned back to see an empty seat behind him and scanned the water until he saw Arnold's head. He pulled the plane back around and stopped in front of Arnold, who climbed back up on the pontoons and into the rear cockpit.

Though waterlogged and catching his breath after his unexpected swim, Arnold could tell that something was off with Smith. He summoned an English doctor, who moved Smith to a bungalow away from the noise of the city. There, he was soon doubled over with cramps. The doctor asked Smith and Arnold to describe everything they had done over the past few days. Once he heard their tale, he told Smith that he was suffering from dysentery, likely a result of drinking the tainted water offered to him in the heat of the lagoon. There was no telling how long it would take for the illness to leave his body.

For the second time, Smith feared that his flight was over. Dysentery, a condition most often associated with wartime, could kill a person in three or four days. Its hours were agony, its victims unable to control their bowels or replenish their bodies with nutrients. With immediate treatment, which consisted mainly of drinking enough purified water to avoid dehydration, the best Smith could hope for was that he'd be idle for just a week, though it would probably be more. He groaned in sorrow, tormented by the pain of losing ground in the race as much as the pain raging in his intestines.

Not far away, the five other Americans woke up to find that a barge had crashed into the *New Orleans* while they slept. Its bottom left wing was nearly smashed in two and barely hung on to the frame. They would have to build an entirely new wing and attach it, which would take several days.

No one wanted to be the one to tell Smith. They all knew that he would fly before he was fully healed as long as he was physically capable of sitting up and keeping his eyes open. He approached life like it were a ticking clock, with each circle of the minute hand a reminder that his time on Earth was limited. Movement eased the burden of knowing that judgment would one day come. The feeling of staying in one spot not only frustrated him as a competitor but gnawed at his hold on the world, leaving him stuck somewhere between purgatory and hell.

The damaged *New Orleans* had to be fixed, no matter how desperately Smith wanted to fly. The squadron would remain grounded until Nelson located the materials and had enough time and energy to rebuild the wing under the boiling sun. In Smith's mind, each second that passed opened the door slightly wider for MacLaren to overtake them. After all, he was exiting the danger of the monsoons while Smith was leading men into it. It didn't take much imagination to see MacLaren reaching Japan and then crossing the Pacific while the Americans struggled against forces they could not control.

The barge that smashed the *New Orleans*, the rain, his own body—it seemed that the conspiracy against him ran deep and was destined to keep him from finding peace. Smith, alone in his bungalow, cried out in the night. He had traveled so far and yet had never felt so close to failure.

CHAPTER EIGHTEEN

Paris Is Waiting

T HE HOURS FELT heavy.

The weight of grand expectations hung on the five healthy American aviators as they labored in the humid afternoon to rebuild the wing of the damaged plane. With help from the welcoming party that had greeted them on the river, they located wood, cloth, and glue and began measuring out enough of each to meet the dimensions that Nelson kept written down in his pocket at all times. The work was hot and slow, giving their minds ample time to imagine what it would be like to return home without fulfilling their promises. They could hear reporters criticizing them for not securing their planes; for the mechanical failure that forced Smith into that lagoon, where he had made the fateful decision to accept water; for being too slow and too mistake-prone to keep themselves out of the path of the monsoons. Of all the sins they would have to atone for, they knew that the one they would never be forgiven for was getting the public's hopes up, allowing Americans to believe in a bright new future that the airplane could bring.

The men worked until they could no longer go on and then were driven to a clubhouse for British officers, built high on stilts as some protection against the abundance of local snakes. There, they made themselves at home, swimming and playing water polo in the pool to escape from the suffocating sun. Harding, who had not comprehended the depths of the cold while they were in Alaska, found that extreme heat also did not suit him, and he took out their map to calculate how many more days it would be until they reached Iceland.

Arnold volunteered to make morning and afternoon excursions to check on Smith, who was recovering in the bungalow of the doctor who was treating him. Never before had their natures clashed so obviously. Arnold appeared armed with stories about the men's adventures in

Rangoon so that his commander—and now friend—did not feel left out; Smith wanted to know only about the condition of the plane and where MacLaren was. As each day passed, he seemed to regain more of his strength. Still, there was no telling whether he was truly healing or simply getting better at disguising his pain in order to resume the race that he lived for.

With Smith recuperating and Nelson testing the repaired plane, Arnold fell into old habits. He sat in a café and watched the local women walk by under vibrant umbrellas, admiring their brightly colored silk skirts, white shirtwaists, and black hair pulled into shiny coils. Come evening, he found himself in nightclubs catering to Europeans who felt a certain kind of freedom granted by their distance from home. "I think Americans miss a lot in life not knowing how to play—they are in too much of a hurry and neglect details," Arnold wrote in his diary that night.

After three days in bed, Smith refused to stay in one place any longer. He thanked the doctor who had attended to him and found his way to the British clubhouse, where he surprised his men with his insistence that they resume their journey. Although he remained weak, he inspected the mended wing of the *New Orleans* and checked on the other two planes. The thought of forcing men to fly in unsafe aircraft was perhaps the one thing that could have swayed him from the race, and he took his time before declaring the machines fit to carry on. The men refueled their tanks and prepared to leave in the morning, having lost four days to what had appeared to be a catastrophic combination of illness and destruction.

In the only nod to his diminished health, Smith let Nelson take the lead position as the squadron taxied out onto the river on the morning of June 25. The three planes maneuvered behind a passing ocean steamer, hoping that its wake would break the grip of the smooth river. The *New Orleans* and the *Boston* both jumped skyward easily. Smith, behind in the *Chicago*, could not seem to free his pontoons. Wade circled back and descended in front of the *Chicago*, grazing the water to churn up wake. Arnold, sitting in the rear seat, could not believe Wade's skill in controlling his aircraft. "To take a heavy Cruiser down and daintily run its pontoons through the water so that they are barely an inch below the surface, and skim along like that for a mile, is the feat of a wizard," he wrote.

The squadron flew over a low, green country of rice fields, headed toward one of the rainiest places in the world during the monsoon season.

Occasionally, farmers and their livestock would look up, startled by the hum of the Liberty engines passing overhead, to see the American pilots waving at them. When possible, Smith preferred flying low. Ascending to greater elevations put more strain on the pilots' bodies, lowering the available oxygen and increasing the bone-chilling cold in their open, noisy cockpits. But he also chose to stay closer to the ground for another reason. Though to all outward appearances quiet and serious, he had a playful streak that he showed only in the air. He loved surprising people he spotted below him, his joy akin to a child hiding around a corner, jumping out, and shooting *Boo!* In the cockpit, where no one could see his face under his goggles and helmet, he wore a broad smile, full of the happiness that eluded him on land.

Smith spotted the first storm clouds in the distance as they approached the shimmering light blue waters of the Bay of Bengal. The sky appeared to have been torn in half, all sunlight on one side and darkness on the other. The rain began falling moments later. It came down steadily at first, coating the fabric of the planes and drowning out the sound of the propellers. Without warning, the storm intensified, as if someone had turned a dial up to its highest setting. Sheets of water descended on the men, lashing their faces and pouring into their goggles until they felt like they were flying through liquid rather than air. The three planes bunched together to prevent losing sight of each other and battled through the heaviest rain they had yet experienced. Pools of water collected in the cockpits, soaking through the seats of their flying suits. Each man increased his grip on the controls, scared that his gloves would slip when he needed them most, as winds from the storm pushed and pulled the planes in every direction.

Then, as suddenly as the storm formed, it vanished. The planes soared into a cloudless sky, their wings shimmering in the sunlight. They landed at Akyab around two in the afternoon. The city, in the British colony of Burma, seemed cursed. MacLaren had been marooned there under its unceasing rain for weeks before he finally escaped, and Smith feared falling victim to the same fate. As soon as they docked, Smith directed his men to refuel and service their aircraft as quickly as possible, aiming to take off again within minutes and reach Chittagong, then a part of British India, by nightfall. He then received a message that the moorings in the city's busy seaport were not yet ready, forcing the squadron to spend the night in Akyab. The specter of MacLaren's long delay hovered over them.

Before retiring for the night, Smith announced that the men would leave the next morning at seven sharp, regardless of the weather.

They awoke to a drizzling rain. Not knowing whether it was a prelude to a more powerful storm, Smith hurried the men into position, and they took off exactly as planned, impressing the British officers who had seen MacLaren struggle for weeks. The long flight the day before seemed to improve Smith's mood and he settled into the lead position. Noticing that the rain appeared heaviest near the shore, he swung the squadron fifteen miles out into the Bay of Bengal, far enough away for them to see crystalline water stretching in every direction below. An hour later they turned north and resumed their path along the coast toward Chittagong. A major seaport since antiquity, the city had appeared on one of the earliest and most influential maps of the known world. Based on the work of Roman geographer Ptolemy, it accurately depicted three continents, stretching from modern-day Korea to the Canary Islands, and included some eight thousand features—cities, rivers, roads, all localized in a rudimentary system of longitude and latitude—that guided the expansion of the Romans as they attempted to conquer the globe.

After the experience of the broken wing in Rangoon, Smith dreaded the prospect of any time spent in a busy harbor. They landed, refueled, and were back in the air within an hour, setting a new personal record for swiftness. They turned toward Calcutta and flew over the vast delta created by the meeting of the Ganges and Brahmaputra Rivers, forming the largest mangrove forest in the world. Known as Sundarbans, the region is often blanketed by wet, heavy mist, obscuring the movements of the tigers that live in its jungles and the crocodiles in its swamps. Before they left for Calcutta, Smith cautioned the others that there would be few places to land in an emergency. The men trailed him as he scanned the landscape for open stretches of water to come down if necessary. Once he passed one, he would aim toward the next possible landing site, hopscotching his way over the impenetrable green forest below.

Shortly after three in the afternoon, Smith spotted smoke rising from the factories of Calcutta, some eighty miles away, and soon could make out small villages, each one seeming to grow larger as they neared the skyline in the distance. The second-largest city of the British Empire, Calcutta was considered the heart of Indian commerce and culture and filled with the largest number of Westerners of any place they had landed since Tokyo. As the squadron edged closer, they could see thousands of people were crammed along the riverfront to watch the arrival of the Americans.

Smith led the squadron low over the crowded docks and up an additional sixteen miles to Port Channing, where they hoped there would be less river traffic. They nonetheless found dozens of small fishing boats and ocean steamers, requiring them to touch down between obstacles. As soon as the men cut their engines, they felt an overwhelming humidity that made it difficult to breathe. They began attaching their planes to their mooring, sweat soaking through their flying suits. By the time they were finished, the men were damp from head to toe, looking as if they had fallen into the river.

The Americans boarded the waiting launch of the governor of Bengal, which began moving downstream toward the center of the city on what soon felt like a riverboat parade. Throngs of people lined both sides of the shore and the decks of passing boats, straining to see the pilots. As they neared the city center, the cheers grew louder. The crowd mirrored the sharply divided city, with British colonists, expatriate Americans, and high-born Bengalis waving streamers and shouting from yachts and balconies and those of lower castes singing songs of welcome in a language that the overwhelmed pilots could not hear or understand.

The Americans checked into the opulent Great Eastern Hotel, where Smith, as commanding officer, was given a bridal suite that consisted of two bedrooms, an office, a reception room, and a large bathroom. Uncomfortable at the luxury and the perception that he was somehow apart from the other men in the squadron, he offered to share it with Arnold, who happily accepted.

Though they remained more than seven thousand miles from the United States, falling back into customs he was familiar with brought out some of the uglier aspects of Arnold's personality. He moved into the suite with Smith and answered a knock at the door to find a bearded man in a turban and long white coat. The man bowed low and asked if the aviators desired a personal servant while in the city. Arnold, thrilled at the prospect, hired him on the spot. Rather than asking the man his name—as would be expected, given that he had demonstrated his fluency in English and knowledge of European customs—Arnold decided to call him Bozo, as if he were nothing more than a stray dog that he had found in an alley.

Reminding the man of his diminished status compared to the Americans became Arnold's obsession. He constantly checked to ensure that his new servant and the other Indian men who worked at the hotel were fulfilling menial tasks. "During our stay in Calcutta, 'Bozo' was busily engaged in seeing to it that some other native pressed our clothes, that still another washed our linen, that someone else brought us suitable viands and refreshment," Arnold wrote, later adding that he wished that he could take the man back with him to the United States and have him on hand at all social functions.

The openness to other cultures and perspective granted by the distance from his own that Arnold had discovered over the long flights across Alaska and Asia seemed to vanish with the reminder of his status. It was as if the exposure to new places and ideas had stretched his conception of the world to its limit, and now, rather than breaking, it snapped back, reinforcing his worst instincts with a sting. As much as the world flight had changed him, he was not ready to fully shed the sense of racial and cultural superiority ingrained since childhood. Arnold, like his country, was a work in progress, his ideals forever at odds with his past. Each step he took forward, away from the isolationism and racism brewing in America, was tentative and at risk of being undone. If he were seen only in glimpses, he could give the impression of a man freed from the narrowness infecting his country or a man who personified America's backward racial attitudes.

Smith did little to stop Arnold's lowest impulses, and he did not praise him when he listened to the better angels of his nature. Though commander and in the position to guide the men under his control, Smith often functioned as an island, set off from others by a stoicism that allowed few insights into his true feelings. As a young man, he had once fought on the side of Mexican peasants looking to create a more fair and free society, hinting at a well of sympathy for the sort of men Arnold would sometimes feel the need to embarrass. But whether due to his focus on beating MacLaren or his discomfort at confronting a man he considered his friend, Smith looked past behavior that he would never have tolerated in himself. He was the fiercest competitor among the six American men in the squadron, yet he still had much to learn about becoming its leader.

While Arnold and the other men distracted themselves in Calcutta, Smith turned his attention to the problem of moving forward. The portion of their flight that took them along the coasts of North America and Asia was now over, and they needed to swap out their pontoons for wheels as they headed across the belly of the continent toward Europe.

British officials offered to send men to help dismantle the American planes, load them onto trucks, drive them to the airfield twenty miles away, and rebuild them there.

Given the heat and the potential for complications, Smith feared that such a plan would take more than a month to complete. Instead, he spent a day coaxing harbor officials and local bureaucrats to find a better alternative. Together, they agreed to land the planes in the middle of the crowded harbor, hoist them by crane into the city streets, and tow them to the sprawling urban park known as the Maidan. To make space for the wide Douglas World Cruisers, city workers temporarily cut down telephone wires and trimmed trees that were in the way.

The following day, thousands of people watched as the American planes slowly rolled down the handsome wide avenues of the Maidan, which one English writer once called "the chief glory of Calcutta." Fifty policemen lined the streets to prevent anyone from getting too close to the aircraft or the aviators, who seemed to have walked out of a movie reel. Three hours after they were plucked from the river, the American planes sat in the middle of a wide green grass field in the heart of the city, where crowds gathered just to look at them.

Until then, most Indians had never conceived of aircraft as anything other than instruments of violence. There were no commercial airlines operating in the country at the time, and the sound of British military planes soaring overhead was common. The buzz of a propeller reminded Indians that they were the colonial possession of a small island, far away, with a population less than a seventh of their own country. The Americans were startled to learn that in India alone, the Royal Air Force maintained more aircraft than the total number of planes in the possession of the US military. When asked why, British officers offered that they were the best deterrent for another uprising. Nearly seventy years earlier, a mutiny by Indian soldiers under British command spread through central India, eventually leading to the death of some six thousand British civilians. British reprisals left at least one hundred thousand Indian soldiers dead and an untold number of civilians. (India would not gain independence from British rule until 1947.)

With Smith in the lead, the squadron got to work dismantling the heavy pontoons, installing the landing gear, and inspecting and replacing parts before the flight to the Middle East. Though policemen were on hand to deter any onlookers, the men had no walls to protect them or their aircraft and felt vulnerable as large crowds came and stared at them. For the first time during the long voyage around the world, the pulse of a city, not the demands of the race or their celebrity, held sway, forcing Smith to adapt to something other than weather. Cows, sacred in Hinduism, freely roamed the park and surrounding streets. Smith told his men to respect the local customs, no matter how inconvenient. A large, fat bull came over to a plane and lay down in the shade offered by its wings. It was joined by a few others who seemed to not notice the six Americans working intensely in the summer heat. Ogden, who had grown up around cows on the farm back home, struggled to follow Smith's orders to leave the animals alone. When no one was looking, he twisted an animal's tail until it bellowed and wandered off away from him. He resumed his work, hoping that Smith had not noticed.

During the long hours in the hot sun, Ogden was peppered with questions from Associated Press reporter Linton Wells, who was sitting under a nearby tree. Wells had followed the squadron since Tokyo. Though Ogden was slow to warm up to the press, he tolerated Wells's company because he offered a measure of familiarity at a time when Ogden struggled to feel at ease in the pulsating city. A trained pilot, Wells was one of the last of a generation of celebrity journalists who blurred the line between adventurers and writers and often became part of the story. He saw himself as a contemporary version of Henry Morton Stanley, who had become famous for his search for missionary and explorer David Livingstone in Africa some fifty years earlier. Determined to travel as far from his hometown in Kentucky as possible, Wells had been on hand to witness revolutions in China and Mexico, served in the navy during the World War, and reported from Tokyo after the great earthquake in 1923.

Nothing, however, compared with the public spectacle of the world flight. Though his editors instructed him to return to Tokyo after the Americans departed from Calcutta, Wells knew that the story would only get bigger as the squadron neared Europe. Wells pictured an epic final sprint against MacLaren with his name on the story that reported it to the world. The problem was how to get there. Traveling from Tokyo to India had been relatively easy, given that the American military wanted reporters on board its ships to share the triumphs of the flight with the nation. The next section of the flight, however, would take it through the interior of the continent, with no easy path to follow. With an air that was somehow both desperate and brash, Wells floated the idea to Ogden of riding in the storage compartment of his plane. Ogden passed his request on to Smith, who gave him a flat no.

Refitting the planes took two days, forcing the American aviators to attend the sort of social events they had tried hard to avoid since Tokyo. On the first night, the American Legion of India hosted a banquet in their honor. Expatriates living as far away as a thousand miles traveled to Calcutta to wish their countrymen good luck. Smith, fearing what would happen if he allowed the men to get caught up in the revelry, told the members of his squadron to leave as early as they could without being rude. The next morning they were working on their planes on the Maidan as the sun came up as some of their hosts from the night before stumbled home.

The following evening, executives of the Standard Oil Company hosted the men for an upscale dinner. While walking back to their hotel in the dark, Smith tripped and fell hard on his side. He refused to acknowledge that he was injured until the following morning, when Arnold noticed him struggling to put on his clothing. Arnold insisted they call a doctor, who discovered that Smith had fractured a rib.

His injury was reported on the front pages of newspapers across the United States, embarrassing a man who hated attention. Rather than wait a day or two to heal, Smith tried to keep to the mission timetable, but it soon became clear that even hoisting something as small as a wrench was excruciating. It could not have come at a worse time. Though they were past the Alaskan ice and the Indian monsoons, there was little in the way of backup if something went wrong during the upcoming flights over the deserts of the Middle East. On the coastlines, at least, they knew a navy vessel could eventually find them; in the blistering, endless stretches of sand, there was no one coming to help. The territory between Karachi (a city in modern Pakistan) and Baghdad was "extremely uninviting from the standpoint of flying," warned a report from an advance officer scouting the path of the American flight. "Along the northern cost of the Persian Gulf, landings cannot be attempted except in the water with any degree of assurance that even the lives of the pilots could be saved."

Noting Smith's diminished abilities, Wells saw an opportunity. Changing his approach, he asked Wade if he could ride along with the flight to help provide additional manpower. The two had forged a friendship over the weeks since Tokyo, bonding over the experience of growing up in the middle of the country. Wade told him that he could ride in the rear cockpit, sharing the seat with Ogden, if Smith agreed to the plan. As soon as he heard what Wade planned to propose, Nelson tried to talk him out of it. Never in their testing had he or Douglas ever considered two men sharing the rear seat. The performance of the plane would no doubt suffer, though Nelson couldn't guess what exactly would happen. He did know, however, that a flight over the desert during a race around the world was not a logical time to start experimenting.

Whether because he was distracted by the pain in his rib or because he recognized that they needed all the help that they could get, Smith reluctantly agreed that Wells could fly with them as far as Constantinople. They were some three weeks behind schedule. MacLaren was pushing ahead through Southeast Asia toward Japan. Smith was desperate and willing to try anything to keep moving. He sent a cable to General Patrick in Washington asking for permission. Wells hurriedly shed nearly all his belongings before Smith had second thoughts or Patrick could respond. He jammed some clothing and his typewriter into a suitcase and arranged to have the rest of his possessions sent to Paris, hoping that he could convince Smith to let him stay on until then.

Thousands of people packed the Maidan on the morning of July 1 as the sun poked through the morning haze. The American aviators, along with Wells, walked toward their aircraft. Wade asked Ogden if he was okay with the idea of sharing a seat. "Suits me," Ogden drawled, though he had no real choice. The two men squeezed into the rear cockpit of the *Boston*. The planes took off over the glistening white dome of the Victoria Memorial and flew north along the Hooghly River. With Smith in the lead, the squadron followed the East Indian Railway toward the city of Allahabad, with the snowcapped peaks of the Himalayas visible in the distance.

What sounded like a plausible plan on the ground revealed itself to be misery for the men in the rear cockpit. For six hours, neither Wells nor Ogden could move an inch. Even though their faces were practically touching, neither man could hear what the other was saying. If they had been able to, Wells might have heard Ogden cursing him with every breath. "If it hadn't been that we were flying high enough to keep fairly cool . . . I believe I should have thrown Wells overboard," a disgruntled Ogden later wrote.

The planes landed in Allahabad just as a long string of camels appeared on the edge of the airfield. None of the fliers except Nelson had ever seen one outside of a zoo. They could not contain their curiosity.

Smith put Wells to work refueling the aircraft in order to make amends to Ogden, and Wade and Ogden convinced the camel drivers to allow them to mount two of their charges. As the men were trying to find their balance, the camels beneath them took off running down the airfield at a speed of some twenty miles per hour. The wide look of surprise and fear on each aviator's face drew heavy shrieks of laughter from their fellow crew members and the local men and women on hand. Wells, meanwhile, worked under the broiling sun, feeding the engines oil and fuel and wiping the grease off the wings. "By the time the ships were serviced for the next jump, I was ready to drop in my tracks," he later wrote. The aviators told Wells that he would make the speeches for them at the banquet planned for them that night.

The squadron, now consisting of seven men, took off the following morning for Ambala, India, into an intensity of heat they had never imagined. Before they left, Wells and Ogden decided to place a board on the seat of the cockpit, creating more space for their torsos to maneuver above the fuselage. But the board also elevated them about eight inches, leaving their heads protruding over the windshield. By the time they landed at another Royal Air Force base that evening, both men were badly blistered by the elements. The British officers who greeted them warned Smith of pilots driven mad by the high temperature and gave them British shorts and light shirts to wear in their cockpits in place of their heavy flying suits.

As they flew over the Thar Desert toward Multan, in current-day Pakistan, a sudden sandstorm obscured both land and sky. Smith directed the other planes to follow him down to an elevation of fifty feet so they could spot the railroad tracks below. Sand tore at the fabric covering the aircraft. Fine granules found their way past the men's goggles, temporarily blinding them. When the aviators took their hands off the flight sticks to wipe their eyes, they were subjected to further punishment as sand pelted their faces. Smith guided them past their landing site without recognizing it and continued for several minutes before realizing his error. He then turned the squadron around, back into the heart of the storm.

Barely able to see, he dipped again and again, sometimes falling to altitudes just a few feet above the desert sand, desperately trying to find the airfield. When he finally located it, he made several passes around it to lead the other two planes down before landing himself. The men climbed down from their cockpits with bloodshot eyes, their faces red and lacerated by the wind. A British officer who greeted them told them that the temperature had reached 120 degrees Fahrenheit before the sandstorm. "It is the hottest place in India," Arnold wrote. "It [is] certainly the hottest place that any of us ever hope to visit in this world or the next."

Still nursing his injured rib, Smith apologized to the waiting British officers and went to rest as soon as the planes were secured. Nelson and Wade, the other two pilots, joined him, leaving the mechanics and Wells as the lone American representatives to a dinner held in their honor. They ate outside at tables laid with fine china and silver and conversed with hosts clad in dress uniforms. A regimental band of Indian musicians played for them. When Arnold learned that the band members had passed up the chance to earn more money at another event in order to be on hand for their arrival, he went over and thanked each man individually, seeming to regain his respect for those different from himself now that he was once again freed from the familiar.

Looking for a way to motivate his men in the face of what felt like an unending desert, Smith told them that if they reached Paris ahead of their current pace, they could have a day of freedom in the city. The following morning, the Fourth of July, the planes were airborne before sunrise. They flew over the brown, sunbaked plains of the Indus River valley, not knowing that below them a team of archaeologists were at the moment discovering the forty-five-hundred-year-old ruins of Mohenjo Daro, at its time likely the most advanced city in the world, complete with two-story homes and a complex sewage system. The capital of the previously unknown ancient Indus people, it had once been home to a population of thirty-five thousand, graced with wide avenues and squat brick buildings that were spread over two hundred fifty acres. The discovery of the ruins, which was not announced until September of 1924, shocked archaeologists with what one called "a long forgotten civilization."

Even in their aircraft, the aviators could feel the heat of the desert floor. They flew higher than they were used to, near the ceiling of their aircraft of five thousand feet, in search of cooler air. In the distance, they could see sandstorms raging on both sides of the valley. When they were about an hour away from their destination of Karachi, spurts of white smoke started pouring out of the engine of the *New Orleans*. Nelson and Harding stood up in their cockpits, trying to gauge whether the plane was on fire. Oil spewed out as if an artery had been cut, and shards of metal flew out and tore holes through the fabric in the wings. Nelson, in the pilot's seat, descended lower, looking for a place to land, but found only baked mud cracked with gaping seams, making it impossible to bring the aircraft down without destroying it.

He increased the throttle to pull the plane higher. More pieces of metal spewed out of the engine as it churned and groaned. A small, hot fragment, no larger than a quarter, grazed Harding's temple when he looked over the side of the plane for a possible landing site. Momentarily dazed, he put his hands to his head, convinced that he was covered in his own blood. Instead, he found warm oil.

Nelson, assuming that any more mechanical strain would make the aircraft combust, slowed until the plane was just short of stalling. The engine kept rumbling and sputtering, oblivious to Nelson's attempt to pacify it. Harding passed pieces of cheesecloth up from the rear cockpit every few moments so Nelson could wipe the oil from his goggles. Barely able to see and with the noxious smell of burning oil filling his nose, Nelson weighed his options. Pulling back any more on the throttle would freeze the engine; pushing it any harder would likely turn it into a fireball.

Somehow, Nelson found a third choice. He slowed the engine and pushed the aircraft's nose down as if he were going to land, gathering speed as he descended for roughly five hundred feet. Then, just as the engine cooled enough to stop gushing oil, he pulled the nose back up and reaccelerated, making up the lost altitude. He leveled out and rode the momentum until the engine heated up and began tossing fluid again, then he repeated the whole process again. And again. And again. For seventy-five miles, he porpoised the *New Orleans* above the desolate landscape, his engine smoking and warm oil spurting into his face.

Smith, ahead in the *Chicago*, circled the landing strip at Karachi so Nelson could have a landmark to aim for. A large crowd watched as he lined up the limping aircraft with the runway and touched down. The plane slowed to a stop and Nelson and Harding jumped out and ran as smoke billowed around them. They were both covered in oil. Trails of blood oozed out of small cuts pockmarking their arms and face. Yet, miraculously, the plane did not catch fire.

Once the smoke cleared, Nelson and Harding walked the length of their aircraft to inspect the damage. It was covered in oil from nose to tail. Dozens of holes from shrapnel punctured its wings. "I will never know how the engine continued to run after dropping an exhaust valve inside the cylinder," Harding wrote in a letter to friends in Ohio. "I could see myself following some camel trail for days through that desert if we had been forced to land."

Keeping the plane airborne was a miracle; making it airworthy again would require another one. Karachi, fortunately, was a repair depot for the Royal Air Force and had extensive parts and supplies for Liberty engines on hand. Concerned that another engine would develop the same problem as the *New Orleans*, Smith ordered the men to swap out all their engines for new ones. The six aviators, along with Wells, parked the aircraft in a corner of the field and spent the evening of the Fourth of July on a British air base, working until it was too dark to see their hands.

As they finished up for the evening, a Rolls-Royce drove up and a chauffeur stepped out and announced that the general in charge of the air base requested an audience with the American squadron leader. Smith prodded Arnold to take his place and slunk to the rear of the group. Arnold stepped into the car, still covered from head to toe in grease. The car pulled up to a white mansion, making Arnold feel like "the ragged urchin in the story books who dreams that he is a prince," he wrote. He walked in wearing his overalls and found himself at the center of a formal party. A British commander stood at the head of the table and toasted his guest. Noting that the Portuguese, French, and British attempts at the world flight were all headed eastward, he said, "You Americans have the reputation of trying to do everything differently from any one else, and here you are flying around the globe in the opposite direction" to hearty laughs.

As Arnold said his goodbyes and thanked his hosts, one of the officers there told him that they had just learned that MacLaren had reached Kagoshima, the city in southern Japan that the Americans had left nearly a month earlier. Arnold hurried back to tell Smith, knowing that he was confirming his commander's worst fears. They had escaped the monsoons only to find themselves stuck in the middle of one of the world's largest deserts with one plane that had holes in its wings and two others that needed to have their engines replaced. They had flown some 12,500 miles, with another 14,000 miles to go. Paris, the city that Smith had hoped would be their reward, now seemed like a distant dream.

CHAPTER NINETEEN

Ruins in the Sand

H UNDREDS OF JAPANESE schoolchildren clad in crisp uniforms stood in formation holding Union Jack flags while staring up into the cloudless sky. Finally, a gray speck appeared on the horizon. A few minutes later the Vicks Vulture landed at the Kasumigaura Aerodrome, about fifty miles from Tokyo. MacLaren climbed down from his plane to a welcome party that included the British ambassador and some of the most powerful officials in the Japanese military. As a marching band played, Admiral Teruhisa Komatsu, himself a minor prince, greeted MacLaren and announced, "We drink to your health and good luck in your great undertaking."

The glad-handing ceremony masked what had been a harrowing twenty-four hours. In Shanghai a few days earlier, Sergeant Andrews, MacLaren's flight engineer, fell ill with a fever and could not go on. After booking a steamship to take Andrews to Japan—a nearly weeklong journey over sea and rails—MacLaren found a local British airman to serve in his place. The man was so unfamiliar to MacLaren that later he did not remember his name. Over the thousands of miles they had flown together since taking off from England, MacLaren and his crew had fused into one unit, able to anticipate one another's actions when they could not hear over the constant roar of the propellers and thrashing wind.

Introducing a new person, especially one who was a mystery, upset the delicate balance, with nearly fatal results. The flight across the East China Sea was uneventful, but shortly after leaving Kagoshima, their first stop in Japan, the British aircraft flew into a consuming fog. Unable to see ahead of them and fearing that they would run into a mountain, MacLaren turned around and plotted a new course that would swing farther out into the ocean, where he expected to have better visibility. Had Andrews been aboard, he would have known that MacLaren often fixated on the route and the weather and left the details of how they would affect the machine to the two other men with him. MacLaren's modifications were slight, adding roughly a hundred miles to the day's journey, and did not require much more than ensuring that the plane carried enough fuel. But the temporary engineer, unfamiliar with the craft and unable to hear MacLaren's shouted instructions, did nothing. His silence allowed the plane to amble on, widening the gap between its fuel capacity and the distance to its intended destination.

The aircraft continued over the Pacific at an altitude of roughly three hundred feet. As the plane neared the rocky coast of Susami, the engine began sputtering as if it had fallen into a coughing fit. Its responsiveness to controls and its power waned. Twenty-five miles away from their destination and no longer confident he could get there, MacLaren landed at the nearest flat field he could find.

Surprised farmers and fishermen, many of whom had never seen an aircraft up close, huddled around the bulky plane. MacLaren and the two other men climbed out to inspect their aircraft. They found nothing wrong—flying over the Pacific, they had simply run out of gas. A few minutes of questioning the small crowd that had gathered revealed that there were no airfields nearby that had fuel. Nor were there any auto shops or factories or anything else that could possibly be of use to their plane. A telegraph operator was available, and MacLaren sent an embarrassing distress call to the airfield nearby for help.

Getting assistance was not as easy as he had hoped. They had left the long footprint of the British Empire, and there were no local Royal Air Force mechanics or supplies to count on. Colonel Broome, the British officer whom Smith had a month earlier assured that the Americans would find a replacement plane for MacLaren, had left on a steamship heading to Alaska, where he intended to deposit supplies of gas and oil to use in the coming weeks.

With MacLaren's options narrowing, the *Asahi Shimbun*, the highly respected Japanese newspaper, offered to send a plane stuffed with gasoline cans to Susami. The civilian pilot, thrown off by the unbalanced additional weight, crashed upon landing yet somehow prevented his aircraft and the dozens of cans of gasoline sitting in its storage bay from igniting. MacLaren and his crew members refilled their machine as quickly as they could and took off for Tokyo. There, the men sat through a welcoming ceremony congratulating them on their progress and made no mention of how closely the British attempt at a world flight had come to ruin due to a simple error.

In the following days MacLaren began overhauling his plane to prepare for the flight into the frozen wilds of the North Pacific. Andrews soon recovered and was ready to resume his duties. The crew had spent months together, but there was no telling how man or machine would respond to the harsh climate they would encounter. They were halfway around the world and remained narrowly ahead of the Americans, who were now delayed in the desert. Each hour that they pushed on would add to their lead, giving them a cushion as they faced the crossing of the Pacific.

FAR AWAY, IN Karachi, Smith and the five men under his command were working on their planes as the sun came up over the flat, sandy plain. Royal Air Force mechanics drove up and offered to help. Smith, ever polite, thanked them for the offer and said the American crew would change their motors themselves. His tone carried neither suspicion nor animosity, but a sense of self-reliance. He had always trusted his gut to steer him, and now, after flying twelve thousand miles with five other men, he put as much faith in the skills of others as he did his own. Slowly, and without perhaps realizing it, he was softening his edges and stepping into his role of commander, leading by showing his men that he believed in them. The squadron, without making it obvious, repaid him in kind, calling him "Smitty" as a term of endearment, erasing the frozen wall he had built between himself and the world.

He allowed few other people into his orbit, making him a mystery to the millions of Americans who followed every stop of the world flight in their daily newspaper. They knew him mainly as the man who had stepped up after Martin's accident, not realizing how much he detested any form of public display. He deliberately held his true self—a man driven by passion, with a sly sense of humor and innate sense of fairness—back under a cloak of shyness. In the papers, he was as famous for his trials—dysentery in Indochina, a broken rib in Calcutta, losing track of Martin's plane in Alaska—as he was for his skills.

One of the few glimpses into Smith as a person came from the unlikely source of Martin himself. After his rescue, Martin went back to the States, gave a few public speeches, and returned to his position at the airfield in Rantoul, Illinois. He remained there for several weeks, no longer in the spotlight he had grown to like. It was there that he received the news that his mother had died in her home outside of Richmond, Virginia, from complications after a surgery. He flew to an airfield north of the city for the funeral, and the following day he took his airplane and circled over his hometown of Liberty, glancing down at the milestones of his childhood below. A reporter for a Richmond newspaper spotted him shortly after he landed and Martin gave him an expansive interview, still in the wistful moments of grief and nostalgia.

"When we started we all expected to finish the trip but Lady Luck was against me," he said. "You have no idea of the terrific weather we encountered. The winds were strong and storms were all about us." He admitted he was following the journey in the newspapers, feeling a daily pang that he was not the one being written about. He knew all the details about how Smith had hurt his rib and read the coverage of how the planes had swapped out their pontoons. It was hard not to imagine himself still up there and flying around the world with his son marking his progress on his map back home, a line that now ended in western Alaska. Despite no longer being a part of the race, Martin said he was convinced that the Americans would beat MacLaren around the world. When asked for the source of his confidence, given all that had gone wrong, Martin responded, "Smith is a good man, though, and will get the flight around in good time."

On the other side of the world, the planes that Martin dreamed about remained idle. As the hours went on, the aviators began to feel like simply departing Karachi would be an accomplishment. Temperatures higher than anything the men had ever experienced made small tasks hard. Picking up a metal tool seared their hands; touching the plane felt like grabbing the rack of a hot oven.

As the men sweated through their overalls, their faces stained with grease and oil, the local American consul approached Smith with a cable in his hand. Smith read that his request to allow Wells to accompany them had been denied. Wells opened his own cable from the Associated Press office in Tokyo, which informed him that he had been fired for disobeying his instructions to return home once the American aviators had left Calcutta.

Wells was out of a job, but Smith faced the possibility of worse. It would be entirely within General Patrick's power to order Smith court-martialed for bringing a civilian passenger aboard a military plane without permission. Wade told Smith that a journalist for the Reuters news agency had erroneously reported that Wells was a stowaway when they had landed in Allahabad. Though they laughed about it, the American aviators had never refuted the story. If they kept up the ruse, it would provide a convenient answer to General Patrick as to how Wells ended up in the plane in the first place. A cover story quickly came together: when the Americans did not hear back from Patrick, Wells climbed into the tiny storage compartment and somehow did not fall out.

Wells was more than happy to go along with that plan. It heightened the image he hoped to cultivate as a fearless reporter willing to do anything for a scoop, even if that meant sneaking aboard a plane that was about to fly over the Himalayas. Smith reluctantly agreed, and he and the other crew members stuck to the fictional account when collaborating with writer Lowell Thomas for a book after their flight was over. (Wells eventually came clean in his first memoir, which was published in 1937.)

The men finished replacing their engines and were up at three in the morning on July 7, hoping to put Karachi behind them. Last-minute repairs delayed them, but at 7:45, they took off into a searing sky. They flew westward over a land seemingly devoid of human life and dotted with date trees. (Today, the region then known as Baluchistan is divided among modern-day Iran, Afghanistan, and Pakistan, and it remains thinly populated.) Arnold, from his cockpit, began cataloging the different forms of sand he saw: sand hills, sand flats, sand storms, sand that appeared to be ancient riverbeds. It was "the most lonesome, barren and desolate place imaginable," he wrote in his diary.

The planes briefly landed to refuel at the small seaport of Chabahar on the Gulf of Oman and were in the air again moments later. Nelson took the opportunity to change out of his heavy flying suit and into a khaki shirt and shorts—at the time a novel fashion worn mostly by young boys—provided to him by British officers to give him some relief from the heat. Accustomed to a full flight suit that protected his fair skin, Nelson did not realize that his knees were now exposed to the sun while he sat in the cockpit and were turning a deep red.

On the flight deeper into Persia, the men passed the halfway point of the race. They trailed MacLaren by a few hundred miles but hoped that the dry weather would enable them to make up the gap. But no matter where they landed, threats seemed to find them. A stop in Bandar Abbas, on the Persian Gulf, was cut short by news that cholera was raging through the native population. The men retired to houses owned by members of the British consulate and prepared to leave before sunup the following day. Sometime after midnight, Ogden, who felt like he was being driven mad by thirst, stumbled in the dark until he found a small hut where jars of water were kept. He spent the remainder of the night there, periodically waking up long enough to drink more water, either not aware or no longer caring about the risk of consuming liquid that might have been contaminated.

Taking advantage of an apparent break in the sandstorms that had downed or delayed other attempts to fly through the region, Smith pushed the men to wake up shortly after three in the morning on July 8, and they were in the air by 5:45 without taking the time to eat breakfast. A stop in the port city of Bushire (now known as Busher) was so short that Smith had the planes back in the air before the sandwiches he had requested from an American consul who met them at the airfield had arrived. They flew over the green gardens of the port city of Basra, in modern-day Iraq, the gleaming water of the Persian Gulf in sharp contrast to the desert sand.

Here, for the first time since they were on the western shores of the Pacific, the men crossed an unseen line back into their own cultural heritage, though they did not seem aware of it. They flew over the light blue dome of the Tomb of Ezra, popularly considered the burial place of a man seen as an important scribe in Judaism, a prophet in some Islamic traditions, and a saint in Catholicism. Not far away lay one of the places that medieval visitors considered to be the site of the Garden of Eden, where the branches of a dead tree—believed by some to be the Tree of Knowledge from which the biblical figure Eve once ate a forbidden apple—hung over the meeting of the Tigris and Euphrates Rivers.

The planes followed the path of the Tigris deeper into the desert. Once they passed the city of Amara, they could no longer spot date palms below. The desert appeared to be flat and empty, stretching endlessly in all directions. The river twisted back on itself, complicating Smith's attempt to fix his position. Soon, they reached the modern city of Hit and the ancient mounds of Babylon. "Here came the captive children of Israel and here Balthazar parked Daniel in the lion's den—now all is sand!" Arnold wrote. Less than an hour later, they flew over what they knew as the Arch of Ctesiphon (now called Taq Kasra), the ruins of an

ancient Persian palace built at least fourteen hundred years ago, before
the Muslim conquest of Persia in the seventh century. Rising 121 feet
above the ground, the building once boasted the largest brick arch in the
world. As the Americans flew above it, its rows of windows and soaring
entryways were surrounded by shrubs and a few palm trees, a ruined
palace seemingly dropped out of the sky onto a blank sheet of sand. At
sunset, the men landed in Baghdad to a large crowd at a Royal Air Force
base and ate for the first time that day. Nelson slept fitfully that night, his
knees badly sunburned.

They attempted to leave early again the next morning but found that
the battery of the *Chicago* was dead. Repairs delayed them until eleven
a.m., and the men took off into clear skies and headed toward the Euphrates. The golden domes of the Al-Kazimiyya Mosque, a shrine and
mausoleum containing the tombs of two of the Prophet Muhammad's
descendants, sparkled in the midday sun as they passed above. Later,
they flew over a series of ancient mounds that they had been told by British officials included the tomb of the biblical figure Nimrod, mentioned
in the book of Genesis as a mighty hunter and by tradition the king who
built the Tower of Babel.

The relics of history, now half covered by sand, struck a chord with
Nelson, who until then had shown little interest in anything aside from
the performance of the planes he had helped design. "Surely this must
be the most fascinating spot in all the world," he later wrote, no doubt
wondering how his own accomplishment in the world flight—if they
won the race or even finished at all—would look to future generations.
Whether due to the desert scenery or the crumbling ancient structures
below, he found himself taking time to enjoy the smaller moments of
the day's flight. He watched as small sand devils—short-lived whirl-
winds that reminded him of waterspouts he had seen while sailing the
ocean—raced across the desert. The unsettled air below made the planes
pitch up and down, yet Nelson long remembered the day as one of the
most content and pleasurable experiences of his life.

The men landed in Aleppo, then under French control, to a crowd of
hundreds of French pilots who insisted on toasting them with glasses of
champagne. After spending a night in a hotel, the Americans were up
at dawn in a motorcade, heading back toward the airfield. They passed
merchants unloading supplies from camel back, and donkeys pulling
carts laden with brightly colored rugs. By six, the planes were aloft, the

men intent on completing a six-hundred-mile flight that would take them out of the desert and into Asia Minor. Nelson watched the shadows of a caravan of camels etched against the desert sand and again found himself in a reflective mood.

"When the airplane comes into its own, as it is sure to do within a few years, one wonders what will become of that most picturesque of men, the desert Arab," he later wrote. "Journeys that take him two months can now be made by airplanes between sunrise and sunset. Within a short time, planes will be so cheap that even the Bedouin sheik will have one, or several. . . . Long before this, we had already become convinced that the airplane is destined to have an immense influence on the peace of the world. The speed with which men will fly from continent to continent will bring all peoples into such intimate contact that war will be as out of date as the cuneiform inscriptions of the ancient civilizations that the shadows of our Cruisers were passing over."

The Americans felt like they were bringing the future with them. Whether they were in Tokyo or Indochina or here in the Arabian Desert, their presence was proof of a new era in which travel from the most barren islands of Alaska to the ruins of Baghdad could be accomplished by a single machine. Pilots stationed at remote outposts of the French and British territories celebrated them not because they had never seen airplanes before or because the Douglas Cruisers were far more advanced than their own aircraft, but because they represented a tangible sense that the world was coming together ten years after the first battles of a war that tore it apart.

Nelson had no way of knowing that on the day that they took off from Aleppo, Brigadier General Billy Mitchell, the man who envisioned the round-the-world flight, returned to the United States from his exile in Hawaii aboard an army transport ship. As soon as his ship neared the Golden Gate, a squadron of Army Air Service planes flew out to greet it and circled over his ship as it steamed toward the San Francisco waterfront. Though the army would not yet confirm it, the newspapers reported the rumor that Mitchell had been chosen as commander of McCook Field in Dayton, Ohio, which he planned to make the largest air base in the world, expanding it to five thousand acres, next to the field where the Wright brothers tested and perfected their Flyer. As soon as he stepped off the ship, Mitchell harangued local reporters about the need for a municipal airfield in San Francisco. "He is a favorite of the flying force, an aviator of ability himself, and an enthusiastic student of aviation and its progress," a newspaper noted.

Though he had not met them all, Mitchell knew his legacy rested largely on the six American men then in progress on the world flight. He followed each day's reports and often asked friends in the British or French military for any information or gossip that was not public knowledge. He was both a big dreamer and a big talker, and he used his ability to command a room and flitter between social classes as ways to feel close to a race that he had to publicly distance himself from. He could not have been more different than Smith, the man now in position to make his dream a reality.

In the desert, the clear weather held, letting the American squadron make up time. They flew six hundred miles one day and seven hundred the next, erasing the hours lost due to Martin's disappearance in Alaska and to the maladies they suffered in Asia. With Smith in the lead, the squadron of planes followed the Berlin–Baghdad Railway through the snowcapped Taurus Mountains. The planes flew in a single file at five thousand feet through a narrow mountain pass, their wings nearly scraping the rocks on both sides.

When they came out on the other side of the mountains, they were in Europe. As they flew toward Constantinople, they could see more than a hundred miles in each direction, gazing over poppy fields and vast rows of corn to the south and the silver sliver of the Bosporus Strait, linking the Aegean Sea and the Black Sea, to the east. Behind them lay the last brown edges of the desert and a sense that it was all a daydream. Despite the brutal heat, their last few days had largely been without worry from politics or the pressure of public attention, granting them the freedom to enjoy themselves.

Now, as they neared the airfield in Constantinople, the men felt a return of the sort of nationalistic tension that had been absent since Tokyo. Just four months earlier, the Turkish assembly had formally abolished the caliphate, smothering the final embers of the Ottoman Empire and replacing it with a secular republic. The fragile new government, however, was naturally suspicious when the United States asked for permission to fly over its airspace and land three planes piloted by military fliers in the country. Turkey refused entry to the Americans until just before the squadron arrived and demanded that they stay on an additional day in Constantinople so that Turkish military officials could inspect the planes.

Smith's insistence that they push themselves to move as quickly as possible since leaving India was paying off, and the men found themselves ahead of the schedule they had laid out in Calcutta. As a result, no one in Constantinople had known they were coming, and the men landed to a near absence of fanfare. By chance, the American ambassador and a small cadre of military officials had just arrived at the airfield, intending to set up for the squadron's appearance a few days later.

The men quickly serviced their planes and then found themselves with the novel sense that they had nothing to do. Smith suggested they go to a restaurant and the six men sat in cheerful anonymity eating succulent fresh lobster from the Black Sea, amazed that it cost just ten cents a plate. The three mechanics turned the conversation to the question of which country they visited so far had the most beautiful women, and Arnold made the argument that the Americans he had met in Shanghai could not be topped. Harding told the assembled men that he'd read that the romance between the Prince of Wales and a Romanian princess had fizzled out, and he intended to meet her when they reached Bucharest. Later that night, the men went to a boisterous nightclub run by Russian refugees that made the clubs they had gone to in Los Angeles in the days before the mission launched look like Sunday school. Smith, out of his element, focused on the fact that the club's owners, once likely highborn Russians, were not above getting their hands dirty. "Some of these dyed-in-the-wool, rolled-below-the-knee, boyish-bobbed Slav aristocrats were washing dishes and peddling cigarettes," he wrote. "All honor to them for working for their living."

Smith found himself more at home the following day when the squadron toured the Hagia Sophia, an ancient Eastern Orthodox church transformed into a mosque in the fifteenth century. For a thousand years it had stood as the largest cathedral in the world, and it was now surrounded by four soaring minarets. Though the son of a preacher, Smith did not wear his faith on his sleeve, and he found himself more drawn to the stillness of the immense space than to its collection of holy relics. "We saw wide, quiet spaces, fluttering doves, rich carpets on the flagstones—in short, an air of strength and serenity which was very impressive," he later wrote.

The calm was not enough to pull his mind away from the race, however. As soon as they returned to the airfield, Smith approached the

Turkish military officials and explained their need to hurry due to the race with MacLaren. The men had flown 15,282 miles and had another 11,000 to go. Perhaps sensing that Smith posed no threat, they permitted the men to continue.

The planes were in the air before dawn on July 12, following the course of the Dâmbovița River toward Bucharest. They passed over ruined villages and fields pockmarked with shell holes and discarded barbed wire, unhealed wounds still remaining six years after the guns finally stopped and ended the Great War. Again when they landed, there was no one to greet them. Relieved at not having a crowd, the men began refueling while Smith found a telephone to notify the American consul of their presence. The overwhelmed man appeared an hour later, confessing that he thought they were hundreds of miles away.

That evening, Harding was devastated to learn that the Romanian royal family was at their summer castle in the Transylvanian Alps but had invited the Americans to come and stay the weekend with them. For the rest of the trip, the other men teased Harding over how close he had come to what they called his "happily ever after."

Smith would not let up. He had the men ready to fly by dawn the next morning, thanks in part to the city's well-equipped airfield. Arnold noted that Bucharest seemed to have more airplanes ready for service than all of America. From there, each stop seemed to come in rapid succession, blurring the line between one place and the next. July 13, they were off for Budapest before the sun came up, and they landed six hours later to a sparse crowd, thinned out by rumors that the Americans were not coming after all. Soon, they were in Vienna. From the air, they could see thousands of people clustered at the airfield. They landed to find a huge number of Americans, seemingly all of them in the city on vacation and intent on getting a picture of the now-famous world fliers. After complying with a half dozen individual requests for photos, Smith announced that the six aviators would line up in front of their planes and stand still for a few minutes for anyone who wanted a picture and then would get back to work. "In spite of this, until dusk, and indeed long after, for the amateur photographer is not particular about lighting conditions, the kodaks clicked," Arnold later wrote.

The men slept in a luxurious hotel that night in rooms with twenty-foot ceilings and chandeliers hanging above their beds. In the morning, they ate a breakfast of raspberries and cream and teased Smith about his decision to serve them eggs Vienna for every meal when they were stuck in Alaska. Smith ended the reverie by noting the time, plunging them back in the present. They took off at 5:30 on the morning of July 14 and flew into dark skies and heavy rain. Smith brought the planes low, again fearing that they would scrape a mountain in the heavy fog. He followed the winding path of the Danube River into the Black Forest mountains of Germany. The men landed in Strasbourg long enough to refuel and took off again without visiting the city.

As they flew on toward France, Wade and Arnold both felt the strange sensation that they had been there before. During the war, each man had flown in combat missions in these now-pleasant valleys. What they knew as rubble had become peaceful scenes dotted with quaint villages and church steeples that seemed never to have been threatened by bombs. Battlefields carved by trench warfare were now green, and leaves once again grew on the trees. The most startling sight, however, was the smallest: songbirds once again flapping between the trees below. "It seemed difficult to realize that it was in these same skies that . . . thousands [of] our fellow airmen—and many equally gallant enemy airmen also—used to dive down, spitting tongues of flame, to send their adversaries crashing to destruction," Wade later wrote. "Our thoughts were with them as we turned west toward the valley of the Marne, for we realized that it was by their efforts that what we were doing now had been made possible."

A convoy of French fighter planes appeared ahead to guide them into Paris. Fifty miles from the city, they saw the Eiffel Tower poking into the sky and the blinding white dome of the Sacré-Coeur Basilica on Montmartre. When they reached the city, they saw its wide boulevards packed with people, celebrating Bastille Day. They circled once around the city, Wade and Arnold pointing out the landmarks they had known as soldiers during the war, and dipped their wings in salute as they passed above the Arc de Triomphe and the Tomb of the Unknown Soldier, interred on Armistice Day four years earlier. Newsreel cameras and thousands of people waving both French and American flags watched as the squadron landed on an airfield in the outskirts of Paris.

Perhaps because of the ceremony or maybe the fact that they had just completed a record crossing between India and Europe two days faster than d'Oisy had, Smith allowed himself for the first time to be publicly overcome with emotion and demonstrate pride in his accomplishment and his fervor to win the race. Newspaper reporters crowded around, asking him what he thought came next. "We'll be in Los Angeles long before September 1," he told them. "Of course," he added quickly, "we are not racing against time, but just to show the world that the world can be flown. . . . It was toughest getting through from Alaska to Japan. The rest is comparatively easy."

It was a boast that he would soon come to regret.

CHAPTER TWENTY
Cold Winds

THEY HAD NEVER known this level of exhaustion.

Flying from India to Europe in record time, through extremes of rain, heat, and wind, left the American aviators' bodies drained. The physical tolls slowly revealed themselves after the men landed in Paris, as if the pain had taken a slower route across the desert and was now catching up. Nelson found that his legs and neck were so badly sunburned from his decision to forgo his flight suit for shorts that the touch of any cloth felt agonizing, a constant reminder that his Swedish skin was a liability. Wade, numbed by fatigue, fell asleep while sitting in his chair at a formal banquet that evening and continued snoring through dinner because no one could bring themselves to wake him up. Smith, still hiding the extent of his rib injury, winced every time he turned his body, his broken rib aching from the nonstop bumps and vibrations of the long hours in the cockpit. In a photo taken shortly after they landed, all the men beam into the camera except for Smith, who has one arm crossed in front of his body to protect his torso from further insult. That night, when the men finally reached their hotel, Arnold wrote notices and posted them on the outside of each of their doors: "Please do not wake us until nine o'clock tomorrow morning unless this hotel is on fire; and even then unless the firemen have given up all hope!"

The men had trained over cold winter weeks in Virginia to endure the physical pummeling required by a world flight. However, they had no way to prepare themselves for the emotional strain of sudden, global celebrity on a previously unknown scale. The French aviator d'Oisy came closest to their level of fame, and he had stepped off the world stage shortly after he reached Tokyo and fallen back into the sweet embrace of obscurity. The stardom of the six Americans, by contrast, had only burned brighter since they walked in parades in their honor in Japan.

Powerful men who four months earlier would have never cared about these unknown pilots now shuffled their schedules to meet them; thousands of Parisians stood for hours to say that they saw the Americans with their own eyes. "With their arrival in Paris and the approaching visit to England of the American army world fliers, the achievements of the aviators are receiving more attention in the newspapers here than at any time since the daring airmen left America," the Associated Press reported. The modesty of the six men, given their accomplishments, made the French love them even more. "They haven't at all the air of men who have just done things," one woman in the official welcoming delegation told an American reporter. "Our aviation aces would not have taken the honors so shyly as all that."

All their movements were chronicled and studied, as if people thought that by looking at them, they could glimpse what it was like to live in the future. Several audience members noticed when Wade again fell asleep that night at a performance of the celebrated Folies Bergère, as famous for the extravagant costumes that singers wore on stage as for the fact that many of its female dancers were nude. (Josephine Baker, an African American expatriate singer and dancer, appeared at the same venue two years later wearing a skirt made of artificial bananas and little else, causing a worldwide sensation that became symbolic of the spirit of what F. Scott Fitzgerald called the Jazz Age.) "If the Folies Bergère won't keep these American airmen awake, we wonder what will?" the French newspaper *Le Matin* asked the next morning.

General John Pershing, commander of the American forces during the World War, invited the six awestruck men to have lunch with him the following day. "As lieutenants in the army he had seemed about as far from us as the Dalai Lama of Tibet," Wade wrote. "But there in Paris he put his arms around us, told us funny stories, and proved himself a genial host and regular fellow!" The Americans were greeted by "more generals, ambassadors, cabinet ministers and celebrities, than we had encountered in all the rest of our lives," Wade continued. "There were so many of them that we couldn't remember their names, despite the fact that they were all men whose names are constantly in the newspaper headlines."

French president Gaston Doumergue, a centrist who a few months earlier had been elected by the National Assembly in a ceremony at the palace of Versailles, welcomed the American aviators at the Élysée Palace, once the home of Napoléon Bonaparte and the official residence of the French president. The men expected to stay for a few minutes. Instead, Doumergue took a liking to them and insisted that they come with him to the Olympic Games, then underway in Paris. The six men sat at his side in the grandstands, their celebrity outshining both the president and the thousands of track-and-field athletes competing in front of newsreel cameras. As the Americans prepared to leave, Doumergue said he wished to decorate them with the Legion of Honor. Smith politely declined, explaining that the US government would not permit them to accept foreign decorations without the consent of Congress. Instead, Doumergue presented each man with a signed photograph of himself.

Had it been up to the other five men, the squadron would have remained in Paris for a week. Here was the city that had welcomed them as heroes following the war and offered every excitement they could dream of. There was no nationalistic tension like in Tokyo or Turkey, and there seemed to be no limit to the adoration that the French people showered upon them. Unlike America, where aviation was widely considered the domain of castoff daredevils and stuntmen, France had embraced the airplane from its inception and held those who could master the machine in the highest esteem. Even Arnold, who more than any other man on the flight enjoyed tasting the world's buffet of cities and cultures, wanted nothing more than to stay still. "It is an experience I wouldn't take a million for, but I wouldn't start over again for a million," he told a reporter.

Smith had them at Le Bourget, the Parisian airfield, early the next morning. Just days after landing in a succession of desert airfields that were indistinguishable from their surroundings, the men were overwhelmed to find their planes enclosed in gleaming hangars. Nearby, they spotted passengers on their way to board their own commercial flights, a far cry from the groups of soldiers and mechanics that they had become used to seeing on far-flung airfields. Though rudimentary by present standards, Le Bourget was the beginning of a modern-day airport, and it shocked the sensibilities of the Americans who had never seen airline service before. "The era of transport by air is not coming some day in the future, it is here!" Nelson wrote. "Travelers were having their tickets punched for Amsterdam with the same bored expression that you might see on the faces of commuters waiting for the Garden City express at Pennsylvania [Station in Manhattan] or the San Francisco–Oakland ferry."

As they took off for London, two passenger planes flew to their side, also bound for England. Paris soon dropped out of sight. Ahead of them hovered an enormous bank of clouds. Smith led them to seven thousand feet, an altitude higher than they were used to, and they felt the first chill winds of the Atlantic slap their faces. Ogden spent most of the short flight keeping a running conversation going by means of gestures with a woman with a flapper haircut in one of the passenger planes. When they all landed together at the airfield outside London, he was devastated to learn that the woman he had been flirting with had left in the back seat of a chauffeured Rolls-Royce.

All that morning, the single-track trolley connecting the Croydon airfield with the sleepy neighboring village of Waddon was overloaded with passengers, each of them trying to be there when the Americans landed. The first had arrived at dawn with cameras hanging around their necks, churning the village into a state of excitement it had never before known. By midmorning, a large crowd waited at the airfield under some of the dozens of American flags put up in a sign of welcome. London policemen waited in clumps of three or four, underestimating how dense the gathering had become. As soon as the American planes landed and rolled to a stop, dozens of men and women surged past the fluid police lines toward the planes, all clutching autograph books, envelopes, receipts—really, anything that could be written on—that they held aloft, hoping to get the American pilots to sign.

Among the first people in the official welcome party to grab Smith's hand was MacLaren's wife. She introduced herself and anxiously asked if he could tell her anything about the Aleutian Islands, which her husband was now attempting to reach. Smith assured her that he would get safely across the Pacific and apologized for not being able to meet him in person when they had nearly crossed paths in Asia. "I am sorry we missed him, but am glad we could help him," he told her.

As they had in Paris, the Americans charmed the British press. One London paper noted that the men appeared "tanned, lean, and brown," while another said they "looked as fit as men can be, and as likely a bunch of men as could be needed for any adventure calling for high courage, grit and endurance." Smith, particularly, stood out, because he seemed so different than the pompous, headstrong aviators that Europe produced. "Mr. Smith is a typical, clean-shaven young American, with sharp-cut features, less plump now than when he set out on the trip. He seems to always be smiling," the *Daily Mail* reported. "He combines coolness and control over himself and his machine that has marked him out as one of the best type of the American aviators."

The presence of Yankee pilots in London seemed to instill a sense in the British press that the race was over and that MacLaren had lost. MacLaren, at the time, was some three thousand miles behind the Americans in total distance flown and was entering the region that had given them the most trouble. "There was good reason for hoping MacLaren would win," wrote C. C. Turner, perhaps the most closely followed aviation expert in the United Kingdom. "He would now be winning had it not been for mechanical breakdowns."

The ruggedness and reliability of the Douglas-designed World Cruiser as compared with the Vicks Vulture would no doubt change the perception that European craft were inherently superior and lead to a surge of interest in American engineering, he noted. "It is idle to pretend that buyers are not influenced by achievement and advertisement . . . the purchaser demands proof as well as assertion," he wrote. Turner, who only months before had boasted that Britain would rule the skies just as it long had the seas, now all but conceded defeat. The only silver lining he found was that "there is much consolation in the knowledge that this fine bunch of men are almost entirely Anglo-Saxon," he wrote.

None of the Americans were willing to declare victory. They had had too many close calls and knew that more no doubt lay ahead. It would take only one problem—a broken crankshaft, a busted cylinder, a wrong turn in a bank of fog—for their fortunes to turn, perhaps fatally. "[MacLaren]'s got a good deal farther to go than we have, but when he has passed the Aleutian Islands he will be all right. We may be delayed in the North Atlantic," Ogden told a reporter.

They also had more competition. Major Zanni, the Argentine ace, announced that he would leave the next day from Amsterdam on his own world flight attempt, following the same route as MacLaren but in a Fokker-Napier plane, considered the fastest aircraft capable of flying long distances. "Major Zanni is rather late in making his attempt, but anticipates that the superior speed of his machine will enable him to overtake his rivals," a London paper wrote in a front-page story. Smith, of course, would not declare the race over until they were back on the ground in Los Angeles. He seemed animated not just by the idea of finishing the world flight before MacLaren or any other competitor but by completing the journey in a time that would stand as an unbroken record. "We must push on, for we are already behind schedule," he said.

After less than twenty-four hours in London, Smith had the squadron flying north toward the seaport village of Hull. There, the men would once again replace their engines and swap out their wheels for pontoons. The cold North Atlantic lay ahead. The ocean had first been successfully crossed by two English pilots just five years earlier. That flight, however, had left nearly a month earlier than what the Americans were now attempting. American naval ships racing to get into position to resupply Smith and his crew reported that some coves in Greenland were iced over earlier than they had anticipated.

Here was the flip side of the bargain that General Mitchell, when planning the Americans' route, had struck with himself. By flying westward from California, the squadron had been the first to cross the Pacific, adding to the list of records that Mitchell loved so dearly. Yet in doing so, they would have to cross the North Atlantic at a time when the headwinds were far stronger than in the spring, making a difficult assignment even more challenging. Alcock and Brown, the English pilots who had completed the Atlantic crossing, had traveled from west to east, in the opposite direction of the Americans, and they had benefited from the assistance of the then-unknown jet stream, a powerful river of air that travels eastward across the northern sections of the globe. (Even now, with advanced engines, a flight from London to New York takes roughly an hour and fifteen minutes longer than one from New York to London.) In 1841, an American mathematician and professor named Elias Loomis was among the first to theorize that unseen air currents were responsible for the fact that storms in North America typically traveled from the interior of the continent toward the East Coast. There had been little further investigation of the phenomenon, especially in the cold reaches of the North Atlantic, which were inhospitable to scientific study under the best conditions.

Few Americans knew that a Japanese meteorologist named Wasaburo Ooishi was at the moment conducting observations with high-altitude weather balloons at a station about sixty miles north of Tokyo. He announced the presence of bands of swift high-altitude air blowing toward the east in his observatory's annual report in 1926. The finding was ignored by the world scientific community and the aviators who would have benefited most, due in part to the publication's obscurity and also to the fact that the article was written in Esperanto, an artificial language created by a Polish ophthalmologist in 1887 in hopes that a universal system of communication would empower humanity to transcend nationalism.

The US military became aware of the jet stream in 1944, when B-29 pilots on bombing missions in Japan discovered winds rippling by them at 230 miles per hour, causing their payloads to badly miss their targets and their planes to use so much more fuel than anticipated that some ran out of gas and crashed on their return trips. Japanese weapons designers drew on Ooishi's work when attempting to build balloon bombs with detonation timers that they could launch from Japan and hit targets on the west coast of North America. They erroneously calculated that it would take sixty hours for the winds to pull the bombs across the Pacific. The true time was closer to ninety hours, which meant that most of the devices fell harmlessly in the ocean. One bomb, however, landed in southern Oregon in 1944 and killed a pregnant woman named Elsye Mitchell and six children, making them the only civilians to die from enemy hands in the United States during World War II.

No airplanes had ever landed along the windblown rocky coast of Iceland or Greenland before, giving the American squadron no path to follow. Should something go wrong, there were far fewer fishing vessels in the region to help than in Alaska, where crews following halibut and salmon were instrumental in providing weather updates. Passenger steamships had no reason to hug land while crossing the Atlantic and took routes more than seven hundred miles to the south, putting them in no position to help even if called upon. "There are few places on the planet so hard to reach as that icecap of the earth which is quaintly named Greenland," Arnold mused in his diary.

General Patrick, in Washington, found himself in a precarious position. Under Smith, the American squadron had done better than anyone had thought possible. Yet to fail now, when victory seemed so close, would almost feel more cruel, shattering the country's sense that its aviators could compete and win on the world stage. He sent an order to Hull that none of the planes were to take off until each man on the squadron was fully rested and healed. An American mechanic stationed in Hull offered to install radio equipment in the *Chicago* so that the men could communicate with their nearby support ships. Smith refused, citing the burden of carrying an additional 110 pounds when gasoline consumption would already be an issue given the powerful winds.

He wanted to get on with it, to press his advantage and secure their place in history; instead, Smith was told to wait. Worse yet, orders came from Washington that the men were expected to appear at additional banquets in London and be prepared to meet the Prince of Wales (later King Edward VIII) if his schedule permitted. With just their crumpled flight suits and regular army uniforms available, Smith sent Arnold to London by train with enough money to buy suits on Savile Row for all of the squadron. Later that afternoon, Smith and Wade joined Arnold in the city while Nelson, Harding, and Ogden remained in Hull to work on the planes.

Arnold took the lead as the three pilots, dressed in perhaps the finest clothing they had ever worn in their lives, strode through the doors of the Savoy, eager to see if it lived up to its reputation as the most sophisticated hotel in the world. The three American men slipped into a side room, hoping to go unnoticed as the ballroom filled with the uppermost crust of British society. Among the guests were Lord Thomson, the air minister; Sir Hugh Trenchard, the man widely known as Boom; and some of Britain's finest pilots.

As Smith was about to walk into the main room, a man in a crimson coat and a walrus mustache stopped him and told him to wait so that he could announce him. Before Smith could protest, the man bellowed, "Lieutenant Lowell H. Smith," prompting the room to fall silent as every eye in the room turned toward him—his nightmare. Later that evening, after numerous speeches and toasts in their honor, Smith was introduced as the commander of the American flight and brought to the front to address the crowd. He admitted that he found public speaking more difficult than flying around the world and apologized for the absence of the three other members of his squadron. "But you will realize that what we are trying to do is get through, and if they had come here, we should not get away so quickly," he murmured before ending with a toast to MacLaren.

As the men were preparing to leave the Savoy, an aide to the Prince of Wales appeared and asked them to follow him. He led them into an upstairs suite where the prince was entertaining a party of friends. When he noticed the Americans, he introduced himself and chatted with them for several minutes, telling them that he would soon be bound for America himself aboard the *Berengaria*, then the flagship of the Cunard line.

In a sign of his lack of faith in airplanes, he bet each man five dollars that he would reach New York before them.

The following morning Smith and his men were back at the remote airfield, servicing their planes. Nearly every part that could be was removed and replaced. Propellers, cowling, ailerons—all were stripped for untested replacements from the boxes of supplies shipped from Seattle. The gasoline and oil tanks were drained and flushed, the wires scraped and repainted, metal coated with rust-resistant oxide. When they got too tired to go on, the men rested in bare rooms on the grounds of the airfield, protected from the crowds of autograph hunters that would not leave.

Performing maintenance was a poor substitute for flying, and Smith chafed at the long delay. While he respected the need to take care of his plane, he ultimately trusted himself more than he did any machine. No matter what happened in the air, he had always found a way to go on, and he saw little reason why this time would be different. Still, he knew his orders and followed them, even as bad omens began piling up. On July 22, he lifted the *Chicago* up with a crane and heavy chain onto a dolly in order to work on the underside of the aircraft. The plane weighed two and a half tons, well below the chain's six-and-a-half-ton capacity. Even with the assistance, the space underneath the plane was cramped, and Smith and Arnold took turns crawling under it, wrenches in their hands. As the men were switching positions, the chain suddenly snapped and the plane plummeted down. Had it happened a few seconds earlier or later, the accident would have been fatal. Not by nature superstitious, Smith nevertheless felt spooked. "Why it took a notion to break at that particular moment, we don't know," he wrote. The pontoons were badly damaged and were replaced by the leftover set that had been meant for Martin and the *Seattle*.

As he waited for a message that the support ships were in place in Iceland, Smith grew testy and impatient. Each morning, he picked up English newspapers and read of MacLaren's progress through northern Japan. The English aviator was now in Paramushir, the final stop before he crossed over the Pacific and landed on Attu Island. He had the wind at his back and seemingly luck on his side. Since leaving Tokyo, he had not reported any mechanical trouble, and there appeared to be none of the blistering storms that had held the Americans in place some three months earlier.

Once MacLaren passed the Gulf of Alaska, there seemed to be nothing that could stop him. The papers announced that he planned to follow the route of the Canadian railroad tracks that spanned the country like a belt across its waist, making it nearly impossible to get lost. His path, more northerly than the one that the Americans planned to take across the continent, would take him above the booming thunderstorms and tornadoes that threatened any aircraft that attempted to fly across the American plains. Once MacLaren reached Newfoundland, at the tip of eastern Canada, he could fly across the Atlantic in just one day if he needed to, sealing the loss of his rivals.

Smith declined an invitation to a garden party at Buckingham Palace held by King George V and Queen Mary of Teck on the grounds that the go-ahead signal from Iceland could arrive at any moment and he did not want any reason to be delayed. Instead, the American pilots spent a few hours at the nearby Humber Estuary paying their respects at the site of the 1921 crash of the R38-class airship, a British-made blimp that had just been purchased by the United States. At the time the largest craft of its kind in the world, the ship began cracking in half while it glided over a crowd of spectators. Men and objects began falling through its open seams. Two explosions then ripped the remaining structure apart. A twenty-year-old man from Texas named Norman Otto Walker jumped from the falling ship just as it was about to hit the water and became the sole survivor among the seventeen crew members aboard.

After the whirlwind of attention in Paris and London, the men spent quiet moments on the windy shoreline, reminding themselves of what could go wrong. When they returned to the air base, Smith ordered each man to secure extra layers of clothing before they took off for Iceland. Then, with nothing else to do, he waited in his spartan room, quelling his restlessness with regular trips to the radio room, where he longed for a message saying they were authorized to take off.

At night as he tried to sleep, the same thought kept returning to torment him as he was stuck in a purgatory of inaction: somewhere on the other side of the world, MacLaren was pulling ahead.

CHAPTER TWENTY-ONE

Distress Message

H E COULDN'T WAIT any longer.

Each tick of the clock felt like another injury as Smith sat in a cold room at the airfield staring through a window at the clouds above. Every conceivable improvement and chore that could be done to their aircraft had been, leaving him with nothing else for distraction. His fastidious attention to detail delighted the press, who saw in him the sort of modest hero they longed to write about. "The airplanes are clean and freshly varnished and as spick and span as when they started from Santa Monica, California," a local newspaper noted. "British experts have been amazed to see the fliers devote virtually all of their daylight hours for the past twelve days to personally supervising the refitting and cleaning of their machines."

Yet beneath his calm exterior raged a world's worth of frustration, each delay suffered over the last fifteen thousand miles another burden he bottled inside. With his orders to stay grounded, Smith looked for other ways to hasten their pace, for the first time allowing his impatience to show. He sent a message to General Patrick, requesting that all welcoming parties and events planned at their stops in America be canceled until they had completed the race. "Recommend that no entertainment for flyers be arranged until after the finish of the flight, which should be made rapidly to reduce chances of our planes being damaged and to prevent personnel from being relaxed," he wrote, his direct tone markedly different than the deference he had shown to his superiors in Washington at the start of the journey. "Our planes are in excellent condition and everything possible has been done to insure [sic] our success," he added, no longer hinting that he felt the aircraft were ready to go.

Finally, on July 30, he got his wish. Smith had the men up and into their aircraft by four in the morning. They maneuvered each plane into the waters of the Humber and loaded them with fuel and oil. Low fog moved in, keeping them waiting like racehorses in the gate until the sun broke through shortly after 10:15.

Smith led the way on a course that would take them over the North Sea toward the Orkneys, an archipelago of seventy islands off the northern coast of Scotland. Once a launching site for attacks by Viking pirates and until the fifteenth century a part of Norway, the isolated, windswept islands were littered with circular gray stone towers known as brochs that were considered ancient even by the Romans who had invaded the British Isles in the first century. With few trees or villages, the islands seemed to have been little changed by the sweep of time. The only sign of the modern era was a large naval base built in 1904 to buttress the British Empire's defenses in the North Sea from an alarming buildup of German warships. Ten years later, Winston Churchill, then the First Lord of the Admiralty, sent the Grand Fleet—a force of forty modern battleships—through the Straits of Dover to the safety of Scapa Flow, the body of water ringed by the Orkney Islands.

As the three American aircraft buzzed their way northward, the clouds gathered in their path as if intent on blocking them. Smith, in the lead, kept flying lower and lower, feeling himself squeezed by the fog piling down from above. Finally, he decided to climb over them. The planes flew for more than an hour without seeing any of the Scottish countryside below except for one ruined castle that Smith briefly glimpsed hanging over a sheer cliff, a high wall protecting it from any intrusion by land. Later, he often came back to this moment in his mind and talked about the beauty of the isolated spot, so far from the demands of banquets and balls. "When I'm a millionaire, I shall buy it," he joked with Arnold.

The men landed at the fishing village of Kirkwall, on the edge of the North Atlantic. Black smoke poured from the four funnels of the USS *Richmond*, a cruiser now sitting in the Kirkwall Harbor that would serve as one of their escorts across the Atlantic. Given the volatile weather and isolation along a route that would take them farther north than they had traveled while crossing the Gulf of Alaska and the Bering Sea, the US Navy had agreed to station a fleet of seven ships in a chain stretching across the Atlantic to Nova Scotia to help guide the aviators. Each vessel in line would churn black smoke from its funnels an hour before the planes were to reach their location and would continue releasing smoke until they had passed by, essentially sending up airborne bread crumbs for the squadron to follow.

While the planes were overhead, sailors would arrange giant placards on the deck of their ships with codes signaling the last known weather conditions. An *L* represented unfavorable weather at their destination, a *T* signaled good weather ahead, and an *H* warned of dangerous flying conditions. The captain of each ship was told that his crew was responsible for the safety of the planes until they were in view of the next ship in line. Those docked at each stop along the way were to have moorings, fuel, and small boats ready to pluck the pilots out of the water as soon as they had landed. Sailors would keep watch to prevent any damage to the planes or the very real chance that an aircraft could break free from its anchors and drift out into the dark sea.

Heavy fog hung over Kirkland the following day, preventing any hope of pushing onward. Instead, Wade, Harding, and Arnold found a small boat and paddled out to view the half-submerged ruins of the once-fearsome German High Seas Fleet. Some seventy-four German ships with skeleton crews aboard had entered Scapa Flow shortly after the armistice was signed in November 1918. There, the ships sat for months, with dwindling supplies of food and water. Sailors were barred from contact with British civilians and not allowed to step on Scottish soil, nearly inciting them into a state of mutiny.

Fed up with waiting and fearful that the Allies would seize the ships during the drawn-out negotiations of the Treaty of Versailles, Ludwig von Reuter, the German admiral in charge of the fleet, flashed a secret signal to all his ships on the morning of June 21, 1919. Immediately, the crews of each vessel began opening all watertight doors, hatch covers, and portholes—anything to let water in. It took an hour for British observers on land to notice that something was happening, by which time von Reuter's own ship was listing heavily toward starboard. Within five hours, eleven battleships, five battle cruisers, eight light cruisers, and fifty destroyers had either sunk or were sinking, at the time the greatest naval loss in a single day in history. British sailors desperately tried to tow the waterlogged ships toward shallower depths or nearby beaches in hopes of saving them. Fights between the British attempting to board the ships and their crews, who saw sinking their fleet as one last stand of national pride, led to the deaths of nine German sailors. Von Reuter was taken prisoner along with nearly eighteen hundred of his men and held in confinement until 1920.

The small boat holding the American aviators passed between gray smokestacks of sunken warships jutting out of the shallow water like enormous metal reeds. They came upon the wreck of the *Hindenburg*, a destroyer that was once among the most fearsome of the German fleet. The men climbed up its mast and looked down into the clear water at the ship lurking beneath them like a whale. Soon, they found two of its great guns rising from the stern. Arnold and Harding pulled themselves on top of one while Wade scurried up the other. The two men bet Wade that he couldn't jump across the gap between them. "Leigh is always ready to take a dare, and he almost made it," Harding later wrote. He fell into the sea, fully clothed, and had to be helped out.

Once dry and back in Kirkwall, Arnold and Harding lounged on a couch talking with the writer Damon Runyon while records played on a Victrola in the background. Runyon, whose short stories about gritty New York characters became the inspiration for the musical *Guys and Dolls*, was perhaps the most famous sportswriter in America, a man so widely followed that a few nice comments he made about Montana were the lead story in several of that state's newspapers that summer. A month earlier, Runyon had been writing columns about ballplayers that ran in papers across the nation; now he was aboard the *Richmond*, expecting to follow the American aviators through to the conclusion of their flight. In his first stories, he transformed the aviators into the sort of on-the-go figures in his stories. He described Smith as "that tall tanned lean-flanked Californian" and quoted him as saying, "You can't very well fly when you can't see" in the fog, given that "there is no use trying to blast your way through that stuff."

Smith was invited by officers stationed on the *Richmond* for a round of golf and could not find a way to say no. While on the course, the men told him that an Italian pilot, Antonio Locatelli, was making his own attempt to circle the globe and would land in Kirkwall in the coming days. A decorated pilot who had briefly been a prisoner of war and later became a National Fascist Party legislator, Locatelli had grown incensed by the fact that Italy was not yet among the countries vying for the honor of being the first to race around the world and found that he could no longer take it. He secured a German-designed flying boat that had been built in an Italian shipyard, equipped it with a pair of Rolls-Royce engines, and took off with two copilots on July 25.

With neither advance planning nor supplies, he expected to follow the route of the Americans across the Atlantic as closely as possible and then improvise once he crossed the sea. Clear weather in Europe and a comparative lack of fanfare at his landing spots had allowed Locatelli to zip across the continent, putting him on pace to catch up to the American squadron somewhere over the ocean. While he was under no obligation to help the Italian pilot in the event of an emergency, Smith was told to be aware that there would be another plane in the air.

The entry of another competitor—even one whose prospects looked slim—gnawed at Smith. He had withstood the worst weather the world could throw at him, and yet he could not break free from reporters who never seemed to leave them alone. The novelty of flying to new places had worn off, replaced with a deep longing to go home. When asked what his plans were once the race was over, Smith replied that he was looking forward to "a couple of weeks for me in Los Angeles, where my father and mother are, and then I'm going to get up in the mountains of Oregon and hide." Ogden said that he wanted to "take room at a hotel and tell them to call me at 3 a.m. And then when somebody comes to do it, fire a shoe at his head and tell him to go where it's hottest. Oh boy, what a grand and glorious feeling that will be." Nelson had perhaps the easiest demand to satisfy: He wanted to be reunited with his dog, Nome, a blue-eyed Siberian husky currently in the care of friends in Dayton, Ohio. "He's wife and kid and everything to me," Nelson said.

THE CLOUDS CLEARED just enough on the morning of August 2 to justify their first attempt to reach Iceland. The men climbed into their planes after a breakfast of eggs and bacon and dispersed the squalling seagulls who had claimed the machines. They were airborne shortly after 8:30, heading in the direction of the rugged Faroe Islands. Within ten minutes they were captured by thick fog. Soon, they could not see the planes next to them. Smith flew as low as five feet off the water yet could not escape the gray blankness that engulfed him. For a brief moment the skies cleared, but that was immediately followed by heavy rain. Smith climbed to twenty-five hundred feet, hoping to rise above both rain and fog, and began circling in hopes that the other planes would soon appear. A few minutes later, he spotted the *Boston* pulling through the fog bank below him. But there was no sign of the *New Orleans*.

They circled for half an hour, wondering if Nelson had decided to keep flying on their intended path or had suffered an accident and was now stranded in the heavy seas below. Fearing that he had once again lost a member of the squadron in bad weather, Smith turned in the direction of Kirkwall in search of the *Richmond*, which was following along their course. Arnold wrote a terse message explaining that the *New Orleans* was missing and stuffed it into a weighted message bag that he planned to drop on the deck of the ship. But Smith could not find the *Richmond* either. They were soon back above Kirkwall, with no obvious choice of what to do next. Arnold dropped the message bag into one of the village streets where some American officials had been staying, hoping that they would pick it up and telephone the radio operator, who could then alert the *Richmond* to begin searching for the lost plane. The *Chicago* and the *Boston* returned to the moorings they had left that morning and the aviators huddled in a room at the local British air base, waiting for word.

UNABLE TO SEE more than six inches from the cockpit, Nelson and Harding stumbled through the fog. Bursts of turbulent air, known as a propeller wash, gave the only clues that other planes were nearby. Somehow in the confusion, either the *Chicago* or the *Boston* passed inches in front of them. The power of the volatile wake forced their plane to buckle and bounce like a bull attempting to throw its rider. Nelson struggled to remain in control and realized that he no longer knew which way was up. "Once one loses equilibrium in a fog, it is very difficult to regain it," he later wrote. "With fog everywhere there was no basis of comparison and it was difficult to tell whether we were flying north, south, east, west, up or down."

He looked to his instrument panel, which was now indicating that the *New Orleans* was descending in a spin at a great speed. He pulled at the stick, trying to reestablish command of the aircraft as the numbers on the altimeter rolled lower. Finally, just above the water, Nelson straightened the plane out and pulled level into a clearing in the clouds. He pushed on, now under the bank of fog. When he came into the clear sun, he found they were alone. Not knowing what had happened to the other two planes, he circled in the air, waiting for someone else to appear.

Harding, in the rear cockpit, spotted a black speck below them. They dove to investigate and decided that it was Sydero Island, the southernmost of the Faroe Islands. Twenty-five miles later, the skies became perfectly clear and the men saw the first navy destroyer in position to guide their way. Harding dropped a message bag on the deck of the ship, asking for a sign that the other planes had already passed. Sailors on board signaled back that they hadn't. Not knowing whether the other members of the squadron had crashed or been forced to turn back, Nelson fought through another fog belt that obscured the sea below them. That evening, seven hours after taking off from Kirkwall, they landed in a cove near the tiny village of Hornafjordur, surrounded by ragged black mountains and icy-blue glaciers that menaced in the distance. Sailors from the *Raleigh* who had earlier that day built the first temporary radio station in the village announced to the waiting world that the crew of the *New Orleans* had made it.

The *Chicago* and *Boston* were in position to take off by 9:30 the following morning. The sky, which the day before had been swollen with fog, was a deep cobalt blue that made the earth feel new. Movie crews cranked their cameras, and nearby steamships blew their whistles as the two planes took off again for Iceland. An unexpectedly stiff breeze on their tail pushed them through the air at speeds of over a hundred miles per hour. Arnold, in the rear cockpit, periodically turned to his right to keep tabs on the *Boston*, which buzzed just a few yards away.

An hour and a half into the flight, Arnold again looked to the right expecting the *Boston* to be there. Instead, there was only sky. Smith and Arnold twisted in their seats, scanning for any sign of them. They spotted the other plane well below them to their left and apparently gliding in for a landing in the open ocean. Smith banked and circled as close as he could while Wade, in the *Boston*, landed between the peaks of mountainous waves. From their position above, Smith and Arnold registered what had happened: the *Boston* engine's oil pump had failed, leaving the plane smothered in oil and casting a glimmering trail in the water.

As soon as he touched down, Wade stood up in the cockpit and began signaling frantically for Smith to stay airborne rather than attempting to land next to him. From his vantage point, Smith, who could see large waves rocking the floating airplane, at once understood Wade's message—it was better to have one plane down than to have two crews stuck in the middle of the ocean without any method of calling for help. Smith circled once to confirm Wade's intentions, then sped toward the Faroe Islands. They noticed a telegraph line once they neared Sydero Island and followed it until they reached a village. While he flew, Smith wrote notes describing Wade's stricken plane, its location, the time of landing, and the conditions of both sea and wind so that naval officers could estimate how far they would drift in the open ocean before they could be found. Arnold dropped one message bag in the village near a building that appeared to house a telegraph.

Smith spotted the USS *Billingsley* steaming through the bay. He flew low over the ship while Arnold hoisted a message bag and aimed for the deck of the ship. He missed by several yards. Smith circled around again for another try. Arnold tied his life preserver to the remaining message bag and tried again. This bag, too, sailed clear of its mark. A sailor on board dove overboard and fished it out of the chilly sea. Smith circled, watching as the captain grabbed the paper out of the sailor's hand and read it on the deck. "Wade forced down, motor gone," it read. "Needs immediate help. Sea growing."

A sailor standing next to the captain immediately ran toward the ship's control rooms. A moment later, clouds of dark smoke poured from its funnels as it darted ahead. "Never have I seen a vessel jump into high speed so quickly," Arnold marveled. "Later we learned that she had traveled so fast she burnt all the paint off her stacks."

Smith and Arnold raced toward Iceland through rain and fog. They flew low, just fifty feet off the water, and for three hundred miles tried not to think about Wade and Ogden stranded with no means of communication and few supplies. The cruiser that was supposed to guide them toward their destination was far out of position, leaving Smith flying by compass over the open sea with nothing to confirm that they were on the right path. Finally, they spotted the village of Hornafjordur below. They landed, moored alongside the *New Orleans,* and reunited with Nelson and Harding, who helped them refuel their plane as the moon rose above them.

Once finished, the four men squeezed into a fisherman's hut, warmed only by blankets. There, under a frigid sky of stars, they waited anxiously by a lone radio for any word of their missing friends.

Chapter Twenty-Two

Disaster

THE DIAL SWUNG to zero.

As Wade piloted the *Boston* over the foggy ocean toward Iceland, he looked down at his instrument panel to see that the aircraft had lost all of its oil pressure. The new Liberty engine, which he and Ogden had installed in England, was now running without any form of lubrication or cooling, causing friction between its parts and dramatically increasing the chance of a fire. There was nothing he could do but try to land immediately. Each additional second that he remained in the air was a gamble, placing all his chips on the idea that the plane would not combust and leave him in the cockpit of a fireball over the Atlantic with no land in sight.

He glided down from an altitude of five hundred feet toward the surface of the ocean. Only when he was nearly on top of the water did he realize how deceitful the sea was. Waves that appeared smooth from a high vantage point revealed themselves as rolling hills, ready to smother whatever came in their path. He attempted to touch down on the peak of a wave, hoping that he would have time to maneuver into a better position before the next swell hit and swallowed him up. Ever since they started in California, the other pilots had admired Wade's handling of the Douglas World Cruiser, the way he coaxed it through deft turns and touches that left them in awe. Yet even with his mastery of the craft, he could not prevent it from slamming down onto the water with a force that surged through it like the blast of a shotgun. The left pontoon nearly wrapped itself around the lower wing, while two vertical wires snapped, leaving the upper wing sagging and at risk of collapse.

Ogden climbed out of the rear cockpit and made his way along the edge of the fuselage, water lapping at his feet, to inspect the sizzling engine. Hot oil lay splattered across both wings and was now leaking into the ocean, turning the water a sickly shade of purple. He expected to find that the oil tank had burst. Instead, he found it nearly full. There was only one possible explanation: the oil pump had failed. With no means of repairing it while at sea, the men had to hope for a rescue if they were to survive.

The *Chicago* flew off in the direction from which they had come. Wade and Ogden, now without any ships or landmarks on the horizon they could use to orient themselves, tried to keep their ship from drifting too quickly away from the spot where Smith would tell the navy ships to search. They pulled the anchor from the storage compartment and heaved it overboard as the plane continued to be tossed by the sea. Within minutes, both were seasick. Dizzy and trying not to vomit, the men climbed onto the wings and repaired the vertical wires, reinforcing the structure of the plane so that it could ride out the waves without crumpling. They then curled back into their cockpits, hoping that the cramps and nausea would pass. Rising and falling with each wave, they called out to each other, hearing in each other's voice the reassurance that they were not alone.

Over the next two hours, they did not see a single living thing. The sea was empty of driftwood, giving them no clues as to how far away from land they were. Eventually a seagull landed near them. Ogden grew excited by the prospect that they were near a shore until Wade reminded him that gulls could fly more than a hundred miles out to sea. Fearing that they would be adrift overnight, Wade told Ogden to get some sleep so that he could be ready to take a turn keeping watch once the sun went down.

A wisp of smoke appeared on the horizon at two in the afternoon, some three hours after they had last seen the *Chicago*. Wade crawled onto the top wing and waved a sheet of canvas while Ogden fired rounds from their flare gun. The ship appeared not to move, dangling just in range of view. The men shouted and waved for thirty minutes until it sank back beyond the edge of the sea, never to be seen again. "Up to this moment our spirits had been high," Wade wrote. "We had felt sure that it would not be long before a boat would pick us up. But now we realized that a ship has to be fairly close in order to see a speck such as we were, bobbing about on twenty-foot waves . . . never in our lives had either of us felt so lonesome, so helpless."

Rain began drizzling down. A heavy bank of fog closed in from the northwest. The men wished that they were in a rowboat rather than a damaged plane just so they could feel like they had some way to fight the current. Unable to stand the sense that he could do nothing, Ogden climbed back along the edge of the plane into the storage compartment and came out with a small National Geographic Society map of the world that they had carried with them since Santa Monica. He pulled it into his cockpit and sat there, estimating the distance they were from the coastline of Norway and how long it would take for the winds to carry them to its shores if the plane remained intact despite the thrashing waves.

Another hour went by. The seagull flew away. They could see nothing now except for the water around them. The sea became choppy, threatening to lap over the wings and make the aircraft buckle under the force of the waves. The men said little, each lost in his own thoughts. Wade began imagining the faces of his relatives and close friends, wondering if he would ever see them again.

Suddenly, so far away that they could not tell whether it was real or a dream, a small puff of black smoke slowly curled into the air. With the fog threatening to turn toward them, the men knew that it could be their last chance of rescue. Ogden yanked one of the wooden supports from the back of the fuselage and attached a strip of fabric to it to make a large flag. He climbed up on the upper wings and waved it as hard as he could while Wade shot the last remaining flare into the sky. When the flare gun was empty, he grabbed the rifle and blasted rounds into the air.

The boat turned, its movements so subtle given the distance that it made them doubt their own perceptions. Listing between belief and fear, the men did not move until they confirmed that it was indeed coming their way. It was a Scottish fishing boat, the *Rugby-Ramsey*. The captain came alongside the stranded Americans, seemingly oblivious to the fact that the men were in an airplane miles from any shore rather than in a seagoing vessel. "Do you want any help?" he asked. "Well, I should say we do!" Wade replied. The fishing crew grabbed a line of rope while the captain tried to get closer to the plane. Just as they were about to throw the line to Wade, a large wave came through and pushed the plane into a position looming above the stern of the boat, threatening to smash both vessels. After a few frantic seconds the *Boston* fell into the trough of the next wave, pulling it away from a collision. Anxious at the close call, the captain attached the line to a small float that he towed in a circle until Ogden could reach out and grab it.

The boat began towing the limp *Boston* toward the Faroe Islands. The lithe, wooden frame of the aircraft was no match for the ferocity of the swells. Each time the boat scaled the face of a wave, the *Boston* swung back and forth like a kite trying to catch the wind. The line then grew taut, jerking the aircraft forward and pushing the pontoons underwater with a sound that crackled like a machine gun. For half an hour, the cycle went on, the plane yanked one way and then dunked moments later.

The USS *Richmond* came into view. Wade and Ogden stepped into a small launch sent from the ship and soon climbed aboard the destroyer. Weary from the hours at sea, Ogden did not notice the charged iron railing used to ground the antennas of the ship's radio and brushed against it, severely burning his leg. While a medic tended to him, sailors from the ship drained all of the aircraft's remaining gas and oil, hoping to lighten the load before bringing the plane onto the deck and returning it to Kirkwall for repairs. A large sling dropped down from the crane on deck, and the sailors wrapped it around the belly of the *Boston*. "I can recall the feeling of joy that swept over me when I saw our beloved plane rising off the water," Wade wrote.

With a sickening groan, the crane started to bend under the weight of the waterlogged airplane. The plane fell hard onto the water, feet away from where sailors had been just moments before. A quick inspection of the craft revealed that its pontoons were crushed, putting it at risk of sinking at any moment. Its propeller was cracked and holes appeared in the fuselage and wings.

Sailors surrounded the aircraft, working fervently to keep it afloat. Men climbed aboard with veneer, fabric, and buckets of thick, pasty glue known as dope, making emergency patches wherever possible. Wade and Ogden pulled everything they could off the plane, emptying the storage compartment and throwing tools and spare parts into the small launch that rescued them. No matter what they did, it continued to sink. Growing desperate, Wade and Ogden began sawing off the wings and pontoons, willing to try anything to disassemble the craft and make it light enough to pull onto the deck. A violent wind rushed in, tossing one of the sailors stripping the plane overboard. Two men jumped into the freezing water and grabbed him before he was pulled away by the current.

It was too dangerous to go on. Wade, Ogden, and the sailors returned to the deck. Running out of options, the captain decided to tow the aircraft to the closest shore in the Faroe Islands and take it apart there. Officers aboard the *Richmond* urged Wade and Ogden to eat, but they were too anxious about the condition of their plane. Despite the wind and rough sea, they stood on the stern of the ship watching the *Boston* as it was pulled through the ocean. It bounced and tumbled on the waves, yet appeared to withstand the blows. The two men drank cups of hot coffee in silence, wondering whether their flight was over. Shortly before midnight, Wade sent a radio message to Smith alerting him that the *Boston* would need extensive repairs and a new engine. Finally allowing themselves to believe that their aircraft would endure despite its damage, they left the deck and fell asleep in their quarters. Though there were numerous reporters on deck, "not one of them bothered us with a single question that night," Wade wrote. "It was very decent of them."

The *Richmond* steamed through the night, pulling the *Boston* through the darkness. At dawn, sailors on deck saw that the plane's front spreader bar had collapsed, squeezing its pontoons together. Rather than gliding through the water, the plane now jolted and bounced, more a skipping stone than a seaplane. Shortly after five in the morning, the captain of the *Richmond* woke Wade up with the news that, given the plane's condition and the large rocks coming ahead, continuing to tow the *Boston* might imperil the *Richmond*. What's more, if it remained on the surface of the water, it would become a risk to other vessels in the area. The responsible thing to do, the captain said, was to sink it.

Wade stared ahead, processing what he had been told. Then he spoke. "The hardest words I ever had to [say] were to the ship's captain: Abandon the airplane," Wade later wrote. As the sun climbed in the morning sky, he and Ogden helped cut the towline. The plane, now without any support, rocked on the surface of the water through a series of waves. It then slowly began taking on water. Within minutes, it capsized, sending its nose under the sea and its pontoons high in the air. Wade and Ogden, on deck, could now see the underside of the plane, their first glimpse of the view that thousands of people around the world had seen as the *Boston* flew over them. The cockpits were quickly submerged, and the plane fell fast into the deep. Soon, there was no sign of the aircraft that had safely taken two men over three-quarters of the globe. The *Richmond* turned toward Iceland, the unspoken pain of Wade and Ogden's journey ending hanging over it as the destroyer cut through the choppy waters.

When the *Richmond* radioed the news that the *Boston* had been lost, Smith, never talkative to begin with, fell into deep silence, as if fighting an internal battle. It had been nothing but bad luck that Wade and Ogden had chosen that particular engine to install in their plane out of the four that lay waiting for them in England. The complete overhaul of each aircraft, which had seemed so reasonable a few days earlier, had introduced a risk that Smith had not seen coming. There was simply no way to know if another newly installed part would fail on the two remaining planes the next time they took to the air. It felt like the men had been whisked back to the early days of the flight, when a cascade of damaged parts kept them tethered to the ground and ultimately doomed Martin and his aircraft. "We were all torn between two emotions," Arnold wrote in his diary. "One of relief that Wade and Ogden were safe, and the other of sorrow that after coming 20,000 miles they should so suddenly lose their plane through absolutely no fault of their own."

The squadron—now down to four men—spent another night in Hornafjordur, where a local businessman coaxed them into attending a performance of native Icelandic songs sung by a choir of young blond girls in traditional costumes. "They were all charming, but [we] were thinking far too much about Leigh and Hank to enjoy ourselves as we should have done," Arnold wrote. Though he now doubted the new parts installed in each aircraft, Smith chose to fly on, no doubt expecting there to be more supplies available in the capital city of Reykjavik some 290 miles away, where five American destroyers were in port.

The two planes fought through a headwind so strong that at times they felt like they were suspended in the sky. Below them, they could see the ruins of shipwrecks piled up along the rocky coast. Upon reaching the city, Arnold looked down to see monstrous swells pushing through its outer harbor that he felt no plane could survive. Smith and Nelson led their planes into a sheltered cove and nestled them down between hundreds of boats that had taken refuge there, surprising the welcoming party who were waiting for them at the harbor.

The men anchored their planes and approached the seawall to find a crowd of twenty-five thousand people cheering their arrival. A few minutes later, the *Richmond* steamed into the harbor. Wade and Ogden appeared on the small launch, and the men of the squadron reunited on the deck just as the prime minister of Iceland strode up to greet them. "Poor old Wade put his arms around Lowell and his eyes filled with tears," Arnold wrote. "Although we were overjoyed at seeing them again, there were lumps in our throats as we thought of their hard luck and the fate of the *Boston*." Reporters swarmed around the men, yelling out questions. "It was a tough break" after five months of flight, Wade said.

"When the four planes left America the Army hoped all four would re-turn. But it's all in the game. We did our best."

Smith found himself with a math problem: They had six aviators but only two planes. When Martin crashed the *Seattle*, the squadron pro-ceeded without him rather than give up before it had left US territory. Abandoning Wade and Ogden after so long, however, seemed cruel, no matter how much Smith burned to finish the race. Once again, his inter-nal poles were at odds with each other. His sense of fairness ultimately proved stronger than his desire to push ahead. While the other men ser-viced the two remaining planes, Smith sent a message to General Pat-rick requesting that he ship the prototype Douglas Cruiser that the crew members had trained on in Virginia to Newfoundland. There, Wade and Ogden could rejoin the flight before they reached the United States, giv-ing them each the hero's welcome they deserved.

Of course, the *Chicago* and *New Orleans* had to make it that far. Na-val ships attempting to get in position in Greenland reported that some coves were frozen solid, making it impossible for the planes to land at their designated supply stops. The long delays in Alaska, in India, and in England were catching up to them. It was as if they had flown across two continents just to find the door to the Atlantic firmly shut.

Failure, which Smith had sensed chasing him like a shadow since Santa Monica, had never felt so inevitable. They had crossed the Pacific, braved Asia, and reached the farthest edge of Europe. As he paced the Reykjavik seawall with barbed, snowcapped mountains nearly engulf-ing him, Smith began to ask himself for the first time whether a flight around the world was truly possible. The Portuguese could not make it past Hong Kong; d'Oisy, the French flier, gave up before trying to cross the ocean. MacLaren alone knew how much they had been through to get this far.

At that moment, he was attempting to fly from Nikolski, in the Russian-held Komandorskis, to Bering Island, the spot where the Amer-icans had touched down and nearly set off an international incident. The plane took off in a swift wind and soared though clear skies over one hundred miles of open water. As they neared the island, the British aviators found dense fog in their path, snatching the color from the sky. Soon, MacLaren could no longer see the wings of his plane. The aircraft, which had been traveling at an altitude of around three thousand feet, descended as low as MacLaren dared to go. It skimmed the water, riding gusts of wind that left it traveling at over a hundred miles per hour—an unnerving speed when the men could see only a few yards ahead. Mac-Laren had to make a choice. Somewhere in the fog loomed the cliffs of Bering Island. Yet making a forced landing here, in the angry sea, would likely doom their aircraft, finally ending their world flight. The seconds passed by, heading deeper into the fog. Finally, MacLaren shouted an order to his pilot, Plenderleith, to bring the ship down.

The plane hit the ocean at the crest of a swell. Its top wings immediately shattered and came off, leaving the body of the aircraft spinning like a top. Fabric tore off the lower wings, and the ailerons were shorn off. Once it lost its momentum and slowed to a stop, the plane seesawed back and forth, the tip of the remaining wing on each side dipping into the water as it rocked. Had it not been for the *Thiepval*, a Canadian fishing trawler there to provide support for MacLaren's flights, the three men would have drowned. Once pulled to safety, MacLaren used the ship's radio to announce to the world that his flight was over. "Wings, flats, and tail smashed and as no spares available necessary to abandon flight," he wired to London. "Hull and engine salvaged and taken aboard by the *Thiepval*."

For the second time, a British attempt at a round-the-world flight had come up short. Of any nation, it had seemed to possess the combination of elements—landing sites, supply chains, technical know-how, and bravado—required to make the dream of global air travel a reality. Failing to meet the expectations of the British Empire weighed on MacLaren, who had left London months ago assuming that he would be catapulting himself into a higher echelon, one that his education and background seemed to demand of him. "For the sake of the Air Forces I am sorry I have failed, but the conditions were almost impossible for flying," he wrote to the Air Ministry in London. His embarrassment now known worldwide, MacLaren sank into a small room aboard the *Thiepval* and did not come out as it steamed westward toward Unalaska, bringing him by sea over the route that he had once hoped to travel by air.

Mercifully, the British press blamed the aircraft rather than the pilot. "Had the machine held out they would no doubt by now made the coast of America," one London paper wrote. Noting that d'Oisy had been unable to complete a cycle of the globe and two of the four American planes were now demolished, it continued that "MacLaren and his gallant comrades have therefore failed in good company, and though they thus come short of success, their efforts reflect nothing but the highest credit upon them and the British Air Service to which they belong." Editorials ran in American newspapers lauding MacLaren as a worthy competitor. "There are few achievements in the annals of flying to be compared with that which Major MacLaren has accomplished," the *Virginian-Pilot* wrote. "The misfortune which forces him to abandon his flight just as his American rivals are sweeping into the home stretch of the globe circling marathon will arouse the sympathy of the American people as MacLaren's pluck and daring have aroused their admiration."

The race finally seemed to be the Americans' to win, if only they could escape Iceland and find a way around the frozen coves blocking their path through Greenland. The Danish government reported that the ice conditions were worse than they had been in decades. Icebergs, some taller than steamships, were spotted a hundred miles south of their normal domains. A day's delay turned into two, then three. Before long, three became nine. And still the count went up, a multiplying effect that began to feel like an omen. Newspaper reporters, bored at their confines on the *Richmond* and losing interest in the novelties of Iceland, began asking Smith if the Americans, too, were going to throw in the towel. The questions became rumors, which seemed close enough to the truth that reporters began betting on the chances of any of the planes reaching North America. Even though they personally liked the pilots, the challenges of the leg ahead—one of the longest of the full flight, with perhaps the worst weather and the most ice—were too great for some writers to put money on American success.

"The world flight of the Army aviators is believed to have reached its crisis, and grave doubts exist here as to whether it will be completed," the *New York Times* reported from Labrador, the fliers' intended destination in the far northeast corner of Canada if they were able to successfully cross the ocean. "It seems to be a very serious situation . . . I am not all sure that [it] can be done," a lieutenant in the US Army Signal Corps told the paper.

Smith, who normally kept his passions hidden, struggled to prevent his frustration at not moving forward from veering into recklessness. He sent a message to General Patrick urging him to permit them to put wheels on the planes and attempt to fly directly to Labrador, bypassing Greenland entirely and aiming for the continent of North America wherever he could find it. He received no response and remained stuck in a picturesque town that now felt like his personal prison.

Two weeks after the Americans reached Iceland, Locatelli, the Italian pilot, landed in the Reykjavik harbor. The Americans greeted him and began inspecting his plane. A monoplane that had one set of wings rather than the two on the Douglas World Cruiser and an all-metal hull, it seemed a futuristic and more lethal machine than their own, as if it were the predator that had finally caught up to its prey. "It appeared to be the most efficient plane for long-distance flying that we had ever seen," Arnold wrote. Locatelli and his copilots—intense, well-dressed, and righteous in their cause—were warmly greeted by newspaper reporters desperate for something new to write about after days spent getting stonewalled by Smith.

The presence of a competitor evaporated the last ounces of Smith's patience. He had the four-person American crew up before dawn and in their planes, ready in case of a favorable weather report. When word of clear skies came at ten a.m., Smith taxied the *Chicago* farther out into the harbor. Powerful swells tossed the aircraft, making it difficult to keep his hands on the controls. Each plane was loaded to capacity with fuel to fight the wind, making them heavier than at any other time on the flight. Smith attempted to take off but could not free himself from the waves. When Nelson, in the *New Orleans*, tried to accelerate, a large wave broke against its nose and snapped the propeller in two. Another wave hit the *Chicago* and ripped loose its spreader bar, threatening to crumple it like the *Boston*. Defeated, Smith signaled to return to the dock.

That evening, Smith and the American aviators dined with the Italian crew. Prodded by the same sense of obligation that had made him ensure that no pilots under his command in the forests of Oregon were lost, Smith invited Locatelli to fly alongside them toward Greenland once the weather cleared so that he could be under the eye of American ships should something go wrong. Locatelli immediately agreed.

For the next day and a half, the four remaining Americans worked without stop on their planes, using spare parts on the *Richmond* to coax them into service. Smith went over the route in his head, mentally taking himself where his plane would not. They would fly 835 miles over ocean and ice fields, with little hope of rescue if they fell into the water. Arctic winds sweeping down over the ice caps would pummel them. For a landing site, they had a temporary airfield that had been built by army scouts over the last few days next to a secluded cove. They would be the first pilots to test whether it was free enough of ice to land.

As the exhausted men walked back to their hotel under the midnight sun of summer, a sailor handed them a sheaf of messages announcing that the weather conditions were at last favorable for flying. Without stopping to eat or sleep, they turned around and climbed into their cockpits. By dawn, the planes were climbing out of the harbor, followed closely by Locatelli, on what Smith had told the men would be the most dangerous leg of the entire flight.

Within minutes it was apparent that Locatelli's aircraft was painfully faster. He attempted to stay with the Americans, circling and stalling in order to hold off on his speed. Eventually, however, the exercise grew frustrating, and he wagged his wings in farewell. He shot ahead toward Frederiksdal (modern-day Narsarmijit), at the southern tip of Greenland, leaving the *Chicago* and *New Orleans* buzzing behind. They lost sight of him within minutes in the misty sky.

After about an hour and a half, they flew over the *Richmond*, the first in the line of navy ships meant to guide them. Dozens of sailors and reporters sat in grandstands on its deck, straining to see the men. Arnold, noticing the crowd, stood up in his cockpit and blew kisses to the audience below. "You might live a thousand years and never get the kick out of the existence that few fleeting moments today produced for us aboard the *Richmond* when the round-the-world flyers rose out of the sunny sky, parading their planes past the cruiser with a startling flourish," Damon Runyon wrote. Smith spotted the *Billingsley* an hour later. Sailors had painted the words *Good Luck* in huge white letters on its deck. Two hours after that, they reached the *Barry*, which was carrying Wade and Ogden toward Nova Scotia. Two flags hung from its mast, a signal that dangerous weather was ahead.

The fog gathered within minutes. Smith and Nelson dove below it, skimming the whitecaps of powerful swells. The water, the fog, the ice—if it had not been for adrenaline, the men later said, they could have frozen to death in the cockpits. Sweat dripped from their foreheads, forming icicles. Though they were supposed to keep flying straight for another 160 miles to reach the last ship in the caravan, Smith swung toward the Greenland coast, hoping that the fog would lift closer to the shore. For roughly seventy miles, they flew just above the huge, dark waves, not sure if they were going in the right direction in the fog.

The monstrous form of an iceberg appeared in the grayness ahead of them. Then another. The plane was flying at a speed of ninety miles an hour. The fog seemed to grow more dense as it closed around them. Freezing gusts of wind that Smith estimated at sixty miles per hour made it impossible to stick to the course of a single line. Smith and Nelson realized that they were in the midst of a swarm of icebergs, all the size of small mountains. Each announced itself with just seconds to spare. In their cockpits, Smith and Nelson pulled their controls to the left or the right, dodging each giant only to find another lurking behind it. "Three times we came so suddenly upon huge icebergs that there was no time left to do any deciding," Smith later remembered. "We simply jerked the wheel back for a quick climb, and were lucky enough to zoom over the top of it into the still denser fog above."

The wingtips were no longer visible; the propeller was nearly shrouded. Once over each obstacle, Smith plunged downward again, seeking an opening in the gray mist. The heavy weight of the fuel for the long trip made flying high enough to crest over the fog impossible. Each man harbored the fear that he, too, would make the same mistake as Martin and plow into an unseen peak. Here, there would be no hunting lodge to tide them over, no cannery to save them.

Smith peered back to see the *New Orleans* behind him. The two planes dipped again, now inches above the water. Suddenly, they saw ahead of them a wall of white. Flying by instinct alone, Smith banked as hard as he could to the right. His left wings seemed to graze the edge of the iceberg. Arnold instinctively covered his head with his arms, preparing for a crash, and shouted, "Hold on, God!"

Somehow, the plane remained airborne. They could no longer see the *New Orleans*. The wind was too strong and their own propeller too loud to hear any sounds that would indicate whether Nelson had cleared the iceberg or crashed into it. Turning back would mean facing the ice field again and risking the two planes smashing into each other in the consuming fog. After glancing at his compass, Smith aimed the *Chicago* toward what he thought was the closest shore. "We had no time to think of anything but our own problem right then," Smith later wrote. "Things were happening fast—faster than they had ever happened in all our lives."

For another hour they slalomed between icebergs and shadows that appeared to leap out at them from the fog. Finally, they saw the looming outline of cliffs, their sign they had reached the mainland of Greenland. The ice did not relent as they edged closer to the shoreline. A few times, Smith reflexively swerved the plane just in time to see that they had dodged an iceberg by ten feet or less. Later, he would ask himself how he had known that it was there. "Perhaps it was a sudden icy draft from the berg, like the cold hand of death, that would cause us to turn our heads," he thought.

The *Chicago* reached Cape Farewell, a place that scientists later identified as the world's windiest region. They flew northward along its west coast for a few miles and soon found themselves bathed in clear sky. For the first time, they took in the high mountain ranges that guarded the coast. The desolate scene had terrified sailors attempting to lay a telegraph line that would connect North America and Europe and made them ache for home. "The rocks resemble spires or minarets," one wrote. "They look very bleak, and are calculated to frighten the observer and give a sad thought for all Greenland."

Smith scanned for a way forward. Fog lay directly on top of the water, blocking everything below an altitude of roughly fifteen hundred feet from his sight. Instead, Smith flew above the clouds, using the peaks jutting into the sky to check his course. They finally reached where they thought Frederiksdal should be and looked for an opening in the fog. They circled several times, waiting for their chance. "The All-Wise Providence, who had already spared our lives a dozen times on this day's journey, parted the clouds for us so that there was a shaft of light extending down to the sea," Smith later said.

Below them they spotted a boat puffing out black smoke. It was a Danish Coast Guard cutter, the *Island Falk*, which was blaring its whistles and firing its guns to signal the plane. Smith, however, could hear nothing over his engine. He descended through the cloud drift and landed in the rough water at the mouth of a fjord. The plane fought the current for several miles upstream and reached their mooring buoys under the shadow of a snowy mountain.

A Danish officer came to greet them and asked where the *New Orleans* and Locatelli were. Smith told him that he had lost them both in the fog. The two Americans climbed out of their cockpits and began refueling and inspecting their plane without saying a word. Neither man needed to. "So narrow had been our own escape that it seemed hardly possible that Providence could bring them through in safety also," Smith wrote. "We simply couldn't see how any one could be as lucky as we had been."

CHAPTER TWENTY-THREE

The Crossing

H E DIDN'T WANT to allow himself to believe.

The sky remained silent. Seconds, minutes, hours—Smith had lost the ability to keep track of time while dodging the icebergs, each moment crashing headlong into the next—passed, and still there was no sound of an airplane engine carving through the fog above them. Then, a murmur. It grew louder, circling around them like a ghost in the darkness. Smith, standing on the makeshift airfield, had told himself that there was no way that Nelson could have flown through the field of icebergs and not hit something. Letting faith back in felt cruel, as if he were setting himself up for an even deeper fall. Yet the buzzing kept gaining in strength until it was so intense that it seemed like he could reach out and grab it. "It sounded like a hymn of triumph," Smith wrote. "No choir of celestial angels could have sounded half so beautiful."

For ten minutes the unseen plane flew in circles above them as Nelson searched for a break in the clouds. The fog slightly shifted, giving him the sliver he needed to bring the *New Orleans* down. When he landed, he caught his pontoons on the crest of a large wave, damaging one slightly. It was the only mark on his aircraft after threading through the iceberg field.

While Smith had opted for the security of land when confronted with the threat of icebergs, Nelson had swung his plane thirty miles out to sea. With Harding in the rear cockpit, he looked for Smith when they reached Cape Farewell. When they did not spot him, they began to worry that Smith had crashed into an iceberg or a mountain along the coast. Finding their commander alive in Greenland was as much a shock to them as their survival was to Smith and Arnold. Together, the two planes had nearly crossed the Atlantic, making the first flight from Iceland to Greenland. "We just flew in every possible direction until God sent us the right one," Harding later said. The exhausted crews sent a radio message from the Danish ship to the *Richmond* announcing their arrival. Then they immediately went to bed, having been awake for roughly forty-two hours.

Neither Smith nor Nelson was in any condition to fly the following day. The fog that nearly killed them hung low over the fjord, preventing them from taking off even if they wanted to. While Smith rested, Arnold passed the time admiring the skills of the native Inuit men who were guarding their planes. Arnold watched as each man took to the sea in a small kayak that "seems to become a part of him," allowing them to hunt with stunning accuracy, Arnold wrote. "They are good-natured, cheery people, and, thanks to the Danish government, they are still practically free from the taints that usually come with the white man," Arnold wrote.

The four Americans worked on their planes in the fjord the following day while icebergs floated less than a hundred yards away. While they refueled and replenished their engines with oil, the top of one iceberg began to wobble and then slowly toppled over, leaving the men spellbound. An inspection of the *Chicago* revealed that the aircraft's pontoons had been punctured by cakes of ice that slammed into them while it was moored at its buoy overnight. There were no cranes at the makeshift airfield that could pull the plane out of the water for repairs.

Smith began undressing. He took off his flight suit and plunged into the cold water with watertight patches in his hand. He dove under the aircraft, searched for the cracks in the pontoons, and resurfaced, panting and blue. He took a few breaths, then disappeared again beneath the plane and slowly sealed its skin. When he could no longer feel his hands, he came up and rubbed oil over them, desperate for any barrier from the ice. Still, he kept on working, until the pontoons were once again safe to use.

The men were quickly running out of supplies at the emergency air base and needed to get to the *Milwaukee*, a naval cruiser stationed one hundred fifty miles westward near the town of Ivigtut. After receiving a report that the weather was clear at their destination, Smith and the squadron prepared to take off into the fog. They taxied between icebergs in the fjord, aligning the space they needed for liftoff with gaps in the ice. Once airborne, they flew for two hours along the bleak coast, feeling all the while like they were about to lose control in the wind. "Nearly every time we rounded a mountain, a terrific gust would strike from the shoulder of a fjord and knock us all over the sky," Arnold wrote.

While the Americans pushed onward, the world's attention remained on Locatelli, the Italian flier, who had not been seen since he sped away from them shortly after they left Iceland. To reach Greenland, he would have to pass through the same field of icebergs and fog that the two Americans had. If he was alive, he had a window of just a few days before he froze to death.

Five of the US Navy ships accompanying the American flight across the Atlantic began a search through swollen seas over an area roughly the size of Maryland, looking for any signs of the pilot or his aircraft. Two search parties with dogsleds set out along the coast of Greenland. For three days they searched, to no avail. By midnight on August 23, the destroyers *Billingsley* and *Reid* were running low on fuel and food and were sent to ports in Europe for fresh supplies. The three other ships—the *Richmond, Raleigh,* and *Barry*—kept up the search, though their stocks too were dwindling.

Late on the night of the twenty-fourth, the captain of the *Richmond* prepared a request that he intended to radio to Washington. It recommended they call off the search, return, and admit that Locatelli was dead. The *Richmond* cut through the darkness 125 miles east of Cape Farewell. As the captain prepared to send the message to the radio operator, a lookout rang an alarm. He had spotted a flicker of light on the horizon, so faint that it seemed to be a dream.

The *Richmond* sped toward the spot and fired a red flare into the sky. The crew waited as the greens and blues of the northern lights swirled above them. A few moments later, a red flare popped up in the dark sea as if to answer. The searchlight of the ship danced along the horizon as officers, sailors, and reporters rushed to the deck, half dressed, with disheveled hair and overcoats and blankets pulled around them for warmth. A small object bobbing like a cork appeared in the glare of the light. The ship fell silent as the spotlight operator struggled to keep the beam in place. When it found the object again, the men on deck could see the red, white, and green rudder of the Italian plane. Its crew of four men stood waving at them across the frigid waters.

Sailors threw out a line and pulled the exhausted and seasick Italian crew aboard the *Richmond* in cargo nets. Once on deck, they covered them with blankets and plied them with hot coffee. When he could speak, Locatelli admitted that he had not seen the destroyer when he fired the flare gun, but was just making sure that he knew how to use it.

The appearance of the *Richmond* out of the darkness was "like the first thread connecting us with life again," he said.

Mechanical trouble had forced them to land in the heavy fog. They found that they could not take off again in the rough sea and were taken more than a hundred miles by the currents. With no way to steer, they rammed into icebergs and were battered by waves. They feared the craft would soon start leaking. If it did, there would be no way to escape. Death would come painfully slowly as they sank into the dark water inch by inch.

By the time of their rescue, their plane's wings were shattered and its engine was bent, preventing it from ever taking to the air again. In order to get it onto the deck of the *Richmond*, American sailors had to shear off the remaining splinters of its wings and slice off its nose. Locatelli pulled his few personal effects and an Italian flag out of the aircraft. Then he asked that the sailors return it to the ocean and burn it rather than allow it to sit in its weak condition.

He remained on the deck watching as fire consumed the aircraft, displaying no visible emotion beyond tightening his jaw muscles as the flames grew larger. He did not speak while the embers of the plane sizzled on the dark water and finally went out, ending his attempt at flying around the world. "Luck was not with us," he said aloud to no one and headed to his bed for the night.

By the next morning, he had forgotten his faults and was looking ahead to his next triumph. He wired congratulations to Smith and began asking the naval officers aboard the *Richmond* when a ship would be able to take him back to Italy, where he said he would begin preparing to be the first person to fly over the North Pole.

The *Chicago* and *New Orleans* landed at the tiny village of Ivigtut. The area's indigenous population was supplemented each summer by about one hundred and fifty Danish miners, who used the brief respite from ice and the unsetting summer sun to extract cryolite, a rare mineral found almost nowhere else on Earth that was used in the production of aluminum and as the color yellow in fireworks. The emergency supply base built at Ivigtut was the "last and most barren" of those they reached during their long flight around the world, Nelson later remembered. The arrival of the *Milwaukee* and the four American aviators overjoyed the miners, who had grown accustomed to the seasonal solitude. That evening, the sailors aboard the *Milwaukee* invited the miners to watch a movie on the deck of the ship during a drizzling rain. The men howled with laughter at the slapstick comedy. "These un-melancholy Danes of Greenland never miss an opportunity of celebrating," Nelson wrote. "If a boat comes in, they have a party. If a boat goes out, they do the same."

Ahead of the aviators lay one more flight over 560 miles of open water to Labrador, on the coast of Newfoundland. Smith, who mistrusted the engines that they had installed in England, put the squadron to work replacing them with backups that arrived on the *Milwaukee*. The men worked out in the open as hard rain fell on them, unbothered by the wet weather. "We had long ago grown accustomed to such trifles as being soaked to the skin," Arnold wrote.

The main problem was the gnats. As soon as the rain stopped, tens of thousands of insects appeared in dense black clouds. They flew up the men's noses and into their eyes, and they buzzed in their ears in such numbers that it was impossible to concentrate on anything else. It got to be so bad that the men couldn't work. They draped netting over their heads and tied it around their necks. "They were the most troublesome brutes you ever saw—worse than tropical insects," Arnold wrote.

With the new engines in place, Smith pushed the planes through a few test flights, hoping to find any weakness that would cause another accident like the one that left Wade and Ogden stranded in the *Boston*. Satisfied, he told the men to be ready as soon as the weather was favorable. On the night of August 28, the miners, sailors, and aviators gathered for a large feast to celebrate Arnold's twenty-ninth birthday, which they followed with another movie shown on the deck of the *Milwaukee* under the glimmering northern lights. In Arnold's pocket was a message from his mother that came via the ship's radio operator. "To Lieutenant Arnold— Happy Returns," she wrote. He pasted the slip of paper in his diary that night, alongside one from the officers aboard the Danish ship *Island Falk* that read simply, "Thirty drinks." They were "royally entertained— deluged, in fact," at the party with the miners, Arnold wrote in his diary. Afterward, they visited the *Island Falk*, which had sailed from Frederiksdal and anchored at Ivigtut, and ended the night "with the usual and inevitable result," Arnold wrote the following day, no doubt nursing a hangover.

The weather turned and prevented the men from attempting another takeoff for the next four days. Storms raged across the northern Atlantic, threatening their supply lines. On the other side of the ocean, near the fliers' destination in Labrador, sailors battled sixty-mile-per-hour winds

that threatened to smash a cache of fuel drums floating in a cove into
the rocks. Had the fuel been lost, the American world flight attempt
would have been delayed for at least seven months, until spring, given
the increasingly savage weather, and perhaps permanently. With the fate
of the now-famous pilots in the balance, Lieutenant George Noville, the
son of a wealthy and well-known hatmaker, set out in a small boat in
Canada with two men under his command to recapture the 450-pound
drums rolling through the icy water. They fought against the storm for
five hours, finally lashing the fuel barrels together and dragging them to
the beach. There, they stayed awake for the rest of the night in drenched
clothing with neither food nor fire. The nearby *Richmond* sent them a
tent and supplies the next morning. The men's bravery "saved the world
flight from indefinite postponement," the *Atlanta Constitution* cheered.

As the storms raged, Smith had time to ruminate on the speeches,
banquets, and public appearances that he knew would accompany their
successful return to the United States. Getting through Tokyo and Paris
had been difficult enough; now he would have millions of eyes of his
own countrymen staring at him. He sent a second message to General
Patrick in Washington requesting that "no entertainments, receptions,
or escorts be arranged for them previous to the completion of the round
the world flight by arrival of planes on the Pacific coast." Again, he received
no response.

On August 31, the storms relented and the sky turned clear and calm.
Shortly after four a.m., the four men climbed into their planes and began
warming up their engines. Smith, in the *Chicago*, attempted to take off
from the fjord but could not break free from the smooth water. After two
hours his plane rose slowly into the air, as if reluctant to be tested again.
Nelson followed close behind. Half an hour later, the planes flew into
fog and came out of it minutes later to find an iceberg directly ahead.
Both easily banked around it and continued through skies so clear that
they could see navy patrol boats stationed along their route thirty miles
before they reached them.

The planes passed the last patrol boat two hundred miles from the
North American coast. The skies were glorious, as if welcoming the men
home. Suddenly Smith felt his engine sputtering. His momentum bucked
like they had hit something. He scanned his instrument panel and found
the gasoline dial plummeting before his eyes. He craned his head to the
side, trying to see whether the plane was leaking fuel. Satisfied that it was

not, he guessed that the motor's main gasoline pump had failed. Smith pulled back the throttle. The engine, now thirsty for fuel, shook violently, threatening to stall. Hot oil began leaking out of the nose of the plane, smearing the sides of the aircraft. There was only one way left to send gasoline into the engine and give it enough power to make it to the shore. As a failsafe, Douglas had installed an emergency wobble pump in the rear cockpit of each World Cruiser that pulled liquid from the reserve tank and fed it by gravity into the engine. Designed as a last resort, the pump was operated purely by hand. If they were going to survive, Smith realized, then they would have to manually force each gallon of fuel into the engine as they soared over the final hours to North America.

Smith turned around in the cockpit to find that Arnold had already stripped himself to the waist and had his hands on the handle of the pump. He began pumping, knowing that their lives depended on it. When he pushed down, the engine hummed; each time he paused, it wobbled, as if one step closer to dying. The pump had become an iron lung, allowing the aircraft to breathe. Arnold pumped with his right arm as Smith kept them on course, every second punctuated by the rhythmic upstroke and downstroke of the pump. Arnold saw nothing of the world beneath him, felt nothing in his body, while Smith piloted the plane through ice fields and wind. After months of sampling all that the world had to offer, his focus had narrowed to one small piece of equipment that meant the difference between flying above the clouds and crashing into the ocean below.

He pumped without stopping for an hour until his arm grew numb from exhaustion. Fearing that he would soon no longer be able to lift his hand, he made a sling with his belt and attached it to the pump. He grabbed the sling with his other hand and carried on, now using both arms to press down. A few minutes later he felt a burning pain between his shoulders from where the sling dug into his skin. He grabbed a handkerchief, tied it around his neck, and kept going.

Sweat poured from his body despite the cold air. Each time he stopped for a second to catch his breath, the engine slowed and began to falter. In the front cockpit, Smith attempted to keep the plane steady. He looked at his control panel and saw that the earth-inductor compass, then considered the leading edge of technology, was no longer working. He and Arnold were fully on their own, unable to rely on anything but their own bodies to save them. With water stretching out in every direction as far as he could see, Smith aimed for the westward sun, betting that land was going to appear in that direction eventually.

They were an hour away from Ice Tickle, their destination on the Labrador coast, when they hit forty-mile-per-hour winds that forced Arnold to pump harder. The success of the trip, the pride of American aviation, their own lives—all of it now depended on the strength of a man who had been a backup on the flight, more interested in partying his way through the world than in proving it wrong. It was moments like these that he had dreamed of as a child, pushing him onto countless theater stages in hopes of adoration. Yet here he was, far from any spotlight, with no audience to play to. At a time when everything rested on him, Arnold found himself fortified by a deep sense of obligation, fearing letting Smith down more than crashing into the cold water below. He had flown around the world, enjoying all the pleasures he could find, only to realize that his most important performance was to be there for his friend. "Les has the strength of a lumberjack, otherwise he could never have done what he did," Smith later marveled. "It is wonderful what guts will do for a man."

Finally, after a 560-mile flight that lasted six hours and fifty-five minutes, Smith noticed puffs of black smoke rising from the *Richmond* sitting in the harbor. The ship's shrill whistle echoed and ricocheted off the rocks of the barren coves. Newspaper reporters crowded the deck of the destroyer, on hand to document the first successful westward crossing of the Atlantic. "The planes swept from the ocean like huge gray gulls, and flying low over the broad expanse of water, circled until they dropped their bright yellow buoys and floated lightly in the green water under the shelter of lofty ridges of rock," the Associated Press wrote.

The reporters soon learned from Smith how Arnold had kept them alive. A writer for the *San Francisco Examiner* found it poetic that, just one day before Labor Day, elbow grease had kept an extraordinary dream alive. "Underneath every wild piece of spectacularity, behind every fantastic achievement of romance and imagination, is some such piece of ordinary stupid fatiguing routine pumping-work," he wrote. "Such is the man driving rivets for a skyscraper, the bookkeeper adding figures for the big corporation, the sailor hauling a wet rope, the housewife cooking breakfasts and washing dishes. To some minds, it takes the flare out of romance; to others, it puts romance into the commonplace."

A naval scout plane attempted to take off from the cove below to escort them to their mooring but could not fight through the rough water. Instead, a small launch came out from the *Richmond* and waited as the men moored their aircraft to the buoys. The captain carried messages of congratulations. President Calvin Coolidge wrote that the squadron's "return to North American soil after circumnavigation of the world by air is an inspiration to the whole nation . . . your countrymen are proud of you."

Arnold, once a man who could not wait to let the world know how great he was, downplayed his efforts both to others and himself. "It was necessary to use the emergency hand pump—and four hours of that is hard on the arm" is all he said about his heroic feat in his diary that night, not elaborating on the fact that he had been unable to move his right arm after the men landed and had to undergo two hours of strenuous massaging by the ship's doctors before he could bring a fork to his mouth to eat.

Overcoming countless challenges, the men had safely returned to North America. They hugged each other, too overwhelmed by the moment to say anything for posterity. "We were just too darned happy for words," Smith later wrote. He was handed a second message, addressed to him alone, that came from Dwight F. Davis, the acting secretary of war. "Your bravery, hardihood and modesty have been worthy of the highest traditions of the army," he wrote. "More particularly to you, as a member of the flight, I desire to say that your courage, skill and determination have shown you to be a fit successor to the great navigators of the age of discovery."

A new era had begun.

CHAPTER TWENTY-FOUR

Home

THEY HAD NO idea what was in store for them.

When the American aviators had left Los Angeles five months earlier, their attempt to circle the world by air was considered a novelty, a literal flight of fancy that had little practical chance of completion. Packed crowds greeting their arrival in Tokyo, Paris, and London hinted at their celebrity but gave no indication how they were seen closer to home. Now, by finishing the race when all other nations had failed, the aviators were about to learn that they had been transformed into some of the most famous people in the country, taking their place among the movie stars America churned out to the waiting world. The send-offs they had in Seattle and Los Angeles paled in comparison to the full, gleaming glare of fame that burned on a level never before reached by men who a few years earlier were fixing cars, digging ditches, or selling pianos to make ends meet.

The first clue of their lost anonymity came in the isolated confines of the *Richmond* the day they landed in Ice Tickle. Although hungry and hoping for rest, the four remaining members of the squadron were called for a dinner with the crew of the ship at five o'clock. At six, they dined again with an audience of newspaper reporters hanging on their every word (the closest thing to a usable quote they pulled from Smith was his observation "The world flight is practically ended"). And at seven, they were called to the admiral's cabin for another private dinner, their third and last of the night. Smith, exhausted by the attention, feared it would be an omen of what lay ahead.

The next morning, they were up early repairing their planes and washing the oil off the *Chicago* and did not know that their pictures were on the front pages of newspapers nationwide. "With their arrival yesterday on the Atlantic coast of the North American continent the round-the-world-fliers of the United States Army Air Service completed the most marvelous achievement in the history of aviation to date—the virtual encircling of the globe in heavier-than-air machines," the Associated Press wrote in an article that greeted readers everywhere from the hills of Macon, Georgia, to the shores of Honolulu. The banner headline "Fliers Land on Continent" ran across the width of the *Minneapolis Morning Tribune* in four-inch-tall letters. In Lincoln, Nebraska, an editorial writer luxuriated in the blissful feeling that the underdog United States had proved itself superior. "In every respect Lieutenants Lowell H. Smith and Erik Nelson measured up to their large responsibilities and have written another glorious page in the history of American military achievement," he wrote. "Aviators of seven nations attempted it. America, alone, will realize her ambition." In London, the *Times*, too, picked up on the sense that the world's attitude toward America and Americans would be changed by the success of the flight. "American airship and the American nation are reaping a well-deserved reward," it noted. "The triumph of the Americans doubtless will be all the sweeter because they showed that particular generosity to their unsuccessful rivals."

The few who did not get caught up in the moment were relegated to the sidelines, their questions of why the successful completion of a world flight mattered yelled into the wind. "It can be done, apparently, but what of it?" asked a columnist for the *Alliance Times-Herald*, a small weekly paper in Nebraska. "[I am] strongly inclined to rank the victory with that of the man who went over the Niagara Falls in a barrel."

There was, of course, still the matter of crossing North America, which itself was not without risk. In his race across the United States a few years earlier, Smith had seen two men die while trying to cross the Rocky Mountains. Other pilots routinely lost their lives as they attempted to deliver the mail or find their way home in rough weather. Reaching their final destination on the West Coast required the aviators to cross the Midwest in late summer, a period when monstrous thunderstorms engulfed the plains, bringing the wrath of hail and wind.

MacLaren, who landed via steamship in Vancouver, British Columbia, the same day that the *Chicago* and *New Orleans* touched down on the other side of the continent, held out the small hope that something would prevent the squadron from reaching the West Coast. "I'll try again unless the Americans make it," he told reporters after he docked, not yet recovered from a tumultuous voyage in which his steamship ran into a fierce storm and left him wondering if the elements were determined to take his life one way or another. "If they succeed, there's no use of anybody else trying it."

The question of where, exactly, the race would end had hovered in the background of the flight for several weeks, as if the schedule makers in Washington did not want to tempt fate by putting anything down on paper. Los Angeles felt like the obvious end point, given that the squadron had taken off from Santa Monica's Clover Field. San Diego threw its hat into the ring, arguing that the initial test runs of the Douglas World Cruisers had taken off from its airfield, making it the true starting point. Seattle, however, became Washington's choice. General Patrick routed the flight path to terminate there, eliminating the twelve days that spring that the planes had been stuck undergoing repairs and final testing on the shores of Lake Washington from the records and making it appear that the American flight was that much faster.

Los Angeles—and all of California—was incensed. Letters of protest from the chambers of commerce in nearly every Southern California city poured into the White House, all calling on President Coolidge to do something. Friend Richardson, a former newspaper publisher and Quaker who had been elected California governor the year before on a platform of cutting spending, sent an official telegram to the White House to register his indignation. "California feels, with some justice, that flight can only end at official starting point to be complete." The *Los Angeles Times* ran articles on the decision every day for weeks, pleading the case to anyone who would listen. "Why, when Los Angeles was the actual starting point of the flight, should she be robbed of the glory of the finish?" asked one editorial. "Was not the flight made in Los Angeles–made planes, and did not 100,000 Southern California people gather to give the aviators the greatest send-off ever recorded? How can a circle be complete when the ends don't meet?"

On September 2, the two planes took off from Ice Tickle on a three-hundred-fifty-mile journey to Hawke's Bay, Newfoundland, where the destroyer *Ashburn* was waiting with fuel. They followed the coast through fog, skipping above the waves and at one point missing a steamer by just thirty-five feet. When the skies cleared, they spotted dozens of shipwrecks lying against unforgiving rocks, littering the coast with more wreckage than any other place they had seen other than Alaska. Fishermen waved up at them as they passed over colorful fields of small, striped buoys, each one marking a lobster trap.

Somewhere in the waters below them sped the navy cruiser ship *Lawrence* carrying a cargo of newspaper correspondents and photographers who had had more than their fill of the desolate Labrador landscape and were eager to return to new assignments in warmer places. While stuck in Canada, one *New York Times* reporter complained, "There are no trees or bushes or any living thing. There are no roads, no automobiles, no railroads . . . there are no cities, no towns, no villages." What the inhabitants did have, besides the occasional polar bear, were the region's namesake breed of dogs, some of which were smuggled aboard the ship by reporters as souvenirs. "One bought by a newspaper correspondent did not have its eyes open and is being fed by a nursing bottle," the *Times* reporter revealed.

Along for the ride as well were Locatelli and his men, who had accepted invitations to appear at the Waldorf Astoria in New York City before what was expected to be a crowd of admiring Italian Americans. As the *Lawrence* charged through the waters at an unheard of forty knots— equivalent to nearly forty-five land miles per hour—Locatelli, once an officer in the Italian navy, shouted his congratulations to its crew. "This is the fastest I have ever traveled in any navy or commercial craft through the water," he told a reporter for the *Cincinnati Enquirer*. "It is a marvelous performance."

The *Chicago* and the *New Orleans* reached Hawke's Bay nearly six hours later. After waiting for the fog to burn off the next morning, they were in the air again by eleven. Soon, they passed the *Richmond* and the other ships that had acted as their convoy across the Atlantic, all of them heading home. As they circled over the crowded commercial harbor at Pictou, their destination in Nova Scotia, they spotted a familiar plane floating below: the prototype Douglas World Cruiser, now rechristened the *Boston II* and with the squadron's emblem on the side.

The *Chicago* and *New Orleans* landed as every steamship and barge that had a whistle blew it to create an ear-rattling shrill. Cheering Canadians lined the shores, which were decorated with bunting and flags, while children held up signs that read *Welcome, World Fliers* and kilt-clad men played bagpipes. On the shore, Wade and Ogden were the first to greet them, and the six men, now reunited, were swiftly put into open-air cars and became the star attraction of a parade through the small city's downtown. At the end of the route, each aviator was prodded to stand up and give a short speech. It was "the first taste of the reception that was to follow us now all the way back to Seattle," Nelson wrote.

With the *Boston II* now with them, the squadron aimed south. Ahead lay the city of Boston, which had been given the honor of being the first to welcome the fliers back to American soil. A sudden rain squall followed by thick fog decreased visibility to just a few feet, forcing the men to leapfrog over trees and rocks that suddenly appeared in their path. Smith, fearing that they would hit tragedy just before their goal, waved off the idea that they needed to reach Boston that day and instead had the three planes land in the sheltered waters of Casco Bay, Maine, just off of Mere Point. Locals who spotted the planes came out in motorboats and put them up in summer rental cabins, freshly emptied out after Labor Day. Reporters eventually caught up with the fliers and rushed to the local store that had the town's one telephone line to call in copy while a Boy Scout troop guarded the planes.

The men, shocked at the outpouring of attention from everyone they came in contact with, did not want to leave. "We all remembered the mere passing interest which the American public had taken in [the flight]. . . . After all, the receptions given us in foreign countries were accorded us mainly because we were representatives of the Air Force of the United States of America who had been entrusted with an important and somewhat spectacular mission," Nelson wrote. "So as we winged our way down from Greenland we simply took it for granted that our countrymen would look upon our flight much like they had looked upon others, and little did we dream that what in some respects was to be the most thrilling part of our journey still lay before us."

A strong wind the following morning forced the men to refill their tanks, which was easier said than done in remote Maine. By noon, the squadron was ready to leave. An escort of ten planes, led by General Patrick, flew with them the two hours to Boston. They descended low over the city, amazed at the sight of tens of thousands of people crammed along the harbor and atop Bunker Hill. Fountains of water spouted from fire boats below as warships fired twenty-one-gun salutes. As soon as they landed, the six men were taken ashore in a small navy boat and their planes were lifted onto a dock to make the final switch between pontoons and wheels.

Someone in the welcoming committee shoved a microphone in Smith's face as soon as he stepped on shore. He looked at it with a blank stare, finally asking, "What am I supposed to do with this thing?," not realizing that his comments were being broadcast live to the crowd and over national radio. "General Patrick, or somebody, explained that Mother and Dad were out in Los Angeles listening in and that I was supposed to make a little speech," Smith later wrote. "I simply said: 'Hello, folks, I'm glad to be home,' and let it go at that."

For as long as Smith could remember, flight had been his way to escape the social demands of the world; now his skill had turned him into a public spectacle, and Smith felt lost as he struggled to adjust. "Whenever I get in front of these [microphones], my gas pump refuses to feed, lung compression drops to zero, my heart starts to knock, and the old think-box freezes," he later wrote. He had no way to escape. The six men were loaded into limousines and followed a cavalry guard through packed streets to the state capitol building, where they were officially greeted by the governor of Massachusetts. The mayor of Boston presented them with the keys to the city and inscribed watches; an American Legion group gave them swords; a citizens' group gave them silver bowls. Then they were back in the cars, following an escort of police on motorcycles to Boston Common, where a stage had been set up for them. Reporters shouted questions as they posed for photographs, and Smith again made a short speech that was broadcast on local radio to an audience that likely included a seven-year-old in the nearby suburb of Brookline named John F. Kennedy.

Shortly after Smith finished, a tall man in a tweed suit and a white straw hat strode up the side of the stage and introduced himself as Archibald Stuart-MacLaren. The British flier had arrived a few days earlier by train and wanted to be on hand to greet the American pilots who had been instrumental in getting a replacement plane to him. He thanked them and told them that he would soon be returning home, where he would begin to plan another world flight. "That's the English spirit," Smith wrote.

That night, each man was given his own suite at the luxurious Copley Plaza Hotel. Their telephones rang constantly and reporters shuffled in and out. A telegram from King George V in England arrived congratulating them on a "heroic undertaking," followed by one from the Prince of Wales. A radio microphone was set up, and each aviator gave a short account of the flight. "Messenger boys arriving every minute, and bell boys dashing around—the place was a madhouse for a while," Arnold wrote in his diary that night, reveling in the fun.

That evening, Arnold, Harding, and Wade slipped into the Majestic Theatre for a performance of the musical *Poppy*. Along with them was MacLaren, who found that he enjoyed the Americans' company even if they had bested him. At the end of the production's second act, W. C. Fields, the star of the show, came forward with his costar Madge Kennedy and told the audience that the world fliers were in attendance. A spotlight was turned on the box in which the men sat, and the audience stood up and cheered. The orchestra joined in, playing the "Star Spangled Banner." In a turnabout for a man who had once dreamed of his own name on a marquee, Arnold rose and gave a speech, thanking the crowd and cast members for the reception. "It was much easier to fly around the world than to get up to speak," he said. "We have been swept off our feet, and I can only thank you for my friends and myself."

While the other men enjoyed their time in the sun, Smith struggled to find solitude. He grew uneasy and fidgety, unable to anticipate what would happen next. He felt his life sliding off the track and wanted to return to the air, the place where everything made sense. The aviators remained three thousand miles away from their destination, and yet everyone behaved like they had done it. Smith had lived too long and had had too many close calls to tempt fate like that.

His growing discomfort was obvious. An advance officer for the flight, who, along with a photographer, would accompany the men for the remainder of their journey to Seattle, handed Smith a letter from Major Walter Glenn Kilner, one of the top-ranking men in the air service, that was both welcome and warning. "Our countrymen are very proud of you and your comrades and they will be eager to show you their appreciation for what you have done," he wrote. "Some demands will be made upon you which cannot be avoided. In these cases, remember that the Air Service is just as anxious as you to bring your wonderful undertaking to a quick and successful conclusion, but the eyes of the entire country will be critically focused upon you and your comrades and any show of resentment to what you may justly consider as unnecessary interference with the purpose of the flight will be noticed and commented upon."

The spectacle continued the next day. More than thirty-five thousand people crammed the streets leading to East Boston, where Logan

Airport—itself little more than a muddy field, three years away from its first scheduled passenger service—had opened eleven months earlier. Whole families came, many of whom had never seen an airplane up close, as hot dog vendors pushed carts through the crowd. "Small boys were everywhere, very much excited, intensely interested in planes and everything connected with them," the *Boston Globe* noted, devoting several pages to the arrival of the fliers. Countless men and women watched as Nelson tightened the bolts of his engine behind a security line of policemen and soldiers. "These are certainly confident-looking airplanes," one man told reporters. "They're powerfully built and they look substantial. The old-time machines were flimsy in comparison with these planes."

On September 8, Smith led the three planes down the runway at Logan Airport and up toward New York City. They flew over Arnold's hometown of New London, Connecticut, where a festival was going on in celebration. Ten planes joined them as an escort at Bridgeport, and the armada soon flew over Manhattan through clear blue skies and passed by the outstretched torch of the Statue of Liberty. When the aviators landed at Mitchel Field, the crowd of more than fifteen thousand mobbed General Patrick's plane, thinking it was one of the world fliers'. The planes in the squadron had to circle the runway twice as policemen cleared the field.

In a short speech in front of a crowd that included the Prince of Wales, Senator James Wadsworth Jr. told the aviators, "The world never forgets its pathfinders. Those who trod the wilderness and cross the seas filled with dangers are never forgotten by posterity." While he was speaking, police officers formed circles around each plane to prevent souvenir hunters from cutting off pieces of fabric and pocketing any equipment that could easily come off. That night, the men crowded into a small theater in Manhattan and heckled each other as they watched a montage of newsreel footage taken of them throughout the world.

The following day they flew through a driving rain over Philadelphia alongside an escort of planes, then headed toward Baltimore. When they were eight miles away from the city, Nelson's engine suddenly failed and he came down in a pasture. As the other planes circled, Nelson climbed out and found that one of the gears had been stripped. President Coolidge was waiting for them in Washington, so an escort plane landed next to the *New Orleans* and its pilot climbed out as Nelson climbed in. He took off, leaving Ogden with the downed plane and orders to fix it.

The squadron passed over downtown Baltimore, where the roofs of downtown office buildings were crammed with people looking for them and factory whistles shouted their greetings. An hour later, they landed at Bolling Field, where President Calvin Coolidge had stood waiting for them in the rain for nearly four hours. The president had passed the time inspecting the planes lined up at the airfield. At one point he tugged on a propeller, sending air service officers rushing forward to warn him that he was about to lose an arm. When aides asked him if he would like to leave and attend the other events on his schedule that day, Coolidge reportedly said, "Not on your life, I'll wait all day if necessary." The president shook hands and posed for pictures with the world fliers, then listened as Smith showed him the aircraft and explained how they worked.

While they were talking, General Billy Mitchell—the man who had envisioned the world flight in a Hail Mary attempt to save American aviation—appeared in full uniform, including riding crop. For once in his long career, he did not immediately walk over to the crowd of reporters to make himself part of the story, nor did he join the aviators whose lives he had changed. Instead, he kept quietly to the side and watched, taking in the scene. The most powerful man in the nation was feet away, standing in clear awe of pilots whose lives had been all but anonymous six months earlier. American-built planes, which would not have existed if not for Mitchell and his idea of a world flight, were now the envy of the world. America, which had seemed destined to be left behind, now had a chance to shape the future that Mitchell saw coming.

The following days were a whirlwind. In Arlington, Virginia, the aviators dropped flowers at the Tomb of the Unknown Soldier, dedicated three years earlier, then rode in a parade down Pennsylvania Avenue. In Dayton, Ohio, the squadron landed at McCook Field, not far from where the Wright brothers had tested their aircraft, and were swarmed by men they had been stationed with before being chosen for the flight. Out of the crowd came Martin and Harvey, who congratulated them on completing the circuit that they all had started. Harding was mobbed by his fellow mechanics, and Nelson happily reunited with his dog, Nome.

They then followed a circuitous path westward, dipping as far south as El Paso, Texas, in order to avoid the summer thunderstorms over the Rocky Mountains, and continuing westward to Tucson, where they received gifts of Navajo blankets at a banquet held in their honor. On

September 22, Smith took the lead as the planes soared into the morning sun, with the purple peaks of the Rincon Mountains behind them. As Smith flew over the desert that he had once raced across in an automobile, he scanned ahead for the familiar landmarks of home. "We had been gone a long time," he later told a reporter. "We had crossed vast continents and distant seas. We had passed through experiences where we lived a lifetime in a day. . . . Now it seems like a dream."

The crowd at Rockwell Field in San Diego spotted the planes just before ten in the morning. On the ground, Smith's mother stood on tiptoe waving her handkerchief with tears in her eyes while her husband beamed next to her. "I'm proud, and I don't care who knows it!" he yelled to the sky. When the planes landed, Smith's friends hoisted him in their arms and began parading him around. "Let me down, fellows, I want to see my mother first!" he shouted. That night, the men slept under the red roof of the Hotel del Coronado, listening to the sounds of the ocean, knowing that they were the only people in history ever to fly across it.

When the squadron reached Los Angeles the next day, a crowd estimated at between one hundred thousand and a quarter million people crammed onto Clover Field. The men were mobbed. Spectators knocked down the fences and police officers who stood in their way. When the melee was over, parts of Smith's shirt had been clipped off by souvenir hunters, and Harding had three cracked ribs from being embraced by a large, overenthusiastic man he never saw again.

Nelson searched for Donald Douglas in the crowd, yelling, "I want to congratulate that boy! He sure does know how to build airplanes!" Editorial writers nationwide hailed Douglas as a genius, and the vanguard of more to come. "European aeronautic authorities belittled the American Machine," a columnist in Dayton, Ohio, wrote. "They maintained that airplane design had not yet reached a state of perfection where metals and fabrics could stand the comparatively sudden changes from Arctic blizzard with gales and zero-minus temperatures to the monsoons and burning heat of the Asiatic deserts. Performance has silenced these critics." Douglas, in an essay published a few days earlier, wrote that the benefits of the American flight would soon extend to living standards the world over. "Such a flight and other attempts of a similar character will hasten the day when the general public will use with confidence the unquestionable advantages of aviation and thus add more years to man's life and more wealth to the world," he wrote.

Douglas Fairbanks and Mary Pickford, the two most famous actors in the country, welcomed the men on a stage decorated with a globe fashioned out of flowers. A reporter stopped Harding on the way to a hotel that night, and he could barely contain his excitement. "Gee whiz, what a wonderful reception this is," he said. "Kinda thought that we'd had so many that nothing could make much of an impression, but this sure got under my hide . . . it seems to me now that it wasn't more than a week or so ago that I rode down here every day to go down to the Douglas Company and look after my ship." That night, the men fell asleep in hotel rooms holding copies of the *Los Angeles Post-Record* and its editorial addressed to them: "You are young, now. The glory and the satisfaction of achievement is yours. But in other days and years to come, when you are old men and memories take the place of achievement and world-flying has become an everyday instance, a great contentment shall be yours. You were the first!"

The final days of the flight were hazy, even to the men who lived them. When they were outside of San Francisco, Wade's battery died and he had to make an emergency landing in a fairground. A young man in a truck drove up to the airplane and offered to take any parts out of his engine that Wade needed. Wade saw the battery was similar enough to work and was soon back in the air. San Francisco, alone out of the cities they visited, offered no parades or speeches, though the mayor gave each man a check for $1,250.

They pressed on and soon saw Mount Rainier in the distance. At Smith's signal, the planes spread out in formation so that no plane was ahead of the others. The squadron landed that way on September 28, 1924, touching the ground at Sand Point Field in unison before a crowd of fifty thousand. When asked by a reporter for his first reaction to completing the flight around the world, Smith said, "We would not undertake another world flight for a million dollars, unless ordered to do so, now that it is over. . . . All of our big worries are over, with the exception of making speeches."

Someone noticed Martin standing in the sea of people and a great chant went up for him to join the pilots on the stage. He finally agreed, weeping as he reached the microphone. "I don't belong in this celebration," he said. "I came here just as one of you to honor and greet these men." The crowd again chanted his name, and he choked back tears. "I realize better than any of you, the courage, hardihood and stick-to-itiveness that these men needed to complete the flight. I certainly hate to face this crowd today for if my flight was a disappointment to you, it was a much keener one to me."

In the following weeks, the men crossed the country on a train tour, celebrated as heroes wherever they went. In Ohio, they met Orville Wright, who was fifty-three at the time and living a quiet life in the home he shared with his sister, Katharine. In Chicago, the mayor of the city gave each man his own Packard during a rally at the packed Chicago Auditorium. Finally, they returned to Dayton, where each man said his goodbyes and left for his next assignment.

They had flown a total of 26,345 miles over 363 hours and 7 minutes, averaging 72.5 miles per hour. Over 175 days, they had been the first to fly across the Pacific; had braved icebergs and deserts, mountains and swamps; had nearly been killed by engine failure and disease; had been greeted by kings and fishermen, soldiers and mothers; had lived to tell the tale of crossing the Atlantic through fog; and had returned to Seattle to show the world that it could be done.

"Other men will fly around the earth," an admiral said when they landed in San Diego. "But never again will anybody fly around it for the first time."

EPILOGUE

"The Fight Is Just Beginning"

A COLD JANUARY rain dripped down the rotunda of the Capitol Building as a black car carrying Wade and Arnold eased to a stop. Reporters in dark suits and fedoras, oblivious to the weather, called out questions as the two aviators stepped out of the vehicle. In the four months since they had landed in Seattle, their celebrity had grown. The two men were now in the middle of a lecture tour, delighting crowds city by city with tales from their flight. Two days earlier, they were at the Hotel Walton in Center City, Philadelphia, telling the members of the chamber of commerce that the city would fall behind if they did not have a municipal airport. The day before that, they were in Boston, talking from noon to night about the coming age of aviation.

Now, as they walked along the marble floors of Congress, they readied themselves to face an audience that was not going to be as friendly. Put on the spot by Billy Mitchell's criticisms of the nation's air capabilities, the House of Representatives had called an inquiry into military spending on aircraft and whether it was adequate to meet the needs of a future war. If the men made a good showing in front of the House panel, it could mean millions of dollars for aviation, fulfilling the promise of their flight. Failing to provide solid answers to barbed questions, however, could make their accomplishment seem like nothing more than a stunt, signifying once again that Americans were willing to do anything for attention.

Clad in their dress uniforms, Wade and Arnold entered the packed hearing room. Congressional representatives and spectators alike applauded as they took their seats at the long table facing the panel. Over the next hour, Wade and Arnold described how their flight around the world had changed their perception of what aircraft could do. No longer was it out of the realm of possibility for a plane to cross the Pacific,

Wade said. Now the question was how many planes there would be and how quickly they could strike. "Where there is air, airplanes can go," he said. "If the route differed little from ours, flight could be made at any time and there are no obstacles to large fleets making the trip. Fleets of planes can fly over the Pacific from the American mainland to Asia in forty flying hours."

The committee members asked if there was the potential for air attacks against the United States. The world flight "proves that such a thing is possible," Arnold replied. The answer hung in the air. Protected by the width of two oceans, America had always thought its fortress of distance allowed it to choose whether to be a part of the world community or remain in isolation. Now the country's own pilots had proved that its hopes that it could be forever left alone were foolish. Left unsaid was the fear that Japan, the country that had welcomed the world fliers with a parade down the streets of Tokyo, would use the speed and stealth of airplanes to further its military ambitions at the expense of the United States.

Over the following weeks, the focus of the inquiry shifted to Mitchell. The success of the world flight swelled his sense of what was possible, and he began arguing that any military dollar not directed to aviation was wasted, a sign of either incompetence or greed among the military elite. Though he was a student of the future, Mitchell never learned from his own past. Before he knew it, he was committing the same mistakes as before, with similar results. He antagonized those whose support he needed, too full of righteousness to mollify another person's ego. His career stalled at a time when the world flight should have given it momentum. By March, he had said too many impolite things and made too many barbed comments, and he found himself demoted to colonel. He was unfazed. "The fight is just beginning," he told reporters.

He set up demonstrations before congressional representatives simulating aircraft attacks on battleships and ground troops, at one point bragging that the machine gunners could tear only one small hole in the fabric of a plane's wing while the plane dropped bombs capable of sending a ship to the bottom of the sea. Despite the mounting evidence of his support, he lost some of the few friends he had left in positions that mattered, and the inquiry ended without any increase in funding. "He was too dogmatic, too audacious, too reckless in his conclusions," the *New York Times* wrote in an editorial. The beat reporters still liked him, if only because he made good headlines.

Mitchell stewed throughout the summer. In August, the navy attempted the first nonstop flight from the US mainland to Hawaii. Two flying boats took off from San Francisco and flew slowly past Alcatraz Island and into the winds blowing through the Golden Gate. Within hours, they had run out of fuel. After losing track of the support ships stationed along the route, the aircraft landed in the Pacific, and drifted for ten days until they reached Hawaiian shores. Weeks later, the USS *Shenandoah*—the first rigid airship built in the United States, and the first in the world to be filled with helium—was on a tour of Midwest state fairs when it ran into a sudden early morning squall in rural Ohio and crashed, killing fourteen of the forty-three men on board.

Two aviation disasters, one on the heels of the other, pulled Mitchell out of his cage. He went on the offensive again, using the newspaper reporters who hovered around him to get Washington to listen. "These incidents are the direct result of the incompetency, criminal negligence and almost treasonable administration of the national defense by the Navy and War Departments," he said. "The bodies of my former companions in the air moulder under the soil in America, and Asia, Europe, and Africa, many, yes, a great many, sent there directly by official stupidity."

The War Department court-martialed Mitchell within days, charging him with "conduct of a nature to bring discredit upon the military service." The trial was a public spectacle. Letters poured in voicing support for Mitchell from all parts of the country. Mitchell's wife, Betty, often made a show of pulling out stacks of envelopes and writing replies during courtroom breaks. Others took to live props. Cowboys from Texas sent a turkey and offered their services to guard him as he testified. Another day, the humorist Will Rogers sat in the gallery to show his support of Mitchell, who had given Rogers his first ride in an airplane.

Yet little of it mattered. The military court focused on the charge of insubordination, not the validity of Mitchell's criticisms. "Is such a man a safe guide?" asked the prosecution in its closing remarks. "Is he a constructive person or is he a loose talking imaginative megalomaniac?" Finally, the court tribunal—which included a young Douglas MacArthur—delivered its verdict: a suspension of rank, command, and duty and a forfeiture of all pay for five years. Rather than face such an indignity, Mitchell resigned. Though his onetime antagonist Theodore Roosevelt Jr. occasionally called and asked for his thoughts on aircraft and tactics, Mitchell felt his influence wane over the following decade. He grew bitter, falling deeper into resentment as he felt the world he had hoped to build slip away.

PERHAPS BECAUSE HE was solely focused on military aviation, Mitchell missed the signs that the future he was describing had already arrived. In the happy afterglow of the world flight, in February 1925, Congress passed the Kelly Act, which allowed the US Post Office to pay private air companies to deliver the mail, with the rates based upon weight.

Rarely has a bill that seemed so trivial had such a long tail of consequences. Within months, dozens of airlines formed, each of them looking to benefit from the first subsidy of commercial aviation in the nation's history. In Michigan, Henry Ford created the Ford Air Transport Service and was awarded the first contract to carry mail between Detroit and Chicago. In Macon, Georgia, the company that would eventually grow into Delta Air Lines was formed. In St. Louis, the Robertson Aircraft Corporation—which would one day become American Airlines—began carrying mail with a young man named Charles Lindbergh as its chief pilot. In New York City, Pitcairn Aviation—the ancestor of today's United Airlines—started as a service bringing letters and packages from Manhattan to Atlanta. The Kelly Act "was an aviation Magna Carta, for it turned virtually the entire job of flying the mail over to private contractors who would bid for the mail routes," aviation historian Robert J. Sterling wrote.

Few individuals benefited more from the surge of money flowing toward aviation than Donald Douglas. The round-the-world flight cemented his reputation as a young genius, and within months of the flight's conclusion he was widely described in newspapers as "the internationally known airplane builder." He signed new contracts with the navy and the Army Air Service, delivering 25 cargo planes and 246 observation planes that were variations of the World Cruiser.

Commercial aircraft soon followed. In 1934, Douglas introduced the DC-3, the first passenger aircraft that could cross the country. The nation fell in love with the idea of safe speedy travel, a futuristic dream where passengers could eat steak and drink cocktails while cruising in the sky. Americans took to the air in record numbers, bolstering corporate profitability while allowing companies to reduce costs. Orville Wright came to inspect a DC-3 when it stopped near his home in Ohio. "They've built everything possible into this machine to make it a safe and stable vehicle of the air," he said. More than thirteen thousand DC-3s were built, and some remain in use as cargo planes today.

With the successful world flight as his calling card, Douglas began expanding his company, building manufacturing plants throughout the Los Angeles area and testing them over fields of palm trees and orange groves. Over the next two decades, Douglas Aircraft grew from a sixty-person operation to the fourth-largest company in the country, its office buildings so big that secretaries put on roller skates to deliver mail through the sprawl. At the height of production, during World War II, the company's El Segundo division alone employed more than 21,000 people, many of them women working on assembly lines capable of churning out twelve planes a day. Thanks in large part to Douglas Aircraft, the United States built approximately 300,000 planes between 1941 and 1945, an exponential increase for a nation that had fewer than 3,000 military aircraft at the time of Pearl Harbor.

The company's business cards carried a logo depicting three planes circling the globe, a constant reminder of the world flight that had proved the superiority of American engineering. Douglas sold the company to McDonnell Aircraft in 1967, forming what was known as McDonnell Douglas. The newly formed defense company retained the spirit of the Douglas logo, replacing one of the airplanes with a missile. A hundred years later, the remnants of the world flight can still be found at Boeing, which bought McDonnell Douglas in 1997. Its logo now depicts a stylized plane and globe, an homage to the flight that once made Douglas a household name and changed the world's opinion about the quality of American aircraft.

FOR NINE MONTHS in 1924, the world's attention was focused on a handful of pilots willing to test whether it was possible to circle the globe by air. But the race to fly around the world involved many more people than those who sat in the cockpits. In the following years, as the airplane played a greater role in swaying the course of history, the men involved in the world flight scattered in different directions. General Patrick, who approved Mitchell's idea of a world flight, retired as chief of the air corps in 1927. He died at Walter Reed Hospital in Washington, DC, in 1942 at the age of seventy-eight. The US Air Force's base at Cocoa Beach, Florida, was named after him in 1950, and is now known as Patrick Space Force Base. Donald Douglas died in February 1981 at the age of eighty-eight. Public parks in Long Beach and Santa Monica are named in his honor. Douglas Aircraft's El Segundo plant, in the shadow of Los Angeles International Airport, was remade into the Los Angeles Air Force Base in 1962 and now houses the Space Systems Command of the US Space Force.

Billy Mitchell, the prophet of American aviation, died in 1936, still worried that his country was doomed to fall behind in aviation. Five years later, the Japanese attacked Pearl Harbor in just the way he had foretold. Nearly twenty-four hundred Americans were killed and twenty-one ships were either sunk or significantly damaged. A total of 347 aircraft were damaged or lost, cleaving more than a tenth off the American military's total airpower in the span of a few hours. Twenty-three years after America burned its surplus aircraft in Europe because it saw no need for them, the country found itself in a war defined by airpower. The nation raced to adapt. Four months after the Japanese raid, sixteen American bombers led by James Doolittle attacked Tokyo, a mission meant to both inflict revenge and show that America had the capacity to fight back in the air. Mitchell had been right, though no one had listened.

Mitchell's attempts to warn others turned him into a sort of folk hero after the war. The film *The Court-Martial of Billy Mitchell* premiered in 1955, with the actor Gary Cooper in the role of Mitchell. The film was nominated for an Academy Award for best story and screenplay but ultimately lost to the musical *Interrupted Melody*.

The world flight touched lives far from America as well. Pedro Zanni, the Argentine pilot who attempted to follow MacLaren's route in a faster plane, got as far as Japan but turned back because of the weather over the Pacific. He died in January 1942. Brito Pais, the Portuguese aviator who saw his flight as an echo of his country's great age of exploration, worked as a flight instructor for several years and died in a plane crash in 1934. Antonio Locatelli, the Italian pilot, caused riots in New York City when he spoke at the Waldorf Astoria following his rescue in the North Atlantic. He eventually returned to Italy and rose through the Fascist Party, pushing for the country to expand its empire by invading Ethiopia. At an air base in Lechemti in 1936, he was killed when his squadron was attacked by Ethiopian guerrilla fighters in what became known as the Lechemti massacre. A shelter in the Tre Cime Natural Park in the

Italian Alps is named after him. Georges Pelletier d'Oisy, the French pilot who became a world sensation, attempted to set records for other long-distance flights, including the fastest from Paris to India, and briefly became an actor. He died in Morocco in 1953.

Archibald Stuart-MacLaren, who nearly won the race, returned to England and was seen as a cautionary tale for falling short of British expectations. In interviews and speeches, he told audiences that he was in the end beaten by fog alone. A successful flight would have made him a national hero and perhaps led to a knighthood. Instead, his career stalled, and he received no further promotions. By 1925 he was back at a Royal Air Force base in Egypt. He retired in 1930 due to a heart condition and died in Portugal in 1943 at the age of fifty-one. In an irony for a man who hoped to fly for the glory of England, his most ardent supporters were Americans, who realized how close he had come to succeeding. "MacLaren's effort was a splendid sporting attempt," the 1925 *Aircraft Year Book* noted. "His organization and supply arrangements were necessarily inadequate. That he got as far as he did was regarded as remarkable under the circumstances."

The eight American pilots who were part of the record-breaking flight scattered in the years following their unexpected victory. Alva Harvey, Martin's mechanic, was a test pilot for the B-17 Flying Fortress, which went on to drop more bombs than any other American aircraft during World War II. He later flew US diplomats to Moscow during negotiations for the Lend-Lease program. He retired from the air force in 1957 and died in 1992 in Virginia.

Martin, who survived alongside Harvey in the Alaskan outback, remained popular in the army despite the crash that prevented him from completing the world flight. He rose through the ranks and was eventually put in charge of air defenses in Hawaii. With a colleague, he wrote a confidential report identifying the vulnerability of Pearl Harbor to an early-morning enemy air raid. The report's conclusions were ignored and the additional aircraft he requested sent elsewhere. Following the Japanese attack in December 1941, Martin was briefly relieved of duty. A commission headed by Owen Roberts, a justice of the Supreme Court, exonerated him of any responsibility and he spent the remainder of the war in Washington State, supervising training for bomber pilots. He died in 1954 and is buried in Arlington National Cemetery, next to his son.

Leigh Wade, the fashion-forward *Mayflower* descendant who gave the order to sink his plane in the Atlantic, resumed his life as a test pilot. In 1940, he attempted to fly from New York City to Rio de Janeiro, then worked as a sales executive for Consolidated Aircraft. Following Pearl Harbor, he rejoined the service and served at an air base in Cuba. He died in 1991.

Ogden, who had rarely left the South before being picked for the world flight, discovered that he loved the thrill of exploration. He and Wade briefly attempted to become the first to fly to the North Pole in 1926, racing against crews headed by Richard Byrd and Roald Amundsen. He remained famous enough that in 1928, articles announcing his engagement ran in both the *New York Times* and the *Los Angeles Times*. After running a short-lived company called Ogden Shuttle Airlines that flew between Southern California, Nevada, Arizona, and New Mexico, he worked at Lockheed Aircraft for years. He retired from the company in 1965 and died in 1986.

Erik Nelson, who helped Douglas refine the World Cruiser, quit the army in 1928 at the age of forty in frustration due to his relatively low rank and slim possibility of promotion. He joined Boeing as a sales manager. The day after Pearl Harbor, he reenlisted at the age of fifty-three and helped create maintenance plans for the first B-29 squadrons in India and China. He retired in 1946 with the rank of brigadier general and became an adviser to Swedish Intercontinental Airlines. He died of cancer in Honolulu in 1971 at the age of eighty-one.

Harding, the Southern mechanic who could not comprehend the extremes of heat and cold he endured on the world flight, spent the rest of his life in temperate climates. Among his stops were Dallas, where he sold aircraft accessories. He died in the beachside city of La Jolla, California, in 1968. The US Air Force spread his ashes over the Pacific.

Leslie Arnold, who saved Smith's life and his own by operating a hand pump for hours, leaned on his gregariousness to become an executive at several airlines, including the forerunner of Trans World Airlines (now a part of American Airlines) and Eastern Airlines. He married the silent-film actress Priscilla Dean in 1928. During World War II, he headed the army's air freight program in Europe and was responsible for ferrying supplies to Normandy during the D-Day invasion in 1944. He died in his home in New Jersey in 1961 at the age of sixty-six, less than a hundred and fifty miles from the hometown he always wanted to escape.

Lowell Smith, the reluctant commander of the flight, slipped into the background as soon as he could. He remained in the military for the rest of his career, though his ability to fly was hampered after a propeller sheared off part of his middle finger in Honolulu in 1925. With his hand badly mangled, he calmly stepped back and said, "Shut her off, Sergeant, please."

In the early 1940s, he served as the commander of Davis-Monthan Air Force Base in Tucson, which was built on the same spot where his squadron had landed near the conclusion of their world flight. There, he oversaw training for bombing groups in World War II. Throughout his life, speed—whether he was behind the wheel of a race car or in the cockpit of an airplane—served as the release valve for the emotions he never allowed himself to show. In a bitter irony for a man who had helped lead his country into the future of transportation, he fell while on a horseback ride through the nearby Santa Catalina Mountains in 1945 and died shortly after. He was fifty-three years old.

Though it was impossible to fathom when the round-the-world flight was on the front page of newspapers around the globe, the drama of the race and the triumph of the aviators involved began to fade from the public's mind within a few years, overshadowed by faster planes and bigger personalities. Lindbergh's solo flight east across the Atlantic in 1927 eclipsed their accomplishment, making him the most famous pilot in the world. As they grew older, the surviving members of the squadron closely followed the Mercury and Apollo space programs, seeing in the lives of the chosen astronauts parallels to their own experiences a generation earlier. "These orbital flights are enough to make one want to continue living at least long enough to enjoy space travel personally," Wade wrote in 1967.

The planes, which outlasted the best European aircraft and convinced Americans that flight was the nation's destiny, are all that remain. The burned wreckage of the *Seattle* was discovered in 1967 and is on display at a small museum in Alaska. The *New Orleans* sits in the Museum of Flying in Santa Monica next to the runways where it once took off on the flight around the world. And the *Chicago* until recently could be found on the floor of the Smithsonian's National Air and Space Museum in Washington, DC, often overlooked by visitors crowding around nearby attractions such as Lindbergh's *Spirit of St. Louis* and the Apollo 11 command module. The museum is currently in the middle of a multiyear renovation that will end in 2026. Until then, the plane that once captured the world's attention sits in storage in suburban Maryland, tended to by preservationists who are keeping the machine that changed the nation's future alive.

ACKNOWLEDGMENTS

This book is the product of many hands, all of whom helped me tell the story of a remarkable group of pilots.

Paul Silbermann and Elizabeth C. Borja at the National Air and Space Museum helped field many of my questions and were instrumental in locating digitized versions of Leslie Arnold's diary from the flight. Vanessa Ascough, Archibald Stuart Charles Stuart-MacLaren's granddaughter, kindly shared her family's history and photos. I look forward to her upcoming biography of her grandfather, which she plans to publish in the next few years. Special thanks are also due to Michael Lombardi at Boeing, Ted Huetter and Ashley Mead at the Museum of Flight, and Dr. William Crossley at Purdue University.

This was my first time working with the wonderful team at Mariner Books and HarperCollins and I'm grateful for the care and attention they put into this project. Special thanks to Lisa Glover for shepherding this book from manuscript to the finished product you have in your hands, and to copyeditor Tracy Roe, who not only saved me from many embarrassing errors and typos but was dedicated enough to confirm the phase of the Moon on a particular day in 1924. I am also thankful for Megan Wilson, who managed the publicity for this book, and Tavia Kowalchuk, who steered its marketing.

It all came together under the genius guidance of Matt Harper, who as editor saw this project for what it could be even before I did. I'm thankful for the time he spent going over the many paths this story could take, and for his sense of humor and humility.

If you look at my books—a conversational approach to sleep science; an epic family saga set against the beautiful backdrop of Malibu; a medical thriller rooted in a crisis in public health; a western that explains why a handful of museums have such impressive collections of dinosaur fossils; and this book of adventure and aviation—it can be hard to see a connective tissue. Luckily, I have the support of a brilliant pair of agents I am fortunate to call friends, Larry Weissman and Sascha Alper, who are willing to help me go wherever curiosity takes me. Special thanks also to Jack and Vivian Weismann, who are now rockstars in the eyes of our children, and Josie Freedman at CAA, who has been a champion of all of my books.

I am also thankful for the love and friendship of Diane Randall; Ryan Randall; Emily Davis; Robert, Gina, and Lucy Scott; Tony and Maryanne Petrizio; Sam Mamudi; Matt Craft; Clint and Nina Litton; Lauren Young; Jeff Strickland; and Alan Yang.

Of course, none of this would be possible if not for my best friend and partner, Megan Randall, and our kind and hilarious children, Henry and Isla. Thank you for making my dreams possible.

NOTES

This book rests on the work of academics, historians, and journalists who chronicled the start of the aviation age and covered the round-the-world flight from its inception to completion. I am incredibly fortunate that, though they are all deceased, the fliers themselves have a voice in this narrative. Their thoughts, family histories, and day-to-day actions over the more than 175 days of flying time come from the book they collaborated on with writer Lowell Thomas. Titled *The First World Flight: As Related by Lieutenants Smith, Nelson, Wade, Arnold, Harding, and Ogden to Lowell Thomas*, the book was a bestseller when it came out in 1925. I was lucky to find a beat-up copy on eBay, its pages yellowed but readable. If not otherwise noted, all personal thoughts and scenes involving the aviators are drawn from their own account of their flight.

Another book that I relied on was *Around the World in 175 Days: The First Round-the-World Flight*, by Carroll V. Glines. A former US Air Force colonel before becoming the curator of the Dolittle Military Aviation Library at the University of Texas at Dallas, Glines, through his work, helped provide a sense of the technical aspects of the planning of the flight and the aircraft involved.

1. The Prophet

1   *the soft Hawaiian sun:* "Billy Mitchell's Prophecy," *American Heritage* 13, no. 2 (1962).

1   *the aircraft were surplus:* Maurer Maurer, *Aviation in the U.S. Army, 1919–1939* (Washington, DC: Office of Air Force History, 1987).

2   *a newspaper columnist complained:* "Army in Need of More Flyers," *Nashville Journal*, October 6, 1922.

2   *he would predict that:* Douglas Waller, *A Question of Loyalty* (New York: HarperCollins, 2004).

3   *"very likable and has":* Lester Cohen and Emile Gauvreau, *Billy Mitchell: Founder of Our Air Force and Prophet Without Honor* (New York: E. P. Dutton, 1942).

3   *"Mitchell's realization that Nome":* Maurer Maurer and Calvin F. Senning, "Billy Mitchell, the Air Service, and the Mingo War," *Airpower Historian* (April 1965).

4   *"made such spectacular flights"*: Tom Crouch, "The Aeronautic Society of New York and the Birth of American Aviation, 1908–1918," *New York History* 92, no. 4 (2011).

4   *above the uncaring farmland*: David McCullough, *The Wright Brothers* (New York: Simon and Schuster, 2016).

4   *total of forty-nine*: G. R. Simonson, "The Demand for Aircraft and the Aircraft Industry, 1907–1958," *Journal of Economic History* (September 1960).

5   *"Everything aeronautical coming out"*: "American in World Flight," *New York Times*, July 11, 1914.

5   *"Now the offensive value"*: Alfred F. Hurley, "Young 'Billy' Mitchell and the 'Old Army,'" *Airpower Historian* 8, no. 1 (January 1961).

6   *"not be entrusted with"*: Karl R. Schrader, "'Good Men . . . Running Around in Circles': Benjamin Foulois, Billy Mitchell, and the Fight for the Future of the Army Air Service," *Airpower Historian* 58, no. 3 (Fall 2011).

7   *"No one ever had"*: Anthony J. Epifano, "Heirs to a Proud Legacy," *Citizen Airman* (April 1989).

8   *"the shooting of wild"*: *United States Naval Institute Proceedings* 45 (1919).

8   *"The spirit de corps"*: John Lancaster, *The Great Air Race: Glory, Tragedy, and the Dawn of American Aviation* (New York: W. W. Norton, 2022).

8   *"The General Staff knows"*: John T. Correll, "Billy Mitchell and the Battleships," *Air and Space Forces*, July 21, 2021.

8   *"The Navy doesn't need"*: Samuel F. Wells Jr., "William Mitchell and the Ostfriesland: A Study in Military Reform," *Historian* 26, no. 4 (August 1964).

10   *"the Washington Monument had"*: "2,000-Pound Bombs from Army Planes Sink Ostfriesland," *New York Times*, July 22, 1921.

10   *"is pleasant to remember"*: "Sinking the Ostfriesland," *New York Times*, July 23, 1921.

10   *"I once saw a man"*: "2000-Pound Bombs from Army Planes Sink Ostfriesland," *New York Times*, July 22, 1921.

2. A Reverend's Son

12   *"may break every rule"*: "Dealing with Airplanes," *Los Angeles Times*, October 9, 1919.

13   *More than fifteen thousand people*: "Kelly Re-Fueling Test Is Fatal to Carnival Aviator," *Houston Post*, November 19, 1923.

15   *"Lowell to many people"*: Lowell Thomas, *The First World Flight: As Related by Lieutenants Smith, Nelson, Wade, Arnold, Harding, and Ogden* (Boston: Houghton Mifflin, 1925).

16   *in an air show:* "Captain Smith and His Wrecked Plane," *Oregon Daily Journal,* April 22, 1919.

16   *"a demigod off for":* "Secret Bared As Homeward Flight Starts," *San Francisco Examiner,* July 7, 1919.

16   *"Science has passed another":* "First Photos Rushed to S.F. for 'Examiner,'" *San Francisco Examiner,* July 7, 1919.

17   *"I wanted to fly":* "Flying Parson Takes Chances," *Idaho Statesman,* October 18, 1919.

19   *only African American pilot:* Phil Keith and Tom Clavin, *All Blood Runs Red: The Legendary Life of Eugene Bullard—Boxer, Pilot, Soldier, Spy* (New York: Hanover Square Press, 2020).

3. The Whole World Round

20   *"I looked at the":* Nellie Bly, *Around the World in Seventy-Two Days and Other Writings* (New York: Penguin Classics, 2014).

20   *Mears circled the globe:* "A Run Around the World," *New York Times,* August 8, 1913.

20   *"We affirm that the":* F. T. Marinetti, *Futurist Constitution and Manifesto* (Milan, Italy: Poligrafia Italiana, 1909).

21   *"Around-the-world travelers":* Joyce E. Chaplin, *Round About the Earth: Circumnavigation from Magellan to Orbit* (New York: Simon and Schuster, 2013).

21   *"The opinion of certain":* Eugene S. Ragger, "World Flight First Planned by Belgian in Year 1804," *New York Times,* June 1, 1924.

21   *Italian naturalist and Jesuit:* Thomas O'Brien Hubbard, ed., *The Aerial Ship* (London: Aeronautical Society of Great Britain, 1910).

22   *"I always fancied the":* S. C. Gwynne, *His Majesty's Airship* (New York: Scribner, 2023).

22   *"We will make those":* Murray Simon, "The Log of the Airship America—A Thrilling Record," *New York Times,* November 6, 1910.

23   *"Such an attempt would":* Orville Wright, "Barely Possible to Cross Atlantic in Air, but Attempt Would Be Height of Folly," *Aberdeen Herald,* May 26, 1914.

23   *"The English, who were":* "American in World Flight."

23   *"An airplane in the":* Pete Fusco, *The Crowd Pleasers: A History of Airshow Misfortunes from 1910 to the Present* (New York: Skyhorse, 2018).

23   *announced that he was:* "Beachey to Quit Flying," *New York Times,* March 9, 1913.

24   *climbed into the cockpit:* "Beachey Killed in a Taube Drop," *New York Times,* March 15, 1915.

24 *essentially a flying boat:* Norman Polmar, "The Navy's First," *Naval History* 25, no. 1 (January 2011).

25 *"I rushed outside to":* Brendan Lynch and A. J. Alcock, *Yesterday We Were in America* (London: History Press, 2019).

25 *early aviation writer Henry:* "High Speed in the Air," *New York Times*, February 6, 1916.

26 *took place in 1922:* "Blake for World Flight," *New York Times*, April 28, 1922.

26 *"beset with difficulties":* "World Flight Abandoned," *New York Times*, August 27, 1922.

26 *"Roger decided to achieve":* Geoffrey A. Pocock, *Outrider of Empire* (Alberta, Canada: University of Alberta Press, 2008).

27 *"Their yacht has been":* "Yachtsmen Face Poverty," *New York Times*, September 20, 1923.

27 *"is All Fools' Day":* "Globe-Girdling Flight to Start Easter Day," *New York Times*, March 30, 1923.

27 *"We hold every airplane":* "M'Cook Men to Cross Country, Encircle Globe," *Dayton Daily News*, April 18, 1923.

29 *"Undoubtedly the next war":* "Airmen Throughout the World Owe a Debt to Maj.-Gen. Mason Mathews Patrick," *U.S. Air Services* (February 1942).

29 *"The Air Service has endeavored":* "Air Chief Describes Plans for the World Flight," *New York Times*, January 13, 1924.

30 *"The disadvantages, at this":* Carroll V. Glines, *Around the World in 175 Days* (Washington, DC: Smithsonian Institution Press, 2001).

30 *"surest, quickest, and cheapest":* Glines, *Around the World in 175 Days*.

4. "An All-American Airplane"

32 *"The best airplanes to be":* Glines, *Around the World in 175 Days*.

34 *"individuals who can dream":* Thomas, *The First World Flight*.

34 *"is safety in numbers":* Glines, *Around the World in 175 Days*.

35 *best in the world:* Frederick Johnsen, "Game-Changing Fokkers Served on Both Sides of the Atlantic," *General Aviation News*, December 4, 2017.

35 *without a clear purpose:* Wayne Biddle, *Barons of the Sky: From Early Flight to Strategic Warfare: The Story of the American Aerospace Industry* (Baltimore: Johns Hopkins University Press, 2002).

35 *meant "House of Happiness":* "Miami Springs Mansion Home of Aviation Pioneer Glenn Curtiss Rises from Ashes," *Orlando Sentinel*, May 13, 2010.

36 *Douglas grew up listening:* Joseph E. Libby, "To Build Wings for the Angels: Los Angeles and Its Aircraft Industry, 1890–1936," *Business and Economic History*, vol. 21 (1992).

37 *"a tall, good-looking":* "The Passionate Engineer," *Time*, November 22, 1943.

37 *"was practically no engineering":* Wayne Biddle, "Air Power," *Los Angeles Times*, July 28, 1991.

41 *Wright brothers had perfected their craft:* Lois E. Walker and Shelby Walker, *From Huffman Prairie to the Moon: The History of Wright-Patterson Air Force Base* (Washington, DC: Air Force Logistics Command, 1986).

5. The Proving Ground

43 *impossible to heat in:* House Committee on Appropriations Hearings, US Congress, 1924.

43 *"life was not worth living":* "Court Martial for Two in $43,000 Theft," *Fort Worth Star Telegram*, February 1, 1923.

43 *for nearly half of:* Schrader, "Good Men . . . Running Around in Circles."

44 *taking off from Langley:* "Doomed Airship Called Langley Home," *Virginia-Pilot*, May 28, 1989.

44 *"undoubtedly the finest airplane":* Robert I. Curtis, John Mitchell, and Martin Copp, *Langley Field, the Early Years, 1916–1946* (Langley, VA: Office of History, 4500th Air Base Wing, 1977).

44 *the Johns Multiplane:* Frederick Johnsen, "On Seven Wings and a Prayer," *General Aviation News*, October 31, 2021.

46 *"practicing great circle courses":* Glines, *Around the World in 175 Days.*

48 *"flown nearly every contrivance":* Thomas, *The First World Flight.*

49 *"such a general nuisance":* Thomas, *The First World Flight.*

50 *"boats of any kind":* Glines, *Around the World in 175 Days.*

6. "God Willing We'll Be in Los Angeles in September"

52 *A Santa Barbara newspaper:* "Barbareno Leads World Flight," *Santa Barbara Morning Press*, March 6, 1924.

52 *in their daily work:* "That 'Round the World Flight," *Oakland Tribune*, March 14, 1924.

52 *golden time when newspapers:* Bill Bryson, *One Summer: America, 1927* (New York: Anchor, 2014).

53 *"The men who are":* "To Try to Beat U.S. Air Record," *Mendocino Coast Beacon*, March 1, 1924.

54 *more than thirty-six thousand people:* Timothy Egan, *A Fever in the Heart-land* (New York: Penguin, 2023).

54 *Black Wall Street that:* "What the 1921 Tulsa Race Massacre Destroyed," *New York Times,* May 24, 2021.

54 *last thirty-six prisoners:* Adam Hochschild, *American Midnight: The Great War, a Violent Peace, and Democracy's Forgotten Crisis* (New York: Harper-Collins, 2022).

54 *led by William Dillingham:* Lawrence Downes, "One Hundred Years of Multi-tude," *New York Times,* March 25, 2011.

55 *"deal with many nationalities":* "Circling the Earth," *Los Angeles Evening Express,* March 18, 1924.

56 *Around the Rim Flight:* Miriam Orr Seymour, *The Around the Rim Flight* (Baltimore: Maryland Historical Press, 2002).

56 *"make clear that we":* Glines, *Around the World in 175 Days.*

57 *built a clubhouse on:* "Douglas History-Making Cruiser and Flight Crew at Factory Plant," *Venice Evening Vanguard,* March 1, 1924.

57 *felt the time slipping:* "Plant Rushes Work on Second Cruiser for World Flight," *Venice Evening Vanguard,* March 3, 1924.

58 *to the news that Tuffy:* "Dog Aviator Disappears from Field," *Los Angeles Times,* March 2, 1924.

59 *"almost as epochal as":* "Honor World Flyers at Aviation Ball," *Los Angeles Evening Post-Record,* March 14, 1924.

59 *"God willing we'll be":* "Flyers Hop Off on Attempt to Encircle World," *Fresno Bee,* March 17, 1924.

59 *"physical bond of peace":* "Santa Monica Inaugurates First World Flight," *Los Angeles Times,* March 13, 1924.

59 *"man's greatest conquest of":* "Weather Delays Start; Planes Off at 9:32 A.M.," *San Pedro News-Pilot,* March 17, 1924.

60 *"All her life she":* "Intuition Is Token That Cheers Fliers, Who Hop Off To-Day," *Cincinnati Enquirer,* March 17, 1924.

7. A Shining Light of England

62 *man hurried through the:* "British World Flight," *Guardian,* March 25, 1924.

62 *The school's immaculate grounds:* Roy Hattersley, "Private Pleasure, but No Public Virtue," *Guardian,* July 17, 2007.

63 *Sir Hugh Trenchard:* Russell Miller, *Boom: The Life of Viscount Trenchard, Father of the Royal Air Force* (London: Weidenfeld and Nicolson, 2016).

64 *"My job was to prod":* Rebecca Grant, "Trenchard at the Creation," *Air Force* (February 2004).

64   *"complicated and expensive arrangements"*: John Washington-Smith, "The Flight of the Vulture," *Airplane* (August 2011).

65   *"The striking thing about"*: G. R. Simonson, "The Demand for Aircraft and the Aircraft Industry, 1907–1958," *Journal of Economic History* (September 1960).

66   *a newspaper in central*: "Round the World in Ten Days," *Grimsby Evening Telegraph*, August 4, 1923.

67   *"unless exceptionally bad fortune"*: "Our London Letter," *Evening Telegraph*, July 27, 1923.

67   *staring into the lens*: "World Flight Leader," *Birmingham Gazette*, July 6, 1923.

67   *the world of its authority*: Katherine Howells, "'A Vast Window Display': The British Empire Exhibition of 1924–5," February 22, 2022, United Kingdom National Archives, blog.nationalarchives.gov.uk/20speople-a-vast-window-display-the-british-empire-exhibition-of-1924-5/.

68   *"The British are pretty well"*: Glines, *Around the World in 175 Days*.

68   *"shall watch your progress"*: "British Aviators Hop Off in Flight to Circle World," *Albany Times Union*, March 25, 1924.

68   *"is merely a coincidence"*: "Great Britain Enters Air Race Around World," *Sioux City Journal*, March 26, 1924.

69   *"We're not afraid"*: "British Flyer Is Off on Globe Encircling Trip," *Buffalo News*, March 25, 1924.

8. "Your Sporting Proposal"

70   *"Date of departure our"*: Glines, *Around the World in 175 Days*.

70   *Nelson joined them in*: "Lieut. Nelson On Way to Seattle; Spent Night Here," *Eugene Guard*, March 20, 1924.

71   *in a remote forest*: "Lieut. Sweeley, Commanding World Flight Escort Party, Cracks Plane Near Peel," *Roseburg News-Review*, March 20, 1924.

71   *"We have prepared a"*: "Aviators Resume World Air Trip," *Springfield News-Sun*, March 18, 1924.

71   *"the real work begins"*: "Prepare Planes for Water Trip," *Los Angeles Evening Post-Record*, March 21, 1924.

71   *"The engine worked fine"*: "Correct Defects in Planes," *Tacoma Daily Ledger*, March 24, 1924.

72   *daily updates of MacLaren's*: "British World Fliers Narrowly Escape Disaster," *North Mail, Newcastle Daily Chronicle*, March 26, 1924.

72   *"airboat is greatly admired"*: "British World Flight: Landing Forty Miles from Rome," *Guardian*, March 28, 1924.

73   *"silly waste of time"*: "The Secret Purpose," *Los Angeles Times*, March 23, 1924.

73   *"certainly have the effect"*: "World Flight," *Des Moines Tribune*, April 2, 1924.

74   *"the great god Jinx"*: "Hop Off Delayed One Day," *Seattle Star*, April 5, 1924.

75   *"The Argentine has a"*: "Argentine Flier to Circle World," *Times Union*, April 6, 1924.

75   *Coolidge sent a message*: "Coolidge Cheers World Air Pioneers," *Indianapolis Star*, March 30, 1924.

76   *"I keep wondering what"*: Diary, Leslie Arnold Collection, Smithsonian National Air and Space Museum, Washington, DC.

9. A Useless Rabbit's Foot

77   *a misty Friday morning*: Herbet K. Beals, *Juan Perez on the Northwest Coast: Six Documents of His Expedition in 1774* (Portland: Oregon Historical Society Press, 1989).

78   *"For the last ten"*: Jean Barman, *The West Beyond the West* (Toronto: University of Toronto Press, 2017).

78   *"We seldom tried to"*: Eric Collier, *Three Against the Wilderness* (Victoria, BC: TouchWood Editions, 2011).

79   *"125 miles in fog"*: Diary, Leslie Arnold Collection.

80   *"in my opinion, inexcusable"*: Glines, *Around the World in 175 Days*.

80   *"Lucky to have a"*: "World Flight Mishap," *North Mail, Newcastle Daily Chronicle*, April 1, 1924.

81   *"Depression is gradually wearing"*: "World Flight Delayed," *Liverpool Daily Post*, April 7, 1924.

81   *"Other accidents will in"*: "Three to Go," *Johnson City Chronicle*, April 8, 1924.

82   *"Now the cowling of"*: Diary, Leslie Arnold Collection.

10. Three-Inch Holes

85   *"a most hostile mountain"*: Jonathan Waterman, *A Most Hostile Mountain: Re-Creating the Duke of Abruzzi's Historic Expedition on Mount St. Elias* (New York: Henry Holt, 1997).

89   *"so isolated from mankind"*: "Maj. Martin, Flyer, Safe at Port Miller, Alaska; Plane Wrecked in Fog," *Hartford Courant*, May 12, 1924.

90   *"drowned in Alaskan waters"*: "Major Martin, Daring Airman, Believed Lost, Says Message," *Evening Review*, April 16, 1924.

90   *side of the world*: "British World Flight," *Daily Telegraph*, April 19, 1924.

91   *"The seriousness of this"*: Glines, *Around the World in 175 Days*.

91   *"These flyers are proving"*: "World Flight Is No Child's Task," *Spokane Chronicle*, April 18, 1924.

11. Presumed Dead

94   *"have given their lives"*: "Grave Fear Entertained for Aviator," *Idaho Times-News*, May 2, 1924.

95   *"When we hauled him"*: "Major Martin, Lost Two Days, Is Feared Dead," *Oakland Tribune*, May 2, 1924.

95   *"Those most closely concerned"*: "No Trace of Missing Aviators," *Riverside Daily Press*, May 2, 1924.

95   *"a general belief here"*: Evan J. David, "Clutch of Ice on Ailerons Looms as Menace of Death," *Atlanta Constitution*, May 3, 1924.

95   *"faint ray of hope"*: "Missing Flyer Seen Headed Toward Bering Sea," *Miami News*, May 3, 1924.

95   *"has been practically abandoned"*: E. R. Egger, "Major Martin Dead Is Fear in Tokio," *Des Moines Tribune*, May 7, 1924.

95   *"don't believe in luck"*: Evan J. David, "Lost Aviators Fate Mystery; Flight Resumed," *Minneapolis Star Tribune*, May 5, 1924.

96   *"steamed into the dozens"*: Evan J. David, "U.S. Sailors Fail to Find Lost Flyer," *Des Moines Register*, May 5, 1924.

96   *"These are terrible hours"*: "Faithful Wife Keeps Sad Vigil," *Atlanta Constitution*, May 3, 1924.

96   *"could they be alive"*: "Mrs. Martin Hopes for the Best," *Bridgewater Courier-News*, May 3, 1924.

96   *"her intuition tells her"*: "Mrs. Martin Is Brave Despite Fleeing Hopes," *Miami Herald*, May 3, 1924.

96   *"It is impossible for"*: "Mrs. Martin, Mother of Flyer, Awaiting Word of Son's Fate," *Richmond Palladium-Item*, May 5, 1924.

97   *"sun bronzed and dusty"*: "British World Flight," *Bristol (UK) Western Daily Press*, April 24, 1924.

97   *"made it a race"*: "Damage to Martin's Plane Again Delays World Flight," *Pittsburgh Post-Gazette*, April 29, 1924.

98   *The nation soon learned*: "Doisy Makes Air Record," *New York Times*, April 26, 1924.

98   *"to show France's predominance"*: "France Enters Japan Air Race with Secrecy," *Baltimore Evening Sun*, April 24, 1924.

99   *"It is believed that"*: "Lieut. D'Oisy's Feat," *London Daily Telegraph*, April 28, 1924.

99   *"hurrying along at a"*: "Editorials," *Indianapolis Star*, April 30, 1924.

99   *took off in early:* "World Flyer Not Yet Found," *Macon News,* May 5, 1924.

100 *"when the flight was":* "Flight Should Not Stop, Opinion at White House," *Boston Globe,* May 3, 1924.

100 *"dauntless spirit of America":* "Game Spirit in World Flight," *Long Beach Press-Telegram,* May 6, 1924.

100 *"a sorry start for":* "Perils of the World Flight," *Rock Island Argus,* May 8, 1924.

102 *"Don't delay longer":* Glines, *Around the World in 175 Days.*

102 *"the windiest places in":* "World Flyers Safe at End of 530-Mile Jump," *St. Louis Post-Dispatch,* May 11, 1924.

102 *"dead had seized her":* "Wife of Martin Fights Collapse," *Tacoma News Tribune,* May 3, 1924.

103 *"psychic death message":* "Wife of Flyer Has a 'Warning' Martin Is Dead," *St. Louis Star and Times,* May 3, 1924.

103 *"It would be foolish":* "Mrs. Martin Sure That Major Is Safe," *Los Angeles Times,* May 4, 1924.

12. Dead White

105 *"twisted mass of wreckage":* "Receive Log of Major Martin," *Orange County Plain Dealer,* May 15, 1924.

105 *"forever lost," he wrote:* Frederick Martin as told to George W. China for the International News Service, *Tribune,* May 15, 1924.

110 *"God bless the little":* "Wife Wants Martin to Quit Flying," *Minneapolis Star Tribune,* May 12, 1924.

13. "The End of Everything"

112 *"Attu Island looks like":* Diary, Leslie Arnold Collection.

114 *"pinnacle of post-war fame":* "'Pivolo' Now Hero to French People," *Baltimore Evening Sun,* May 23, 1924.

115 *"never had a honeymoon":* "Statue Even Thought of for D'Oisy," *Roanoke Times,* May 29, 1924.

115 *"are a queer lot":* Diary, Leslie Arnold Collection.

117 *"The hardships endured by":* "Warships' Weary Vigil," *Guardian,* May 16, 1924.

118 *"Will not enter Russian":* Glines, *Around the World in 175 Days.*

118 *"uncommon love for one":* Jacob Mikanowsky, "The Giant Sea Mammal That Went Extinct in Less Than Three Decades," *Atlantic,* April 19, 2017.

118 *and suffering from scurvy:* Kim MacQuarrie, "Kamchatka: Siberia's Forbidden Wilderness," PBS, https://www.pbs.org/edens/kamchatka/bering.html.

119   *a Siberian sailor*: Dean Littlepage, *Steller's Island: Adventures of a Pioneer Naturalist in Alaska* (Seattle: Mountaineers Books, 2006).

119   *"I don't dare mention"*: Diary, Leslie Arnold Collection.

120   *"We knew not how"*: Frank Jacobs, "The Border That Stole 500 Birthdays," *New York Times*, July 31, 2012.

123   *"blazed a trail through"*: "U.S. Army Airmen Make Safe Flight Over the Pacific," *Brooklyn Daily Eagle*, May 17, 1924.

                              14. The Seeds of War

124   *accumulated power in doses*: Kristofer Allerfeldt, "'And We Got Here First': Albert Johnson, National Origins and Self-Interest in the Immigration Debate of the 1920s," *Journal of Contemporary History* 45, no. 1 (January 2010).

125   *son of a farmer*: Alfred J. Hillier, "Albert Johnson, Congressman," *Pacific Northwest Quarterly* 36, no. 3 (July 1945).

125   *"The day the United States"*: *Congressional Record* 50 (1913).

126   *"Our new immigration legislation"*: "Applaud Alien Bill in D.A.R. Convention," *New York Times*, April 19, 1924.

126   *"a challenge to Japan"*: "Jingo Tokyo Paper Hints of 'War,'" *New York Times*, April 18, 1924.

126   *"The seeds of conflict"*: "Japan," *Post-Crescent*, May 16, 1924.

126   *"ought to slap them"*: "U.S. Steel Corporation Head Hits Jap Exclusion Cause," *Bellingham Herald*, May 1, 1924.

126   *"the extreme in restrictions"*: "Urge Coolidge to Turn Down the Alien Bill," *Sioux City Journal*, April 17, 1924.

126   *"disapprove it without hesitation"*: "Coolidge Signs Immigration Bill Despite Exclusion," *Hartford Courant*, May 17, 1924.

127   *nominate Johnson for vice president*: "Albert Johnson—Vice President," *Tacoma Daily Ledger*, May 22, 1924.

128   *"Japan must adopt plans"*: "Japan Watches Airplane Stunt," *Albany Daily Democrat*, May 17, 1924.

128   *"Intelligent Japanese are aware"*: "Japanese Officials Show Anxiety and Jealousy on Subject of World Flights," *Arizona Republic*, June 17, 1924.

130   *"Why does the entire"*: "Why It's Big News," *Long Beach Telegram and the Long Beach Daily News*, May 23, 1924.

131   *architect Frank Lloyd Wright*: Christopher Klein, "The Birth of Lincoln Logs," *History* (February 11, 2016).

131   *"adopted football tactics, forming"*: "Tokio Greets U.S. Heroes of World Flight," *Chicago Tribune*, May 25, 1924.

132 *"Magellans of the air"*: "American World Fliers Grimly Battled Fog and Snow in Crossing Seas," *Daily Oklahoman*, May 25, 1924.

132 *president of the University*: "American Aviators on World Trip Are Feted by Japanese," *Anaconda (Montana) Standard*, May 26, 1924.

133 *in New York City said*: "Radio Review," *Daily News*, June 11, 1924.

133 *"Click! Gates Are Locked"*: *Cincinnati Enquirer*, May 27, 1924.

15. "A Tonic"

134 *heat had melted the glue*: "British Airmen Feel Desert's Heat," *Twin Falls Daily Times*, May 22, 1924.

134 *stuck again due to*: "World Flyer Down," *Windsor Star*, May 24, 1924.

134 *He waited days for*: "MacLaren May Quit Trip," *Lincoln Journal Star*, May 24, 1924.

134 *The heavy plane strained*: "MacLaren Plane Is Wrecked," *Daily Advertiser*, May 26, 1924.

135 *"latest misfortune in his"*: "True Sport," *Grimsby Evening Telegraph*, May 27, 1924.

137 *"assist a friendly rival"*: "Rushing a New Machine to MacLaren," *Guardian*, May 27, 1924.

137 *"the airplane is demolished"*: "French Flyer Ends Journey at Shanghai," *Sacramento Bee*, May 20, 1924.

137 *"had enough of glory"*: "Mme. D'Oisy Is Glad," *Buffalo Enquirer*, May 22, 1924.

142 *"American pluck and ability"*: "America's Progress in the Air," *Virginian-Pilot*, June 8, 1924.

16. Tiger Country

144 *The calm water did them*: Thomas, *The First World Flight*.

17. "The Outlying Borders of the World"

153 *calling the "back stretch"*: "Here's the 'Back Stretch' in World Air Race," *Buffalo News*, June 14, 1924.

154 *"a very keen race"*: Diary, Leslie Arnold Collection.

156 *no longer a threat*: "D'Oisy Lands Near Tokio: French Aviator Successfully Completes Flight from Paris," *New York Times*, June 9, 1924.

156 *way around the impossible*: "Japan Decorates D'Oisy," *New York Times*, June 18, 1924.

156 *immediately promoted to captain*: "D'Oisy Wins Captaincy," *New York Times*, June 23, 1924.

156 *out of the running:* "Portuguese Flight Abandoned," *Guardian,* June 23, 1924.

156 *"to evade the monsoon":* "New World Flight," *Birmingham Gazette,* June 19, 1924.

156 *having narrowly escaped Rangoon:* "British Machine Ready," *Daily Telegraph,* June 23, 1924.

157 *"rather at a loss":* "Editorial," *Baltimore Evening Sun,* June 26, 1924.

157 *"teach millions of landlubbers":* "Teaching Us the Map," *Dallas Journal,* June 18, 1924.

157 *"than perhaps ever before":* "World Flight Succeeding," *Long Beach Press-Telegram,* June 28, 1924.

157 *running a long story:* "S.F. Girl Describes U.S. World Flight," *San Francisco Examiner,* June 24, 1924.

157 *race came from Australia:* "The Pathfinders," *Lithgow Mercury,* June 20, 1924.

158 *"pilots must attempt it":* "Many Obstacles Facing Flyers on Long Jaunt," *Tulsa World,* June 15, 1924.

18. Paris Is Waiting

162 *"miss a lot in life":* Diary, Leslie Arnold Collection.

164 *the city had appeared:* Sneha Bhura, "The Good Old Port of Chittagong: Revisiting Illustration History of Chattogram," *Week,* July 25, 2020.

167 *"chief glory of Calcutta":* "Unbelievable Ugliness—Calcutta's Gory Past Must Be Saved from a Venal Government," *Telegraph,* March 7, 2009.

167 *population less than a seventh:* S. Chandrasekhar, "Population Pressure in India," *Pacific Affairs* 16, no. 2 (June 1943).

168 *A trained pilot, Wells:* Linton Wells, *Blood on the Moon: The Autobiography of Linton Wells* (Boston: Houghton Mifflin, 1937).

169 *front pages of newspapers:* "U.S. Airman Fractures Rib," *Columbia Missourian,* July 1, 1924.

169 *"extremely uninviting from the":* Glines, *Around the World in 175 Days.*

171 *"By the time the":* Glines, *Around the World in 175 Days.*

172 *ruins of Mohenjo Daro:* "Rediscovering the Lost City of Mohenjo Daro," *National Geographic* (October 9, 2009).

172 *"a long forgotten civilization":* Rita P. Wright, *The Ancient Indus: Urbanism, Economy, and Society* (Cambridge: Cambridge University Press, 2009).

19. Ruins in the Sand

175 *Hundreds of Japanese schoolchildren:* "British Flyer Reaches Japan," *Dayton Daily News,* July 7, 1924.

175   *a harrowing twenty-four hours:* "MacLaren Held Up," *Daily Telegraph*, July 7, 1924.

176   *the engine began sputtering:* "British Airman Reaches Japan City on Round the World Flight," *Minneapolis Star Tribune*, July 7, 1924.

177   *calling him "Smitty":* "Jack Harding Happy as Boy," *Los Angeles Times*, September 24, 1924.

177   *source of Martin himself:* "Major Martin Flies to Richmond; Visits Sister," *Richmond Item*, July 6, 1924.

178   *read that his request:* Glines, *Around the World in 175 Days.*

179   *eventually came clean in:* Wells, *Blood on the Moon.*

179   *"the most lonesome, barren":* Diary, Leslie Arnold Collection.

182   *"He is a favorite":* "Who's Who in the Day's News," *Bakersfield Morning Echo*, July 9, 1924.

183   *Turkey refused entry to:* Glines, *Around the World in 175 Days.*

186   *guide them into Paris:* "Army Fliers Reach Paris," *Los Angeles Evening Express*, July 15, 1924.

187   *"We'll be in Los Angeles":* "Home by Sept. 1, Predicts Flyer," *Muncie Evening Press*, July 15, 1924.

20. Cold Winds

189   *"With their arrival in":* "American Airmen on World Flight Win Europe Press," *San Luis Obispo Tribune*, July 15, 1924.

189   *The modesty of:* "Modesty of American Flyers Noted by French," *Washington, DC, Evening Star*, July 20, 1924.

189   *skirt made of artificial bananas:* Morgan Jerkins, "90 Years Later, the Radical Power of Josephine Baker's Banana Skirt," *Vogue*, June 3, 2016.

189   *"keep these American airmen":* Glines, *Around the World in 175 Days.*

190   *"It is an experience":* "World Fliers Greeted by Big English Crowd," *Hutchinson News*, July 16, 1924.

191   *connecting the Croydon airfield:* "U.S. World Fliers at Croydon: Modest Heroes Welcomed," *Daily Telegraph*, July 17, 1924.

191   *"I am sorry we":* "World Fliers Greeted by Big English Crowd."

191   *"typical, clean-shaven young":* "The Great World Flight," *Hull Daily Mail*, July 17, 1924.

192   *"There was good reason for":* C. C. Turner, "World Flights: American Airmen's Fine Performance," *Observer*, July 20, 1924.

192   *"Zanni is rather late":* "Missing World Flight Party Found Safe," *Leicester Mercury*, July 18, 1924.

193   *meteorologist named Wasaburo Ooishi:* Jeff Glorfeld, "Wasaburo Ooishi and the Jet Stream," *Cosmos*, June 13, 2021.

194   *killed a pregnant woman:* Kathryn Tolbert, "When Japanese Balloons Threatened American Skies During World War II," *Washington Post*, February 3, 2023.

194   *"There are few places":* Diary, Leslie Arnold Collection.

196   *The English aviator was:* "Briton Will Continue His World Flight," *Los Angeles Evening Express*, July 18, 1924.

21. Distress Message

198   *detail delighted the press:* "Yankee World Flight Airmen Hop Off Thursday," *Brainerd Daily Dispatch*, July 19, 1924.

198   *"Recommend that no entertainment":* Glines, *Around the World in 175 Days*.

200   *Some seventy-four German ships:* "The Scuttling of the German Fleet 1919," Imperial War Museum, www.iwm.org.uk/history/the-scuttling-of-the-german-fleet-1919.

201   *He described Smith as:* Damon Runyon, "The World Flight Is Again Delayed by Bad Weather," *Coffeyville Daily Dawn*, August 2, 1924.

201   *Locatelli had grown incensed:* "Italian's Progress," *Guardian*, July 29, 1924.

202   *longing to go home:* Haden Church, "Writer Touches on Human Side of Gallant Army Aviators," *Daily Oklahoman*, August 3, 1924.

22. Disaster

206   *dial swung to zero:* Damon Runyon, "Disaster to World Circler Told," *Quad-City Times*, August 5, 1924.

211   *"We were all torn":* Diary, Leslie Arnold Collection.

211   *a local businessman coaxed:* "Flier Dashes Through Fogs into Iceland," *Daily Oklahoman*, August 3, 1924.

212   *Smith sent a message to:* Glines, *Around the World in 175 Days*.

212   *The plane took off:* "Major MacLaren at Behring Isle in World Flight," *Honolulu Advertiser*, August 3, 1924.

213   *MacLaren used the ship's radio:* "MacLaren Safe," *Daily Mirror*, August 2, 1924.

213   *"sorry I have failed":* "MacLaren's Regret," *Evening Express*, August 5, 1924.

213   *"Had the machine held":* "The Abortive World Flight," *Western Morning News*, August 6, 1924.

214   *"There are few achievements":* "MacLaren's Abandoned Flight," *Virginian-Pilot*, August 6, 1924.

214   *"have reached its crisis":* "Gale Hits Labrador Coast: Destroyer Driven Toward Rocks, but Is Turned Back to Sea," *New York Times*, August 10, 1924.

215   *Locatelli, the Italian pilot, landed:* "Off Over Icy Seas," *Kansas City Star,* August 21, 1924.

216   *"might live a thousand years":* Damon Runyon, "Aerial Race Described by Eyewitness," *San Francisco Examiner,* August 23, 1924.

218   *the world's windiest region:* Catherine Brahic, "Earth's Windiest Region Confirmed by Crewed Flight," *New Scientist,* September 4, 2008.

218   *"The rocks resemble spires":* "The North Atlantic Telegraph," *Illustrated London News,* 1843.

23. The Crossing

220   *"become a part of him":* Diary, Leslie Arnold Collection.

221   *the world's attention remained:* "Ships Comb Icy Sea for Italian Flier; U.S. Planes in Greenland," *Washington, DC, Evening Star,* August 22, 1924.

221   *began a search through:* "U.S. Planes Hunt in Vain for Lost Italian Aviator," *Hartford Courant,* August 23, 1924.

221   *search parties with dogsleds:* "Eskimos Being Organized to Hunt for Locatelli," *Baltimore Sun,* August 23, 1924.

221   *searched, to no avail:* "U.S. Flyers Think Italian Failed to Get Through Fog," *St. Louis Post-Dispatch,* August 24, 1924.

221   *a flicker of light:* "Locatelli Rescued; Adrift 125 Miles East of Greenland," *Washington, DC, Evening Star,* August 25, 1924.

221   *fired the flare gun:* "Locatelli and Companions, Worn Out but Not Hurt, Taken from Sea After 100-Mile Drift," *Barre Daily Times,* August 25, 1924.

222   *would soon start leaking:* "Italian Girdler Relates Thrilling Story of Cheating Death at Sea," *Minneapolis Star,* August 26, 1924.

223   *He pasted the slip:* Diary, Leslie Arnold Collection.

224   *the fuel been lost:* "Hero Saves Fuel for U.S. Airmen," *South Bend Tribune,* August 30, 1924.

224   *"saved the world flight":* "Heroic Efforts Save Fuel Oil of World Fliers," *Atlanta Constitution,* August 30, 1924.

226   *"like huge gray gulls":* "World Flyers Complete Hop to America," *Winchester Sun,* September 1, 1924.

226   *an extraordinary dream alive:* "The Hero at the Gas-Pump," *San Francisco Examiner,* September 3, 1924.

227   *President Calvin Coolidge wrote:* "Your Countrymen Are Proud of You," *Daily News,* September 1, 1924.

24. Home

229   *"the most marvelous achievement"*: "Globe Flight Is Virtually Ended by U.S. Airmen," *Tuscaloosa News*, September 1, 1924.

229   *"Fliers Land on Continent"*: *Minneapolis Morning Tribune*, September 1, 1924.

229   *in the blissful feeling*: "Nearing Home Shores," *Lincoln Star*, September 1, 1924.

229   *picked up on the*: "British Praise American Flyers," *Boston Globe*, September 8, 1924.

229   *"It can be done, apparently"*: "What of It?," *Alliance Times-Herald*, September 2, 1924.

229   *"I'll try again unless"*: "Humdrum Finish of British World Flight," *Los Angeles Record*, September 1, 1924.

230   *Los Angeles felt*: "World Flight to End Here," *Los Angeles Times*, July 20, 1924.

230   *Letters of protest from*: "A Reward of Merit," *Los Angeles Times*, September 9, 1924.

230   *"flight can only end"*: "End Big Flight in L.A. Is Plan," *Los Angeles Evening Express*, July 28, 1924.

230   *pleading the case to*: "Governor Wires Coolidge to Have Flight's End Here," *Los Angeles Times*, July 28, 1924.

231   *"There are no roads"*: "Gale Hits Labrador Coast."

231   *"This is the fastest"*: "Hawkes Bay," *Cincinnati Enquirer*, September 3, 1924.

233   *The mayor of Boston*: "Three Swords for U.S. Flyers Await Their Arrival in Boston," *Boston Globe*, September 1, 1924.

234   *A spotlight was turned*: "Three Aviators Guests at Show," *Boston Globe*, September 7, 1924.

234   *"Our countrymen are very"*: Glines, *Around the World in 175 Days*.

234   *More than thirty-five thousand people*: "More than 35,000 Visit Airport to See Planes," *Boston Globe*, September 8, 1924.

235   *"Small boys were everywhere"*: "Wheels Substituted," *Boston Globe*, September 8, 1924.

236   *passed over downtown Baltimore*: "World Flier Is Forced to Land Near Baltimore; Other 2 Reach Washington," *Brooklyn Daily Eagle*, September 9, 1924.

237   *the squadron reached Los Angeles*: "Flyers Home Again and New Epoch Begins," *Los Angeles Daily News*, September 24, 1924.

237   *between one hundred thousand:* "Throng of 100,000 Greets Airmen at Clover Field," *Birmingham Post-Herald,* September 24, 1924.

237   *searched for Donald Douglas:* "Donald W. Douglas Hails Birdmen in Planes He Built," *Daily News,* September 24, 1924.

237   *"belittled the American Machine":* "Young Designer of World Flight Planes Once Held Record for Flying Kites," *Dayton Herald,* August 8, 1924.

237   *"Such a flight and":* "Says Plane Now Takes Place Besides the Auto," *Omaha World-Herald,* August 17, 1924.

238   *barely contain his excitement:* "Jack Harding Happy as Boy," *Los Angeles Times,* September 24, 1924.

238   *editorial addressed to them:* "Greetings to You Fliers, from All Around the World!," *Los Angeles Evening Post-Record,* September 23, 1924.

238   *offered no parades or:* "Opera Star Helps Swell Flyer Fund," *San Francisco Examiner,* September 27, 1924.

238   *"We would not undertake":* "Globe-Encircling Trip of U.S. Army Flyers Is Officially Completed," *Albuquerque Journal,* September 29, 1924.

238   *join the pilots on:* "World Airmen at Seattle," *Bellingham Herald,* September 29, 1924.

238   *weeping as he reached:* "Martin Weeps as Park Crowd Cheers Him," *Seattle Star,* September 29, 1924.

239   *they returned to Dayton:* "Dayton Gives Second Welcome to World Flyers," *Dayton Daily News,* October 4, 1924.

Epilogue: "The Fight Is Just Beginning"

240   *middle of a lecture:* "Welcome for Fliers," *Philadelphia Inquirer,* January 8, 1925.

240   *the packed hearing room:* "Fliers Tell of Record Journey," *Lewistown Daily News,* January 9, 1925.

241   *Now the question was:* "Yank World Fliers Say Pacific Flight Could Be Made in Forty Flying Hours by Fleet of Planes," *Honolulu Advertiser,* January 9, 1925.

241   *attacks against the United States:* "Say Air Fleets Could Reach Asia in 40 Hours," *New York Times,* January 9, 1925.

241   *Left unsaid was the:* "A Reasonable Question," *Sacramento Union,* January 11, 1925.

241   *committing the same mistakes:* "Mitchell Defiant as Air Inquiry Ends," *New York Times,* March 3, 1925.

241   *himself demoted to colonel:* "General Mitchell Demoted," *New York Times,* March 7, 1925.

242 *US mainland to Hawaii:* Jason Ryan, "Ten Days Lost at Sea: The First Flight (and Voyage) to Hawaii," *Naval History* (February 2019).

242 *"directly by official stupidity":* "Mitchell Assails Aircraft Chiefs, Expects Arrest," *Standard Union,* August 6, 1925.

242 *was a public spectacle:* "Aircraft Inquiry Is Abruptly Halted Amid Much Mystery," *New York Times,* February 22, 1925.

242 *"loose talking imaginative megalomaniac":* "Mitchell Halts His Defense, Refusing to Go On with Trial," *Washington, DC, Evening Star,* December 17, 1925.

243 *that seemed so trivial:* David D. Lee, "Herbert Hoover and the Development of Commercial Aviation," *Business History Review* 58, no. 1 (Spring 1984).

243 *"an aviation Magna Carta":* Robert J. Sterling, *Legend and Legacy: The Story of Boeing and Its People* (New York: St. Martin's Press, 1991).

243 *cemented his reputation as:* "Plane Designer for Air-Cooled Motor Vehicle," *Los Angeles Times,* April 26, 1925.

244 *"They've built everything possible":* J. C. Smith, *The Aerospace Age* (Washington, DC: Department of Defense, 1971).

244 *put on roller skates:* "Girls on Wheels Expedite Aircraft Production," photograph, Los Angeles County, between 1942 and 1945, https://www.loc.gov /item/2017854830/.

244 *El Segundo division alone:* Robert Mulcahy, "The Douglas Plant That Became Los Angeles Air Force Base" (Washington, DC: US Air Force, 2012).

244 *Douglas sold the company:* Walter J. Boyne, "The Rise and Fall of Donald Douglas," *Air and Space Force,* March 1, 2006.

245 *caused riots in New York City:* "Greetings to Flier Upset by a Riot," *New York Times,* September 5, 1924.

246 *as a cautionary tale:* Derek O'Connor, "All in the Game," *Aviation History* (September 2010).

246 *"a splendid sporting attempt":* *Aircraft Year Book 1925* (New York: Aeronautical Chamber of Commerce of America, 1925).

247 *articles announcing his engagement:* "Famous Aviator to Wed," *New York Times,* July 12, 1928.

248 *propeller sheared off part:* "Capt. L. H. Smith Loses Finger in Propeller," *New York Times,* July 12, 1928.

248 *"These orbital flights are":* "The First Aerial Crossing of the Pacific," *Aerospace Historian* 14, no. 1 (Spring 1967).

Index

ABOUT THE AUTHOR

David K. Randall is the *New York Times* bestselling author of five works of nonfiction. His last book, *The Monster's Bones,* was named the year's best biography by the American Society of Journalists and Authors. His writing has appeared in the *New York Times,* the *Wall Street Journal,* the *Los Angeles Times,* and elsewhere. He lives in Montclair, New Jersey.